COSMIC
INTELLIGENCE
and
SPIRITUAL
HIERARCHIES

Rudolf Joseph Lorenz Steiner
February 27, 1861 – March 30, 1925

FROM THE WORKS OF DR. RUDOLF STEINER

COSMIC INTELLIGENCE
and
SPIRITUAL HIERARCHIES

Dr. Douglas J. Gabriel

Our Spirit, LLC
2024

OUR SPIRIT, LLC

P. O. Box 355
Northville, MI 48167

www. ourspirit. com
www. neoanthroposophy. com
www. gospelofsophia. com
www. eternalcurriculum. com

2024 Copyright © by Our Spirit, LLC

ISBN: 978-1-963709-05-6

Book cover art by Iris Art

CONTENTS

Cosmic Intelligence

Christ's words are all we need to attain a new Language of the Spirit that allows us to listen to and speak with the spiritual hierarchies that surround us both day and night. Some of the words of Christ are embedded in a mystery language that he told his Apostles could only be understood by them through the help of the Holy Spirit after the fiery tongues of the spirit descended upon them during Pentecost. The Apostles were taught the Language of the Spirit; which is a moral path of development reserved for the select few who could understand the nature of the Cosmic Christ—whereas others were taught through parables and Jesus Christ's example. This moral alphabet of the Cosmic Christ's Language of the Spirit is understood through Spiritual Science as the Sophia of Christ, the Wisdom of Love.

In the third volume of *The Gospel of Sophia, The Sophia Christos Initiation*, by Dr. Tyla Gabriel, we are presented with a variety of 'alphabets of the spirit' that can be developed into a Language of the Spirit. Numerous alphabets are presented from ancient traditions, religions, and even modern writers who present, as it were, the 'rungs of the ladder' of Ascension; for thereby, the human soul can rise into the spiritual world of living, active hierarchical beings who stand ready to assist the winged soul on its path to 'my Father's house which has many mansions.' These spiritual alphabets constitute the basis for a moral language of love that builds the celestial mansions which our souls are destined to accomplish with the help of Christ and the Holy Spirit. These mystery languages reveal the deep wisdom we find when we examine Christ's Ascension and the coming of the Holy Spirit during Pentecost.

1

We hear Dr. Gabriel explain the Language of the Spirit from *The Gospel of Sophia, The Sophia Christos Initiation*, Volume 3, pg. 303.

The Spiritual Language of Human Beings

Once you have constructed your Temple of Wisdom with sturdy pillars of virtue holding its starry dome in space, it will be only natural that you will want to invite the hierarchy into your spiritual abode. This is your wedding day. Here, you join your Higher Self and discover the amazing being that you have always been. The spiritual hierarchies have spoken to you through the aeons in their Language of the Spirit. Your physical and etheric bodies are reflections of the language they spoke to you from the beginning: *the Word*.

Now that you are awakening from your spiritual slumber and becoming conscious of your divine nature, you begin to see, feel, and hear non-physical beings all around you. Your deepest desire is to communicate and reconnect with them. But their language is not an earthly one, so you must find a language befitting an Angel or an Archangel. Your language, like your Temple of Wisdom, will be uniquely yours. You will choose a language that resonates with you and your traditions. It will reflect your individual cosmology, whether it comes from the religious traditions of your family, *The Gospel of Sophia*, the Tarot, or in one of the many different spiritual languages. There is no guru or master at this point who can guide you over the threshold. This is your journey, prepared for you by Sophia, to enter the etheric realm to meet Christ. Once you accept this as your language of communication with the divine, you will become more proficient in using it, especially after much practice. Only one Language of the Spirit is needed, and choosing several languages will not necessarily reap greater rewards.

There are many spiritual languages, and no particular one is exclusively correct. The openness of the initiate is the key to success. As commonly known to seekers of higher knowledge, there are many paths to the mountaintop. Once at the summit, the initiate must learn to fly with her newfound wings of spiritual language.

Spiritual languages can take many forms, indicated by words, symbols, numbers, forms, and functions. Both the ten (10) and twenty-two (22) letters of the human spiritual language describe the active working of living spiritual beings of the hierarchy. We have found our place among the hierarchy with our descent into matter and our ascension back to heaven. The forces of cosmic space have spoken a Language of the Spirit to create us. Now, we are learning a new language to converse with the spirit. This language flows into us from all directions and builds our world. Learning to listen and translate this language is the current challenge of spiritual evolution.

The Mysteries of Twelve are found in the active formative forces of space raying into the human form. These mysteries are accessed through one of many spiritual tools that reveal the true nature of the human being's spiritual constitution as a language of form and force. When the language is translated and taken deeply into the soul, a spiritual dialogue is possible with higher beings and the elemental forces of nature. This is the speech of Nature, or the 'language of the birds' referred to in legend and fairytale. This language is derived by taming the dragon, the combined animal forces of the Zodiac which reside in your head and your astral body of desire.

Psyche and Heracles were good examples of solar initiates who conquered the twelve signs of the Zodiac and brought their astral body of desires under the control of their spiritual nature. They went through trials and learned new languages to overcome the challenges placed before them. This is the perennial story of every budding aspirant who wishes to become an initiate. Offered below are several approaches to languages of the Cosmos for the aspirant to consider. To the untrained and uninitiated, these spiritual tools may be illegible and meaningless, but they provide the initiated with amazing insight and a clear map of the path of moral initiation. Ultimately, the initiate will choose the language that resonates with her personal cosmology and works the best in dialogues with the spirit.

Twenty-Two Sayings of Christ Jesus

It is not only formative forces and letters of an alphabet that are needed to understand a Book of Wisdom. The aspirant also must examine ideas that energize philosophies and the heavenly virtues, driving him upward to meet his Higher Self. Christ's words leave fiery images in our heart that drive our will into loving action in resonance with these images. Christ kindles the fires of the heart through words that create images in our mind and spur us on to loving deeds. Christ's words are living Moral Imaginations that create a moral ladder by which the human spirit ascends. Christ is not only creating archetypal images to emulate, but also giving us virtuous instructions by which to live.

1. "If ye continue in my word, *then* are ye my disciples indeed; And ye shall know the truth, and the truth shall make you free." *John* (8:31-32)

2. "In your patience possess ye your souls." *Luke* (21:19)

3. "Salt *is* good: but if the salt have lost his saltness, wherewith will ye season it? Have salt in yourselves, and have peace one with another." *Mark* (9:50)

4. "And all things, whatsoever ye shall ask in prayer, believing, ye shall receive." *Matthew* (21:22)

5. "Ask, and it shall be given you; seek, and ye shall find; knock, and it shall be opened unto you:" *Matthew* (7:7)

6. "A good man out of the good treasure of the heart bringeth forth good things: and an evil man out of the evil treasure bringeth forth evil things." *Matthew* (12:35)

7. "Lay not up for yourselves treasures upon Earth, where moth and rust doth corrupt, and where thieves break through and steal: But lay up for yourselves treasures in heaven, where neither moth nor rust doth corrupt, and where thieves do not break through nor

steal: For where your treasure is, there will your heart be also." *Matthew* (6:19-21)

8. "But he that is greatest among you shall be your servant. And whosoever shall exalt himself shall be abased; and he that shall humble himself shall be exalted." *Matthew (23:11-12)*

9. *"The things which are impossible with men are possible with God."* *Luke* (18:27)

10. "Do unto others as you would have them do unto you." *Luke* (6:31)

11. "Ye are the light of the world. A city that is set on an hill cannot be hid. Neither do men light a candle, and put it under a bushel, but on a candlestick; and it giveth light unto all that are in the house. Let your light so shine before men, that they may see your good works, and glorify your Father which is in heaven." *Matthew (5:14-16)*

12. ""Suffer the little children to come unto me, and forbid them not: for of such is the kingdom of God. Verily I say unto you, Whosoever shall not receive the kingdom of God as a little child, he shall not enter therein." (*Mark* 10:14-15)

13. "Thou shalt love the Lord thy God with all thy heart, and with all thy soul, and with all thy strength, and with all thy mind; and thy neighbor as thyself." (*Luke* 10:27)

14. "But love ye your enemies, and do good, and lend, hoping for nothing again; and your reward shall be great, and ye shall be the children of the Highest: for He is kind unto the unthankful and to the evil." *Luke* (6:35)

15. "Judge not, that ye be not judged. For with what judgment ye judge, ye shall be judged: and with what measure ye mete, it shall be measured to you again. And why beholdest thou the mote that is in thy brother's eye, but considerest not the beam that is in thine own eye?" *Matthew* (7:1-3)

16. "And as ye go, preach, saying, The kingdom of heaven is at hand! Heal the sick, cleanse the lepers, raise the dead, cast out devils: freely ye have received, freely give." *Matthew* (10:7-8)

17. "Behold, I send you forth as sheep in the midst of wolves: be ye therefore wise as serpents, and harmless as doves." *Matthew* (10:16)

18. "Be ye therefore perfect, even as your Father which is in heaven is perfect." *Matthew* (5:48)

19. "But seek ye first the kingdom of God, and his righteousness; and all these things shall be added unto you. Take therefore no thought for the morrow: for the morrow shall take thought for the things of itself. " *Matthew* (6:33-34)

20. "Blessed are the poor in spirit: for theirs is the kingdom of heaven. Blessed are they that mourn: for they shall be comforted. Blessed are the meek: for they shall inherit the Earth. Blessed are they which do hunger and thirst after righteousness: for they shall be filled. Blessed are the merciful: for they shall obtain mercy. Blessed are the pure in heart: for they shall see God. Blessed are the peacemakers: for they shall be called the children of God. Blessed are they which are persecuted for righteousness' sake: for theirs is the kingdom of heaven." *Matthew* (5:3-10)

21. "For there is nothing covered, that shall not be revealed; neither hid, that shall not be known. Therefore whatsoever ye have spoken in darkness shall be heard in the light; and that which ye have spoken in the ear in closets shall be proclaimed upon the housetops." *Luke* (12:2-3)

22. "But the hour cometh, and now is, when the true worshippers shall worship the Father in spirit and in truth: for the Father seeketh such to worship him. God is a Spirit: and they that worship him must worship him in spirit and in truth." *John* (4:23-24)

The Spiritual Language of Johannes Tauler

The Master Jesus (Zarathustra) as a simple layman known as 'the Friend of God from the Highlands,' or Nicholas of Basle visited 'the Master of Holy Writ' Johannes Tauler of Strasbourg (title: 'Doctor Illuminatus et sublimis,' c. 1300-Jun. 16, 1361 A.D.), and told him: "The single letters of the Holy Writ are killing your soul." The story continues:

> "But the Spirit giveth life. And know, therefore, that if so be you are willing, that same letter which now killeth, will by the power of the Spirit make you alive again. But in the like which you now have, know that you have no light, but are in the night. You can indeed understand the letter, but have not yet tasted of the sweetness of the Holy Ghost. Withal you are yet a Pharisee."

Three friends of God; records from the lives of John Tauler, Nicholas of Basle, Henry Suso, **Mrs. Frances A. Bevan, J. Nisbet & Co., Ltd: London, 1890**

This encounter ultimately led to Tauler becoming the Master's pupil and inspired Tauler to write his *Alphabet of Virtues* as a rare gift to spiritual history. Regarding this, Rudolf Steiner replied to a question concerning the 'Friend of God from the Highlands' in a conversation with the Christian Community priests W. Klein and Emil Bock, in February of 1924:

> "Was the Friend of God Zarathustra?" Rudolf Steiner answered: "Yes."

The Friend of God from the Highlands was a hidden figure in history; as the Master Jesus's incarnations are often very obscure and unknown to historians. In light of this, Rudolf

Steiner once replied to a question concerning the identity of the
Friend of God from the Highland, that he was the Master Jesus/
Zarathustra, who, since the Mystery of Golgotha, has incarnated
during every century. To another question about whether he
was currently incarnated, Steiner said that he was living at the
time in the Carpathian Mountains, 1. and indicated that they
were in spiritual contact. Furthermore, there is a response
by Rudolf Steiner to a question by Wilhelm Rath, Stuttgart,
October 16, 1922:

> "'You see, this is where you have the change to
> Rosicrucianism. It is the same thing that is pointed to in *The
> Mysteries*, a Christmas and Easter poem by Goethe.' Since
> that time Christian Rosenkreutz has become the leading
> personality in the spiritual life of the West. Both he and the
> Master Jesus, the Friend of God from the Highlands, have
> been incarnated in every century since then. They incarnate
> in turns every century, and from that time on the Master
> Jesus has worked along with Christian Rosenkreutz."

*The History and Contents of the First Section of the Esoteric
School*, Rudolf Steiner, *Letters, Documents, and Lectures 1904-
1914* (pg. 203; GA 264)

For further details see:

*The Friend of God from the Highlands: His Life, according
to the records of the St. John's Hospice, the 'Green Island,' in
Strassbourg*, Wilhelm Rath, Hawthorn Press: Stroud UK, 1991

There is an indication by Rudolf Steiner, as given by Ehrenfried
Pfeiffer and others, that the Master Jesus incarnated in the

US around the Civil War in order contribute to the ending of slavery. One can only wonder exactly whom Rudolf Steiner was referring to? One might venture to guess it to be someone inspiring the abolitionist Louisa May Alcott, or *William Mentor Graham* (1800–1886) the tutor of Abraham Lincoln? There are an abundance of apocryphal stories; such as, that he influenced the Christian mystic Jacob Boehme (Jakob Böhme, Apr. 24th, 1575–Nov. 17th, 1624). What we do know is that that Rudolf Steiner met the clairvoyant herb gatherer Felix Koguzki (1833-1909) when Steiner was a young student on the train to Vienna. It was Felix that introduced Rudolf Steiner to his Master in the Carpathian Mountains; whom is referred to by Rudolf Steiner only as 'M' in his Autobiography *The Story of My Life* (GA 28). 'M' told Rudolf Steiner to study the philosopher Johann Gottlieb Fichte (May 19, 1762-Jan. 29, 1814), a founder of German Idealism; and also to study natural science. Furthermore, he encouraged Rudolf Steiner to strive to understand human willpower; and said: 'No unnecessary conflicts.' Fortunately for posterity we have a record given to Édouard Schuré called: *"The Barr Document"* which reports Rudolf Steiner's parting conversation with 'M' in this quaint excerpt from an early translation:

> "If you wouldst fight the enemy, begin by understanding him. Thou wilt conquer the dragon [of materialism, Ahriman] only by penetrating his skin. As to the bull [of public opinion, Lucifer], thou must seize him by the horns. It is in the extremity of distress that thou wilt find thy weapons and thy brothers in the fight. I have shown thee who thou art, now go and be thyself!"

Édouard Schuré, *The Personality of Rudolf Steiner and His Development,* included with the preface to the early edition of what would later become, *Knowledge of Higher Worlds and It's Attainment,* entitled: *The Way of Initiation,* Rudolf Steiner, 1908 (GA 10)

Note:

1. It needs to be said in response to the assertion made in certain sources recently that the German mystic Alois Mailänder was Rudolf Steiner's teacher 'M.' A simple review of the preceding references shows that this is clearly not true. First, it's important to realize that Alois Mailänder was a "simple weaver and factory worker from Southern Germany." In fact, Alois Mailänder is known to have been a mystical illiterate teacher that lived in Kempten, Germany. In light of this, keep in mind that Kempten, Germany is over 900 miles from the Carpathian Mountains where 'M' lived according to Rudolf Steiner. While Alois Mailänder was a remarkable individual indeed, it's very clear that he is not 'M.' Furthermore, Rudolf Steiner's teacher 'M' recommended that he study Fichte; an unusual request coming from an illiterate teacher one would think?

Truly, the taming of the astral body through the perfection of virtue is a path of spiritual development appropriate for our time. Unbridled passions, fears, and mental illnesses rule the modern soul-scape. Seldom do New Age teachings recommend renunciation or austerities as the first step in spiritual development. The great ills of jealousy, envy, greed, sloth, gluttony, hatred, lust and anger are counteracted by the development of faith, hope, charity, industry, frugality, love, and patience. In other words, through the taming of the astral body, the aspirant is able to ascend on a path back to their heavenly home, traveling a road that in this modern era is completely determined by the individual. Responsibility and discipline are its foundation, and devotion and dedication are the elements that encourage the aspirant along their path of individual freedom. For the serious aspirant, there are no excuses for not discarding vices from one's life and developing good habits based on the heavenly virtues. When this is done, spiritual perception can then reveal the heavenly worlds interacting within the physical realm, and sheds light upon the two paths of vices and virtues—dark and light.

Upon receiving this *Alphabet* from the Master Jesus (1346 A.D.), Tauler retreated for two years in silence within a Dominican monastery. His first sermon following this period of silence is reported to have been so spirit-filled that it caused around forty people to faint. The *Alphabet* as a path contains fundamental secrets of spiritual development. For it brings about a complete purification of the astral body, so that it is possible to eliminate all hindrances from it such as egotism, self-will, and personal ambitions. The astral body can then become clairvoyant through the resulting alignment with certain cosmic powers. Tauler's alphabet is an initiation into the cosmic forces of the planetary system and Zodiac. Each letter reveals one secret of a planet or zodiacal sign. Knowledge of how the Logos is incorporated in the Zodiac and planets is the result of such a study.

Tauler's Alphabet leads to a moral language of the spirit that tames the astral body and refines thinking, feeling, and willing into moral super-sensible organs that supplant the normal five senses and replaces them with twelve enlivened senses that can peer through the veil between the material and spiritual worlds. This new type of sense perception is linked to witnessing the moral forces of love that are quietly secreted within everything in the world – *whether human, animal, plant, or mineral.* For all perception changes when Cosmic Love and Wisdom come to live in the heart, mind, and deeds of the aspirant. Ultimately, what is perceived becomes spiritual nourishment for the individual; and furthermore, what the individual does with these 'moral perceptions' can liberate the spirit beings who have been 'enchanted into matter.' Then, everything we think, feel, or do reveals the universal laws of the spiritual hierarchies that interpenetrate all living Nature. As a result, the individual begins to commune with the spiritual world as the moral Language of the Spirit aligns with the Divine Spiritual Plan.

The Alphabet of Johannes Tauler

A pure and godly life begin.

Bad deeds and thoughts avoid and do the good instead.

Cherish the golden mean; restrain yourself.

Demure in thoughts and actions, practice humility.

Egotism and self-will, let them submit to the will of God.

Firm and with steadfast earnestness remain with God and in God.

Godly things most willingly obey.

Hold not onto the Earthly creation.

In your heart strive to practice and meditate on the measure of things, good and divine.

Kourageously and strong, resist the temptation of the flesh and the devil.

Laziness and indifference conquer with force.

Mindful and merciful, exercise love for God and your fellow man.

Nothing desire; begrudge no one, whatever it be.

Order keep in all things and turn all things to the good.

Punishment from the Creator or from the world of the creatures most willingly accept.

Quicken forgiveness for all who have wronged you.

Reason, soul, and body learn to keep pure.

Stay gentle in soul concerning all things that are truly good.

True and faithful be to all human beings.

Unerringly desist from excess of any kind whatsoever.

Xristos, His Life and His teachings—emulate and meditate upon them without ceasing.

Yearning for heavenly solace, entreat our Lady to aid you.

Zealously tame your nature that in all things divinely created you may attain peace.

This type of morality training is at the heart of spiritual development, and Tauler has given a moral alphabet to reach the spiritual world, encouraging a reciprocal relationship and dialogue with the Divine. Human effort is answered by spiritual response; then both realms, the human and Divine receive nourishment. There are many people like Tauler throughout history who share with humanity the wisdom they have gleaned from their own personal Book of Wisdom. Tauler's *Alphabet*, as a Book of Wisdom, works, and so do many others. For spiritual languages can serve as bridges to connect human language to the Language of the Spirit.

Human and Cosmic Intelligence

Rudolf Steiner has indicated that the path of initiation is defined, from one point-of-view, as three stages that raise the initiate into the realms of Angels, Archangels, and Archai through the development of three soul capacities that can turn thinking, feeling, and willing into Moral Imagination, Moral Inspiration, and Moral Intuition. This path of spiritual development will happen gradually for humanity; but the path can be accelerated by initiates, masters, bodhisattvas, and the pure-hearted strivings of the aspirant. These stages of initiation change the aspirant's perception of the inner and outer worlds and develops a dialogue with the angelic realms.

Rudolf Steiner has given wonderful descriptions of these three realms of the three Higher Egos of humanity which will develop in the future. We provide below a summary of Steiner's teachings concerning these three stages of spiritual development.

Stage One: Imagination [Upside Down]

This stage of initiation is called Imagination, and it involves the Consciousness Soul (Spiritual Soul) merging with the Spirit-Self to advance the reincarnating human ego. During this stage we feel our ego outside of our physical body in the world, receiving Imaginations streaming in from the Angelic realm. The ego that we generally experience, we will call the everyday ego, or Earthly Ego, in contradistinction to the Higher Ego and the World Ego. (True 'I') The Earthly Ego is but a mirror image of the Higher Ego. This Higher

Ego was donated to us before 'creation' began. The creation of new egos throughout the evolution of a solar system is the primary intent of creation, as a certain type of 'creation out of nothingness.' Christ has donated all three human egos and is intimately connected to the progress and evolution of them all.

During the Old Moon incarnation of the Earth, objective perception of thought as a living being appeared in the astral body through pictures, signs, and symbols. Human beings were not confused into believing that their thoughts were their own property or that they had created the thoughts out of their own capacities of thinking. Only in our times, by necessity, are our thoughts considered to 'belong' to the thinker. This illusion of thinking as 'personal' and the 'product of human effort' is a recent development for humanity, and has led to the development of false egotism, pride, and evil in the realm of thinking.

Sense perception is observation of things that are essentially made from the thoughts of the Divine Spiritual Beings. Things are thoughts slowed down to provide the illusion (Maya) of solidity so that humans could have a realm of isolation in which to be born as 'new thinkers.' Transforming sense perception into 'food for the gods' is the intent of the spiritual world; that is acted out through the course of human evolution. Through enlivened thinking, called 'Imagination,' higher thinking can be borne by finding eternal truths that are objective, even in the outside world of seeming illusion. Therefore, through partaking of certain qualities these thoughts can rise into the realm of Moral Imagination, called the Manasic realm, or the realm of Spirit-Self; through transformation of the astral body. This transformation occurs because these qualities are aligned with eternal truths; and so, are *objective* and have a basis of reality in both the physical and spiritual worlds.

The personal, everyday ego can be found in the interaction between the seeming center of consciousness inside the human being and the picture of that human being coming to him from the outside world. For example, it takes another human to reflect to us who we are. Our actions in the world, and the response of the world to those actions, tell us much about our ego. We see ourselves through others and find our ego coming to us as our destiny and karma. This 'self-knowing' is the first step in knowing the Higher Ego—*the 'Christ in you.' Colossians* (1:27)

Imagination is the first step of initiation that begins with transforming 'thinking about thinking' into a force of self-knowing. Studying the same processes of thinking that have produced the outer world's laws of nature tunes us into the true nature of the ego both inside of us, and outside of us.

Stage Two: Inspiration [Backward]

The second stage of initiation is called Inspiration or Moral Inspiration. This stage happens when the Spirit-Self (Manas) merges with the Life-Spirit (Budhi) through transformation of the etheric body. The realm of Life-Spirit is where Christ reigns through creating an atmosphere of redeemed etheric life-force of love that nourishes the Spirit-Self through providing the archetypal Higher Ego for the Spirit-Self to wed—*the Christened Group-Soul of Humanity.* This is often depicted as the Virgin Sophia as a bride wedding the Lamb of God—*that is Christ the 'bridegroom.'* This heavenly marriage is found in many religions and spiritual practices. It is accomplished by emptying our being so that spirit can flow into the prepared sacred space made for the 'Christ in you.'

On the path to the second, transcendental ego, we again find the Higher Ego outside of the physical body; which brings the experience of Inspiration (or Moral Inspiration)—*which is like hearing the Music of the Spheres in perfect harmony.* To reach this level of initiation, the initiate must extinguish the pictures that were so abundant in the first stage of Imagination. One must push past the images to the experience of the inner activity behind the thought processes—*to the beings who create thoughts to begin with.* No sense perception is allowed into this realm, only sense-free thinking or spiritual sound. New supersensible organs of perception must be developed to perceive and communicate in these realms. It is there that the Earthly Ego, living in the Spirit-Self, can unite with the Higher Ego of the initiate living in the Life-Spirit. This creates the spiritual anointing of the Earthly Ego that unites with the Higher Ego that was donated by Christ. The initial etheric drops of blood donated by Christ to create the Earthly Ego now send energy to the head; represented as entering the New Jerusalem or the Temple of Wisdom, or the Grail Castle.

In the second stage of initiation, Inspiration, the initiate's Earthly Ego assimilates the 'Christ in you'; and receives inspiration from the Archangelic realm of the Life-Spirit—*as the human etheric body is spiritualized through merging with the Etherized Blood of Christ.* This process is called the 'etherization of the blood' and is a type of spiritual communion which nourishes the spiritual world and the initiate simultaneously. This is contact with the Higher Ego, or Higher Self, as it is commonly called. The experience of the Higher Ego comes from the outside world, and is experienced in the outside world, in a sense looking from the outside toward the inside. Your Higher Ego is developed by your spiritual practice; but the substance of the Higher Ego is taken from the common substance provided by Christ to all Higher Egos ready to put on the 'resurrection body' of Christ. Your Earthly Ego is realized through the outside world coming at you; whereas your Higher Ego is witnessed from the outside world looking towards you. The perspective changes from a dynamic of outward raying in, to one of outward witnessing. One is a type of 'being beheld' whereas the other is one of 'beholding.' There is a distinct sense of 'selflessness' that comes with the Higher Ego that is quite different from the experience of the Earthly Ego.

Stage Three: Intuition [Inside-out]

The third stage of initiation is called Intuition (or Moral Intuition)—*wherein the Higher Ego from the realm of Life-Spirit becomes one with all other Christened beings within the Cosmic Ego of Christ which manifests in the realm of Spirit-Human (Atman).* This Cosmic Ego of Christ is the third, the 'True Ego.' ('Wahr Ich'; 'True I') Again, this True Ego is located outside of the human body and is found only when, through personal effort, the Earthly Ego and the Higher Ego are extinguished. All of the effort to develop the ego and become selfless and Christ-like must then be voluntarily surrendered and annihilated until nothing of the *personal earthly self remains—but without a loss of individuality.* This embodiment of the True Ego (Cosmic/World Ego of Christ, World I) fills the hollow sacred space surrendered for the reception of this being. The awareness of this 'presence' fills the prepared space, a spherical temple called a 'Zodiac.'

When we can empty ourselves and go beyond sense perception, beyond perception of thoughts as beings, beyond the extinguishing of our Earthly Ego and our Higher Ego; we are then ready to be filled by the World Ego of Christ (Macrocosmic I) and become a sphere of stars (Zodiac) that can become co-creative with the Trinity (through Christ) to give birth to a new Zodiac of Ego Beings who will, in time, come to their spiritual birth and development as Christened beings.

This stage of Intuition is one wherein the will of the initiate becomes one with the will of the World Ego of Christ (Macrocosmic I Am). There is nothing of the physical world in this realm. It was from this realm of Spirit-Human (Atman) that the Earthly Ego was born and thus returns; but now, as a creator equal to his own creator over the course of evolution. This mirroring of the True Ego (Cosmic/World Ego of Christ) in the Earthly Ego is the basis of consciousness in the physical realm becoming self-consciousness, higher selfless consciousness, and consciousness aligned with the Cosmic Christ's Ego.

There is no time or space as we know it in the spiritual world; so therefore, the Earthly Ego, Higher Ego, and the True Ego are one and the same, simply divided by time and space. This type of hyper-connectivity through time and space constitutes the path of human self-development from birth to ascension back to heaven. Christ is the perfect example, model, and archetype of what the ego must go through in its entire evolution, from the descent from heaven to Earth, and then, the ascent from Earth to heaven—the story of the prodigal son.

There is much confusion in spiritual circles about the Higher Ego and the True Ego, the comprehensive divine ego. The True Ego is the Cosmic Ego which we are all on a path to gain and recover through grace and mercy. The path to supersensible knowledge proceeds from Earthly Ego, to Higher Ego, to True Ego. Christ is the living eternal archetype of the Human Ego ('Menschlich Ich'; 'Human I') whose only 'true' name is "I Am." The human being is developing upward from below; while Christ is descending from above offering the true "I Am." Christ is both the model and the goal as we make the journey to our own ego; which is fraught with challenges. We need unlimited trust in Christ and the spiritual world to bridge the chasms between these worlds. We need the loving arms of Christ to catch us when we fall into the Abyss. Only trust in Christ can bring us safely across the Abyss. Or, as Steiner says in *Theosophy*, "In order to approach the Abyss as nothing, it is necessary that one trusts that the True Ego will be brought to one out of the spiritual world."

To know that the 'True Ego will be brought to one' from beyond the Abyss is the greatest of comforts and only arises through the grace and mercy of the spiritual world. Then, once one meets Christ, the World Ego (World I), man ascends to his True Ego and no longer experiences Christ outside of oneself but within. This is the culmination of the stage of Intuition. 'Not I, but the Christ in me.'

The True Ego remains in the spiritual world and can only be found there and cannot fully come into the physical world except through spiritual Moral Intuitions. The Earthly Ego works through sense perception to find itself in the outer world. The Higher Ego is the gift of Christ from the outer world alighting in us. The True Ego is a gift of Christ from heaven at the edge of the Abyss. The True Ego can have perception of the supersensible worlds through Intuition and the sense of moral technique that joins with the efforts of Christ, the Lord of Karma.

It is often the case that Western esotericists' tend towards a greater focus on the development of the Earthly Ego; whereas Eastern esotericists' often focus on the True Ego, the heavenly ego that is not tied in any way to material things. A balanced path of spiritual development would use a synthesis of both the sensible and supersensible to develop all three egos.

Rudolf Steiner tells us about the nature of the human ego in the following indication.

The Threshold of the Spiritual World, **Rudolf Steiner, IX,** *Concerning the Ego-Feeling and the Human Soul's Capacity for Love; and the Relation of these to the Elemental World*, **GA 17**

"An over-developed ego-feeling in the physical world works against morality. An ego-feeling too feebly developed causes the soul, around which the storms of elemental sympathies and antipathies are actually playing, to be lacking in inner firmness and stability. These qualities can only exist when a sufficiently strong ego-feeling is working out of the experiences of the physical world upon the etheric body, which of course remains unknown in ordinary life. But in order to develop a really moral temper of mind it is necessary that the ego-feeling, though it must exist, should be moderated by feelings of good-fellowship, sympathy, and love."

The Gospel of St. John, **Rudolf Steiner, Lecture V. Basle, November 20, 1907, GA 100**

"'The Law was given by Moses, but grace and truth came by Jesus Christ.' If we thoroughly understand this passage we shall also understand that deeply significant event in the history of humanity which took place through the appearance of Christ on the Earth. In the earlier lectures of this course we have traced the evolution of humanity in broad outlines, and we have described the way in which the consciousness of the Ego developed in the distant past whole groups and generations of human beings had one Ego in common. From this we learned to understand the long age of the patriarchs. Gradually this feeling of the Ego became limited more and more to the single personalities. We also showed how two spiritual streams made themselves felt in this evolution: the one was the stream of blood-relationship, which endeavored to hold men together by natural ties, and the other, the Luciferic, which made men independent and prepared them for the purely spiritual tie which was to come.

"During the whole period of the *Old Testament* one understood by 'Law' something which brings order into human society from without. After blood-relationship had lost its binding power, men had to be brought into a certain connection with one another by an outer thought-order. The law was perceived as something coming from outside, and this Law which was given from outside holds good until the 'grace and truth,' or devotion and truth, which comes through Jesus Christ, has developed in us from within, the understanding for the true knowledge. Devotion and truth can only develop gradually. Christianity, which is to bring devotion and truth in place of the Law, is only at the beginning of its growth; the further the Earth progresses in its evolution the stronger will be the influence of Christianity on humanity. Humanity is to raise itself to a stage of social life at which each one is drawn, by an impulse arising within himself, to act towards his neighbor as one brother to another. Men could not however, raise themselves of their own power to this high stage of development, and it is the task of Christianity to help them to do this. Men will no longer need any outer law to force upon them this attitude when they have the inner impulse so to act that devotion and truth are the motives for their actions.

"We do not mean to say by the above, that humanity no longer needs the Law; but that which we have described is an ideal, which should be striven for. Gradually men will come to where the harmony of the world will be brought about through their voluntary action, but for this goal to be reached the Power which in the Gospel is called Christ had to step in. In the occult schools it is said of one who, of his own inner power, is able to raise himself into this relationship to all his fellowmen, that 'he bears Christ within him.' In order to understand what we are about to say, it will first of all be necessary to recapitulate once more the real constitution of man. Recall to mind the contents of the third lecture with the aid of the following sketch.

"Through the work of the Ego upon the astral body the latter is transformed into Spirit-Self. But this takes place step by step, through the Sentient Soul being developed first, then the Intellectual Soul, and finally the Spiritual Soul [Consciousness Soul]; then the Spirit-Self pours into the purified and mature Spiritual Soul. In the same way the Ego ['I'] works upon the etheric body, and the impulses which are most effective in this case are the influences of art, religion and occult training.

"There were also occult schools in pre-Christian times, where pupils were trained, so that they were able to look into higher worlds; but this vision only existed among the true pupils in the most hidden occult schools, and even they only at the actual moment of initiation, when the etheric body was separated from the physical body. The raising of a human being, so that he might be able to see in the spiritual world, was called Initiation. In all initiations of pre-Christian times the one who was to be initiated had to be brought into a kind of sleeping state. This sleep of initiation was distinguished from ordinary sleep by the fact that in the latter the etheric body remains united with the physical body, whereas in the former the etheric body was for a short time separated from the physical body. During this time the Hierophant had to keep the body alive. Through the etheric body being separated, it was possible to lead it, together with the other parts, into the higher worlds, in order there to undergo experiences which could afterwards be imparted to the physical brain. That was the method of initiation in pre-Christian times.

"Through the advent of Christ Jesus an entirely new kind of initiation came in. Imagine that a man has transformed the whole of his astral body into Spirit-Self. This Spirit-Self then impresses itself into the etheric body, as a seal impresses itself into sealing-wax, and gives it its imprint. The etheric body is thereby changed into Life-Spirit. When this has come about completely, the Life-Spirit then imprints itself in the physical body and makes it into Spirit-Man [Spirit-Human]. Now it was only through the appearance of Christ Jesus that it became possible to imprint the Life-Spirit directly into the life body; and the experiences undergone in the higher worlds could henceforth be embodied in the physical brain without the necessity of a previous separation of the etheric body. Thus all the pre-Christian initiates had undergone the experiences of initiation outside the physical body; they had then descended again into the physical body and could from that time forward, out of their own experience, announce what had taken place in the spiritual world.

"Buddha, Moses and others were initiates of this kind. In Jesus there had come to the Earth for the first time a Being who, while still remaining in the physical body, could see the life of the Higher Worlds. The teachings of Buddha, Moses, etc., were quite independent of the personality of their agent. Those who accept the teachings of Buddha or Moses are Buddhists or followers of Moses; for these founders of religion only passed on what they had experienced in the higher worlds. *With Christ it is different.* It is only through His personality that His teachings become Christianity, and in order to be a Christian it is not enough merely to follow the teachings of Christianity. Those alone are true Christians, who feel themselves united with the historical Christ. Certain sentences contained in Christian teaching, or something very similar to them, could also be found in that world before Christ appeared; but that is not the point. The essential thing is, that the Christian believes in Christ Jesus, that he considers Him to be the One Who, while walking in the flesh, represents the '*Perfect Man*.'

"In ancient times the statement was often made; 'The initiate is a divine man.' The reason for this lay in the fact that during the ceremony of initiation the initiate was above in the spiritual world with the Spiritual or Divine Beings; He was then the 'divine man.' But one could 'see' the Deity in the physical body for the first time through Christ Jesus—but never before. Thus we have to take the words of *John* (1:18) quite literally: "No man hath seen God at any time; the only begotten Son, which is in the bosom of the Father, He hath declared Him." Formerly the Deity could only be perceived by one who had himself made the ascent. In Christ the Deity had *for the first time* come down visibly to the Earth. This is told to us in the *Gospel of St. John* (1:14): "And the Word was made flesh, and dwelt among us (and we beheld His glory, the glory as of the only begotten of the Father), full of grace and truth." It was also taught in the School of Dionysius [the Areopagite, that was established by St. Paul in Athens. (*Acts* 17:34)]. Christ came to show men the way; they are to become His followers; they are to prepare to imprint what is in the etheric body into the physical body; that is to say, to develop within themselves the Christ principle.

"*The Gospel of St. John* is a book of life. No one who has merely enquired into it with his intellect has understood this book; he alone who has experienced it really knows it. If a man meditates upon the first fourteen verses day-after-day for some time, he will discover the purpose of these words. They are really words which, when one meditates upon them, awaken in the human soul the capacity to see the various parts of the *Gospel*, such as the marriage at Cana in chapter two, the conversation with Nicodemus in chapter three, as one's own experiences in the great *Astral Tableau*. Through these exercises clairvoyance develops in the human being and he can then experience for himself the truth of what is written in *The Gospel of St. John*. Hundreds have experienced this. The writer of *The Gospel of St. John* was a great Seer who was initiated by Christ Himself.

"The disciple 'John' is never mentioned by name in this *Gospel*. We read of him as "the disciple whom the Lord loved," for example in Chapter 19:26. This is a technical expression and signifies the one who was initiated by the Master Himself. 'John' describes his own initiation in the story of the "raising of Lazarus." (Chapter 11). It was only through the writer of *The Gospel of St. John* being initiated by the Lord Himself that the most secret connections between Christ and the evolution of the world could be revealed. As we have already said, the old initiations lasted for three and a half days; hence the raising of Lazarus on the fourth day. It is also said of Lazarus that 'the Lord loved him' (*John* 3:35-36.)

"While the body of Lazarus lay as if dead in the grave, his etheric body was lifted out in order to undergo the initiation, and to receive the same force that is in Christ. Thus the one whom the Lord loved, the one to whom we owe *The Gospel of St. John*, was raised, he was awakened. Not a line in *The Gospel of St. John*, contradicts this fact; the process of initiation is represented in a veiled way.

"Let us now consider another scene in this *Gospel*. In (*John* 19:25), we read: "Now there stood by the cross of Jesus, His mother, and His mother's sister, Mary the wife of Cleophas, and Mary Magdalene." If we wish to understand this *Gospel* it is necessary to know who these three women are. We do not usually give two sisters the same name; neither was it the custom in former times. The passage we have quoted proves that, according to *The Gospel of St. John*, the mother of Jesus was not called Mary. If we search through the whole of this *Gospel* we nowhere find it said that the mother of Jesus was called Mary. In the scene of the Marriage of Cana, for example, Chapter 2, we only read, "the mother of Jesus was there." In these words something important is indicated, something we only understand when we know how the writer of this *Gospel* uses his words. What does the expression "the mother of Jesus" mean? We have seen that man consists of physical, etheric and astral bodies. We must not consider the transition of the astral body to the Spirit-Self so simply. The Ego ['I'] transforms the astral body very slowly and gradually into Sentient Soul, Intellectual Soul and Spiritual Soul [Consciousness Soul]. The Ego goes on working and only when it has developed the Spiritual Soul is it able so to purify it that Spirit-Self can arise in it. The following diagram represents the constitution of man.

Father	7. Spirit-Human	
Son	6. Life-Spirit	
Holy Spirit	5. Spirit-Self	Virgin Sophia (purified Spiritual Soul)
	4. Intellectual Soul	Mary the wife of Cleophas
	3. Astral Body	Sentient Soul – Mary Magdalene
	2. Etheric Body	
	1. Physical Body	

"The Spirit-Man will only be developed in the distant future, and Life-Spirit is also only germinal in most people of the present day. The development of the Spirit-Self has only just begun; it is closely united with the Spiritual Soul (somewhat like a sword in its sheath). The Sentient Soul is similarly united with the astral body. The human being thus consists of nine parts or principles; but as the Spirit-Self and the Spiritual Soul, and the Sentient Soul and the astral body are so closely united, we often speak of seven parts. Spirit-Self is the same as the 'Holy Spirit,' who according to Esoteric Christianity, is the guiding Being in the astral world. According to the same teaching, Life-Spirit is called the 'Word' or the 'Son'; and Spirit-Man is the 'Father Spirit' or the 'Father.'

"Those human beings who had brought the Spirit-Self to birth within them, were called 'Children of God'; in such men "the light shone into the Darkness and they received the light." Outwardly they were, men of flesh and blood; but they bore a higher man within them – for the Spirit-Self had been born within them out of the Spiritual Soul. The 'mother' of such a spiritualized man is not a bodily mother, she lies within him; she is the purified and spiritualized Spiritual Soul; she is the principle who gives birth to the higher man. This spiritual birth, a birth in the highest sense, is described in *The Gospel of St. John*. The Spirit-Self or the Holy Spirit pours into the most highly purified Spiritual Soul. This is referred to in the words, "I saw the Spirit descending from heaven like a dove, and it abode upon him." (*John* 1:32).

"As the Spiritual Soul is the principle in which the Spirit-Self develops, this principle is called the 'mother of Christ,' or, in the occult schools, the 'Virgin Sophia.' Through the fertilization of the Virgin Sophia the Christ could be born in Jesus of Nazareth. In the occult school of Dionysius, the Intellectual Soul was called 'Mary,' and the Sentient Soul 'Mary Magdalene.'

"The Physical man is born of the union of two human beings; but the higher man can only be born of a Spiritual Soul which embraces a whole people. Among all the peoples of olden times the method of initiation was essentially the same. Each initiation had seven stages or degrees. Among the Persians, for example, they were called as follows:—

1. **The Raven.** One at this stage had to bring information from the outer world into the temple. The Raven has always been called the spiritual messenger; for instance in the legend of the Ravens of Barbarossa, and also in the German legends of Odin and his two ravens.

2. **The Occultist.**

3. **The Warrior.** In the occult school the warrior was allowed to go forth and announce the teachings.

4. **The Lion.** The Lion was one who was firmly grounded in himself; he not only had the *word*, but he possessed also the magical forces; he had stood the test which guaranteed that he would not misuse the powers entrusted to him.

5. **The Persian.**

6. **The Sun Hero.**

7. **The Father**.

"Let us consider the title of the fifth degree, the 'Persian,' a little more closely. In all the occult schools an initiate of the fifth degree was called by the name of the people to whom he belonged; for his consciousness had widened where it included the whole people. He felt all the sorrow of the people as his own; his consciousness had been purified and expanded to the consciousness of the whole people. Among the Jews the initiate

at this stage was called an 'Israelite.' Only when we grasp this fact
do we understand the conversation between Christ and Nathanael
(*John* 1:46-49). Nathanael was an initiate of the fifth degree. The
words of Christ Jesus to Nathanael, that he had seen him under
the fig tree, refer to a special process in initiation, namely, the
reception of the Spiritual Soul.

"The following considerations will help towards the
understanding of the inner process of initiation. The individual
'I-consciousness' of man is in the physical world; men walk
the Earth with their Ego. But the egos of the animals are on
the astral plane; each group of animals there possesses an ego-
consciousness in common. There is, however, in the astral
world, not only the ego of the animal, but also the ego of the
body which man has in common with the animals, the ego of
the human astral body. In the Lower Spirit World, we find the
ego of the plants and also the ego of the body man possesses in
common with the plants, the ego of the etheric body. If we rise
still higher, into the Higher Spirit World, we there find the ego of
the minerals and the ego of that part which man has in common
with the minerals—the ego of the physical body. Thus, through
our physical body we are connected with the Higher Spiritual
World. We are here in the physical world with our individual Ego
only. When, in the case of an initiate, the ego of the astral body
is permeated by his Individual ego ['I'], the consequence is that
he becomes conscious in the astral world; he can then perceive
the beings around him there and become active in that world.
He then meets Beings who are incarnated in astral bodies; he
also meets the group-souls of the animals, and the higher Beings
who in Christianity are called Angels. On being initiated still
more deeply, the ego of the etheric body is also permeated by
the individual ego. The consciousness of the human being then

extends into the Lower Spiritual World. There he encounters
the egos of the plants and the Spirit of the Planet. A still deeper
initiation takes place when the individual ego permeates the ego
of the physical body, man then rises to personal consciousness
in the higher Spiritual World. There he meets the egos of the
minerals and still higher Spirits. Thus, continued initiation raises
a man to higher and higher worlds, in which he meets with
higher and higher Beings.

Higher Spiritual World Egos of the Minerals	**Ego of the Physical Body**	**Consciousness in the Higher Spirit World**
Lower Spiritual World Egos of the Plants	**Ego of the Etheric Body**	**Consciousness in the Lower Spirit World**
Astral World Egos of the Animals (also Angels)	**Ego of the Astral Body**	**Consciousness in the Astral World**
Physical World	**Individual Ego**	**Day Consciousness**

"When the individual Ego has gained full control over
the three bodies, it has brought about inner harmony. Christ
possessed this harmony to the fullest extent; he appeared
on the Earth in order that men might develop this power of
inner harmony. In this Son of Man, we see represented the full
development of humanity, up to the highest spiritual stage.
Formerly this inner harmony did not exist, outer laws worked in
its place; this inner harmony is the new impulse which humanity
received through Christ. Man is to acquire the 'Christ capacity,'
that is to say, he is to develop the inner Christ. Goethe said: "The
eye was created by light to receive light"; in the same way this
inner harmony, this inner Christ is only kindled through the
presence of the outer, historical Christ; before His appearance

it was not possible for man to reach this stage of spiritual development.

"Those human beings who lived before the appearance of Christ on Earth are not excluded from the blessings He brought to humanity; for it should not be forgotten that, according to the law of reincarnation, they will come again to the Earth and will therefore have the opportunity to develop the inner Christ. It is only when people forget the law of reincarnation that they can speak of injustice. *The Gospel of St. John* shows the way to the historical Christ, to that Sun which enkindles the inner light in man, just as the physical Sun has enkindled the light of the eyes.

"The ego of the etheric body may be compared to the engineer who builds a motorcar; the ego of the astral body may be compared to the one who drives it; and the ego of the individual to the one who owns it."

Wisdom of Man, of the Soul, and of the Spirit, **Rudolf Steiner, Part III,** *The Wisdom of Man,* **Lecture III,** *Imagination— "Imagination"; Inspiration—Self-fulfillment; Intuition— Conscience,* **Berlin, December 15, 1909, GA 115**

[Imagination]
"How does imagination, first of all, penetrate consciousness? Well, we found it first on the side of the emotions, but there, though it enters consciousness, enters the soul, it does so primarily on the side of the emotions, not on the side of visualization. It is the same in the case of intuition. Intuition can enter the soul-life without providing the possibility of being visualized. Imagination, too, can occur without our being aware of it, in which case we have 'imagination' directly affecting the world of visualizations. Intuition, however, is to be found on the side of emotions...

[Inspiration]
"If we then endeavored to proceed through intuition, which sways the soul, we would not get very far; instead, we must proceed more from the other side, must try to develop imagination, to focus our attention on the imaginative world, in order not merely to wallow in emotions but to arrive at concrete images. If we do that, a sort of contact enters our life between intuition, which is not yet understood but rather felt, and imagination, which still floats in unreality and consists only of images. This contact finally enables us to ascend to the plane we can describe by saying that we have arrived among the beings who bring about spiritual events. Approaching these beings is what we call inspiration, and in a sense we have here the reverse of the processes confronting us in the outer corporeal world…

[Intuition]
"Now, that is the process that takes place in the case of *intuition*. We can put it this way. When we can grasp with our own consciousness something that comes to full expression within this consciousness—not merely as knowledge but as an event, a world event—we are dealing with intuition, or more precisely, with intuition in the higher sense, such as is meant in my book, *Knowledge of the Higher Worlds and Its Attainment.* Within intuition, then, we are dealing with the governing will. While that shrewd psychologist, Brentano, finds only emotions within the soul, not will, because the will does not exist for ordinary consciousness, it remains for the consciousness that transcends ordinary consciousness to find something that is a higher event. It is the point at which the world enters and plays a part in consciousness. That is, intuition…

"When this has been intensified to the point of its full potentiality in life, this transition reveals what we can call the human conscience. All stirrings of conscience occur at the transition from emotions to intuition. If we seek the location of conscience, we find it at this transition. The soul is really open laterally on the side of imagination and on that of intuition, but it is closed on the side where we encounter the impact, as it were, of outer corporeality through perception. It achieves a certain fulfillment in the realm of imagination, and another when it enters the realm of intuition—in the latter case through an event.

"Now, since imagination and intuition must live in one soul, how can a sort of mediation, a connection of the two, come about in this single soul? In imagination we have primarily a fulfilled image of the spiritual world, in intuition, an event that impinges out of the spiritual world. An event we encounter in the ordinary physical world is something that leaves us no peace, so to speak. We try to understand it, then we seek the essence underlying it. It is the same in the case of an event in the spiritual world that is to penetrate our consciousness. Let us consider this more closely. How does imagination first of all penetrate consciousness? Well, we found it first on the side of the emotions, but there, though it enters consciousness, enters the soul, it does so primarily on the side of the emotions, not on the side of visualization. It is the same in the case of intuition. Intuition can enter the soul life without providing the possibility of being visualized. Imagination, too, can occur without our being aware of it, in which case we have 'imagination' directly affecting the world of visualizations. Intuition, however, is to be found on the side of the emotions…

"If we then endeavored to proceed through intuition, which sways the soul, we would not get very far; instead, we must proceed more from the other side, must try to develop imagination, to focus our attention on the imaginative world, in order not merely to wallow in emotions but to arrive at concrete images. If we do that, a sort of contact enters our life between intuition, which is not yet understood but rather felt, and imagination, which still floats in unreality and consists only of images. This contact finally enables us to ascend to the plane we can describe by saying that we have arrived among the beings who bring about spiritual events. Approaching these beings is what we call inspiration, and in a sense we have here the reverse of the processes confronting us in the outer corporeal world.

"In confronting the outer corporeal world we have, so to speak, the thoughts we frame about objects. The objects are given, and we think about them. Here it is the event, the 'object', that appears in intuition primarily as emotion, so that imagination as such would remain in suspension. Not until the two unite, until intuition streams into imagination and visualizations are set free by imagination so that we feel imagination as coming to us from beings, not until then does the essence of the beings stream into us as an event, and what the imaginations have provided flows into intuition. We perceive in the event a content comparable to that of visualizations. These thoughts, for the perception of which imagination has prepared us, we then perceive by means of the event provided by intuition..."

Ralph Waldo Emerson, *Natural History of the Intellect: The Last Lectures of Ralph Waldo Emerson*, edited by Maurice York & Rick Spaulding, Wrightwood Press, Chicago, 2008

"Imagination is a spontaneous act; a perception and affirming of a real relation between a thought and some material fact. Whenever this resemblance is real, not playful, and is deep, or pointing at the causal identity, it is the act of Imagination. The very design of Imagination, this gift celestial, is to domesticate us in another nature. No faculty leads to the invisible world so readily as Imagination. Imagination transfigures, so that only the cosmic relations of the object are seen. Inspiration is very coy and capricious. We must lose many days to gain an Inspiration, and, in order to win infallible verdicts from the inner mind, we must indulge and humor it in every way. We know vastly more than we can digest."

"Happy beyond the common lot if he learns the secret, that besides the energy of his conscious intellect, his intellect is capable of new energy by abandonment to a higher influence; by unlocking at all risks his human doors and suffering the inundation of the ethereal tides to roll and circulate through him. This ecstasy, the old philosophers called an inebriation, and said that Intellect by its relation to what is prior to Intellect is a god. Nothing can be done except by this inspiration."

The Candle of Vision, by A. E. (George William Russell; 1918)

[Imagination]
"Imagination is not a vision of something which already exists, and which in itself must be unchanged in the act of seeing, but by imagination what exists in latency or essence is out-realized and is given a form in thought, and we can contemplate with full consciousness that which hitherto had been unrevealed, or only intuitionally surmised. In imagination there is a revelation of the self to the self, and a definite change in being, as there is in a vapor when a spark ignites it and it becomes an inflammation in the air. Here images appear in consciousness which we may refer definitely to an internal creator, with power to use or remold pre-existing forms, and endow them with life, motion, and voice…
(pgs. 66-67)

"…I asked the librarian who were the Gnostics and if there was a book which gave an account of their ideas. He referred me to a volume of Neander's *Church History*, and there, in the section dealing with the Sabaeans, I found the myth of the proud Aeon who mirrored himself in chaos and became the lord of our world. I believed then, and still believe, that the immortal in us has memory of all its wisdom, or, as Keats puts it in one of his letters, there is an ancestral wisdom in man and we can if we wish drink that old wine of heaven. This memory of the spirit is the real basis of imagination, and when it speaks to us we feel truly inspired and a mightier creature than ourselves speaks through us. I remember how pure, holy and beautiful these imaginations seemed, how they came like crystal water sweeping aside the muddy current of my life, and the astonishment I felt, I who was almost inarticulate, to find sentences which seemed noble and full of melody sounding in my brain as if another and greater than I had spoken them; and how strange it was also a little later to write without effort verse, which some people still think has beauty, while I could hardly, because my reason had then no mastery over the materials of thought, pen a prose sentence intelligently. I am convinced that all poetry is, as Emerson said, first written in the heavens, that is, it is conceived by a self deeper than appears in normal life, and when it speaks to us or tells us its ancient story we taste of eternity and drink the Soma juice, the elixir of immortality." (pgs. 74-76)

[Intuition]
"That sense of a divinity ever present, in act or thought my words do not communicate. The ecstatic, half-articulate, with broken words, can make us feel the kingdom of heaven is within him. I choose words with reverence but speak from recollection, and one day does not utter to another its own wisdom. Our highest moments in life are often those of which we hold thereafter the

vaguest memories. We may have a momentary illumination yet
retain almost as little of its reality as ocean keeps the track of a
great vessel which went over its waters. I remember incidents
rather than moods, vision more than ecstasy. How can I now,
passed away from myself and long at other labors, speak of what
I felt in those years when thought was turned to the spirit, and no
duty had as yet constrained me to equal outward effort? I came to
feel akin to

those ancestors of the Aryan in remote spiritual dawns when
Earth first extended its consciousness into humanity. In that
primal ecstasy and golden age was born that grand spiritual
tradition which still remains embodied in *Veda* and *Upanishad*,
in Persian and Egyptian myth, and which trails glimmering with
color and romance over our own Celtic legends. I had but a faint
glow of that which to the ancestors was full light. I could not
enter that Radiance they entered yet Earth seemed to me bathed
in an aether of Deity. I felt at times as one raised from the dead,
made virginal and pure, who renews exquisite intimacies with the
divine companions, with Earth, Water, Air and Fire. To breathe
was to inhale magical elixirs. To touch Earth was to feel the influx
of power as with one who had touched the mantle of the Lord.
Thought, from whatever it set out, forever led to the heavenly
city. But these feelings are incommunicable. We have no words
to express a thousand distinctions clear to the spiritual sense. If
I tell of my exaltation to another, who has not felt this himself,
it is explicable to that person as the joy in perfect health, and he
translates into lower terms what is the speech of the gods to men.

"I began writing desirous to picture things definitely to the
intellect and to speak only of that over which there could be
reason and argument but I have often been indefinite as when I
said in an earlier chapter that earth seemed an utterance of gods,

'Every flower was a thought. The trees were speech. The grass was speech. The winds were speech. The waters were speech.' But what does that convey? Many feel ecstasy at the sight of beautiful natural objects, and it might be said it does not interpret emotion precisely to make a facile reference to a divine world. I believe of nature that it is a manifestation of Deity, and that, because we are partakers in the divine nature, all we see has affinity with us; and though now we are as children who look upon letters before they have learned to read, to the illuminated spirit its own being is clearly manifested in the universe even as I recognize my thought in the words I write. Everything in nature has intellectual significance, and relation as utterance to the Thought out of which the universe was born, and we, whose minds were made in its image, who are the microcosm of the macrocosm, have in ourselves the key to unlock the meaning of that utterance. Because of these affinities the spirit swiftly by intuition can interpret nature to itself even as our humanity instinctively comprehends the character betrayed by the curve of lips or the mood which lurks within haunting eyes. We react in numberless ways to that myriad nature about us and within us, but we retain for ourselves the secret of our response, and for lack of words speak to others of these things only in generalities. I desire to be precise, and having searched memory for some instance of that divine speech made intelligible to myself which I could translate into words which might make it intelligible to others, I recollected something which may at least be understood if not accepted. It was the alphabet of the language of the gods.

"This was a definite exercise of intuition undertaken in order to evolve intellectual order out of a chaos of impressions and to discover the innate affinities of sound with idea, element, force, color and form, I found as the inner being developed it used a

symbolism of its own. Sounds, forms, and colors, which had an
established significance in the complicated artifice of our external
intercourse with each other, took on new meanings in the spirit
as if it spoke a language of its own and wished to impart it to the
infant Psyche. If these new meanings did not gradually reveal an
intellectual character to pursue this meditation, to encourage the
association of new ideas with old symbols would be to encourage
madness. Indeed, the partial uprising of such ideas, the fact that
a person associates a vowel with a certain color or a color with
a definite emotion is regarded by some as indicating incomplete
sanity. I tried to light the candle on my forehead to peer into
every darkness in the belief that the external universe of nature
had no more exquisite architecture than the internal universe of
being, and that the light could only reveal some lordlier chambers
of the soul, and whatever speech the inhabitant used must be
fitting for its own sphere, so I became a pupil of the spirit and
tried as a child to learn the alphabet at the knees of the gods."
(pgs. 112-116)

Pollen and Fragments, by Novalis (Georg Philipp Friedrich Freiherr von Hardenberg, May 2, 1772–March 25 1801)

[Imagination]
"The Imagination places the world of the future either far above
us, or far below, or in a relation of metempsychosis to ourselves.
The depths of our spirit are unknown to us. The mysterious way
leads inward."

Imagination, Inspiration, Intuition, and the Spiritual Hierarchy

Rudolf Steiner, *Towards the Deepening of Waldorf Education,* **Introductory remarks for the opening of** *The Study of Man,* **Stuttgart Teacher Conference, September 6, 1919**

"We wish to form our thoughts in such a way that we may be conscious that: Behind each of us stands his Angel, gently laying his hands on the head of each. This Angel gives you the strength which you need."

"Above your heads there sweep the circling Archangels. They carry from one to the other what each has to give to the other. They unite your souls. Thereby you are given the courage of which you stand in need. Out of this courage the Archangels form a chalice."

"The light of wisdom is given to us by the exalted beings of the Archai, who are not limited to the circling movements, but who, coming forth from primal beginnings, manifest themselves and disappear into primal distances. They reveal themselves only in form of a drop of light. Into the chalice of courage there falls this drop of light, enlightening our times, bestowed by the ruling Spirit of our Age."

Fifth Gospel, **Volume II, Rudolf Steiner, Lecture II, Cologne, December 18, 1913, GA 148**

"Let us take thought, that is, what we as humans think. At first these thoughts are in our consciousness, but not merely in our consciousness. At the same time, they are in the consciousness of the beings of the next higher hierarchy, the angeloi, the angels.

But whereas we may have one thought, *all* our thoughts are the angels' thoughts. The angels think our consciousness. Thus you can see that when we ascend to clairvoyance, we must develop a different feeling towards perceiving the beings of the higher worlds than is the case in ordinary reality. If we think as we do in the physical-sensory earthly existence, we cannot achieve higher clairvoyance. One must not merely think, one must also be thought, and be aware that one is being thought. It is not easy—for human words have not yet been devised to describe what the feeling about this perceiving is. But to use a comparison: we make all kinds of movements and if we don't observe these movements in ourselves, but in the eyes of another and see there the reflection of our own movements we say to ourselves: by observing in this way we know that we are doing this or that with our hands or with our facial expressions. One already has this feeling at the next stage of clairvoyance. We know in general that we are thinking; but we see ourselves [doing it] in the consciousness of the beings of the next higher hierarchy. We let the angels think our thoughts. We must realize that we are not conducting our thoughts, but that the beings of the next hierarchy are conducting them. We must feel the interweaving, undulating consciousness of the angels. We then receive information about the continuous impulse of evolution, for example about the truth of the Christ-impulse, how it continues to be active now. The angels can think this impulse; we humans can also think and describe it, if we devote our thoughts to the angels so they think in us. We can achieve this by continuous practice, as I described in my book *Knowledge of the Higher Worlds and its Attainment*. From a certain moment on we connect a feeling, a sensation with the words: *'Your soul doesn't think any more, it is a thought which the angels think.'* And when this becomes a truth for the individual human experience, we experience the thoughts about the truths of the Christ-impulse, also other thoughts about the wise guidance of Earth evolution.

"Those things related to the epochs of the Earth's evolution—the ancient Indian Period, the ancient Persian Period and so forth—are thought by the archangels. By means of further [meditative] practice we are able not only to be thought by the angels; but to be experienced by the archangels. You must then come to the point where you know that you are delivering your life to the life of the archangels. In *The Threshold of the Spiritual World* I go into this in more detail: how you have the feeling, when you continue the exercises—I also spoke about this in Munich, using a grotesque example—as if you were to stick your head in an anthill, and the ants are the thoughts in movement. Whereas in ordinary life we think that we think our thoughts, through practice we realize that the thoughts think in us, *because the angels think in us*. And continuing with practice we arrive at the feeling that we are brought to various regions of the world by the archangels and thus learn about those regions. To correctly describe the [ancient] Indian or Egyptian cultures one must understand the meaning of: '*Your soul has been brought to this or that time by an archangel.*' It is as though our life body fluids knew that they support the life process and are carried through the organism as the blood is. Thus the seer knows that he is conducted through the life process of the world by the archangels. But where individual experiences of the soul are concerned, they can only be investigated if the soul gives meaning to the words: *The soul delivers itself as food to the Archai, the spirits of personality.*

"What I just said sounds grotesque, but it is nevertheless true that one cannot investigate such concrete facts as the life of

Jesus of Nazareth before one gives meaning to the words: One is eaten as spiritual food and thus serves the Spirits of Personality. Obviously this sounds like madness to people who live in the outer world. Of course it does! Nevertheless it is just as true as the piece of bread that enters our stomachs becomes our food, and if it could think it would know that its existence has meaning and purpose in that we make it our food. It is just as true that we humans have the purpose of serving the Archai as food. While we walk around here on earth we are at the same time beings who are continually consumed, eaten by the Archai. You will not deny that people in ordinary life don't know this, and that they would call it madness if someone told them something like this. Man is for the Archai what a grain of wheat is for you as a physical human being. Don't only know this theoretically; but live in respect to the Archai as a grain of wheat would live were it to be ground to porridge by our teeth and pass through our pallets and stomach with the awareness: I am human food. Therefore also know: *I am the Archai's food, I am digested by the Archai; that is their life, which I live in them.* To vividly know this means to enter the consciousness of the Spirits of Personality, the Archai. Just as what it means to enter the consciousness of the Archangels when one knows: *Your soul is brought to this or that epoch by the Archangels*; and what it means to enter the consciousness of the Angels when one knows: *My thoughts are thought by the angels.* If we wish to enter the higher worlds, the conditions of experience must be different. It is necessary to be knowingly consumed by the Spirits of Personality if concrete facts such as the life of Jesus of Nazareth in human evolution are to be investigated…."

This means that higher research is not possible without inner pain and suffering. But where individual experiences of the soul are concerned, they can only be investigated if the soul gives meaning to the words: *'The soul delivers itself as food to the Archai, the spirits of personality.'*

Wisdom of Man, of the Soul, and of the Spirit, Part II, *The Wisdom of the Soul*, Rudolf Steiner, Lecture IV, *Consciousness and the Soul Life, (Psychosophy)*, November 4, 1909, GA 115

"It would take days to elaborate that in detail, but the riddles of consciousness will be solved and the whole peculiar nature of the soul life clarified if you start with the premise that the current of desire, love and hate comes to meet you out of the future, and meets the current of visualizations flowing out of the past into the future. At every moment you are actually in the midst of this encounter of the two streams, and considering that the present moment of your soul life consists of such a meeting, you will readily understand that these two currents overlap in your soul. *This overlapping is consciousness.*

"If at any moment of the present you search your conscious soul life, you will find there something that acts out of the past into the future and something that runs from the future into the past. Consciousness can be explained in no other way than by the overlapping of these two streams, and if you will visualize all the damming up that comes about here, you will see that the soul takes part in all that flows out of the past and in what streams to meet that current out of the future. Observing the conscious soul life at any given moment, you will see a certain interpenetration of these two streams. Here are all the conceptions you have brought along, there is everything that flows out of the future into the past, meeting the current of visualizations as interest, wishes, desire, and so forth.

"…Thus, we will designate the current of visualizations, flowing from the past into the future, 'the etheric body of the soul,' and the other, the current of desires, running from the future into the past, 'the astral body of the soul.'

"Consciousness is the meeting of the astral and etheric bodies. You can test this. Try to recall all that you have learned from the research of clairvoyant consciousness about the etheric and astral bodies, and to apply it here. You only need ask yourselves what brings about the damming up, the intersection of the two streams. The answer lies in the fact that the two currents meet in the physical body. Assume for the moment that the physical and etheric bodies were removed. What would happen? The current from the past to the future would be missing, and the other, the astral current, would have an unobstructed course. Now, that is exactly what occurs immediately after death, with the result that during the period of kamaloka consciousness runs backwards. Thus in following our psychosophic paths we rediscover what we learned by way of exact theosophy."

Truth as Cosmic Intelligence

The following summarized indications and quotes of Rudolf Steiner are derived from his lecture cycle entitled: *Metamorphoses of the Soul,* that tells us that the pursuit of truth is truly a pursuit of cosmic intelligence and cosmic consciousness, a type of communion with spiritual beings in non-physical realms. These realms of creative archetypes are similar to the world of archetypes described by the Greek philosophers. Greek philosophers believed that to contact a living archetype you first must spread your wings of soul and fly upward into that rarified realm; then, you could eat and drink the 'nectar' and 'ambrosia' of the gods which endow one with immortality and eternal youth.

Each spiritual truth, summarized and condensed below, is a living archetype that exists in a non-physical world that truth-seekers long to enter. Truth is a spiritual being who has power in the realms of soul and spirit, and also within the physical world; and therefore, is a living building-block in the spiritual body of the aspirant, as well as, the realms of soul and spirit. Truth is represented as the 'dew of heaven' of the Christians, the 'soma,' or 'Amrita' of the Hindus (Sanskrit Amṛta: 'immortality').

According to the ancient epic Hindu scriptures known as the *Mahabharata*, and also the Puranas, and elsewhere, under the direction of Vishnu the devas and asuras worked together for thousands of years to churn the 'Sea of Milk,' the 'churning of the Cosmic Ocean,' in order to obtain amrita, the 'elixir of immortal life.' It was said to be the cause of the conflict between the devas and asuras competing for this amrita the 'drink of immortality.' This amrita can be seen as an imagination of that which is immortal that arises as the ultimate fruit of human activity that will be carried on after Earth evolution.

This vision of truth is also represented the 'Golden Apples of Hesperides' of the Greeks, the 'Golden Bough' of the Hyperboreans, the Hieroglyphic Monad of the Universe, the Norse draught of wisdom from Mímir's head, and the key to the Temple of Wisdom, among other things. There is no end to the appellations of truth. Truth comes from the hierarchical rank of the Kyriotetes, the Spirits of Wisdom. Truth/Wisdom is what orders the entire Cosmos and empowers life in all things great and small. Wisdom is called many names throughout all religions and beliefs and is known as a female Goddess. Her name, Sophia, is the usual way she is referred to in Western Esoteric traditions. Rudolf Steiner calls her, Anthroposophia. The Roman Catholic Church calls her the Holy Spirit, the 'Spirit of Truth,' the 'Comforter' (Paraclete; Greek: Paráklētos) a term that occurs five times in the Johannine texts of the *New Testament* and is often translated as 'advocate,' 'counsellor,' or 'helper.' The great Parthian initiate Mani, the founder of Manichaeism in the 3rd Century A.D. often referred to himself as one of the manifestations of the Paraclete.

The aspirant can take these comprehensive lists of cosmological truths by Rudolf Steiner offered below, and use them as content for concentration, contemplation, meditation, prayer, and as a ladder of moral training that is like a 'Jacob's Ladder' into moral spiritual worlds—the seven heavens. Simply reading, speaking, visualizing, and embodying these truths will advance the aspirant on the quest for spiritual communion with higher beings and the awakening of their own spiritual nature. Truth is like turning on a light that illuminates the path of spiritual development. This path, in the East, is called Sūtrayāna, is the Indo-Tibetan three-fold classification of yānas. A yāna is a Buddhist practice leading to the realization of emptiness. The three yānas of the Sūtrayāna are Śrāvakayāna or Pratyekabuddhayāna, Mahāyāna, and Vajrayāna. This is a path whereby the aspirant spends many years refining their astral body of desires and their etheric body of habits into a continuous practice of thinking, breathing, and living moral principles.

Metamorphoses of the Soul, Paths of Experience, Volume I, Rudolf Steiner, Lecture III, *The Mission of Truth*, Berlin, October 22, 1909, GA 58

"The love of truth is the only love that sets the Ego free and stops self-seeking."

"Truth should be loved and valued from the start."

"An inward cultivation of truth is essential for the progress of the soul."

"A higher truth must be the aim of man's endeavor, while he treats anger as an enemy to be increasingly abolished. He must love truth and feel himself most intimately united with it."

"When the nature of truth stirs the soul to strive for it, the soul can be impelled to rise from stage to stage. Since there is this everlasting search for truth, and since truth is so manifold in meaning, all we can reasonably say is that man must set out to grasp truth and to kindle in himself a genuine sense of truth. Hence we cannot speak of a single, all-embracing truth."

"By cultivating a sense of truth in his inner life man will be imbued with a progressive power that leads him to selflessness."

"Truth is best served when the seeker leaves himself out of the reckoning."

"It is just when a man lovingly immerses himself in his own soul that his soul is strengthened and an ascent to higher stages of the Ego comes within reach. The outstanding element that the soul may love within itself, leading not to egoism but to selflessness, is truth. Truth educates the Intellectual Soul. While anger is an attribute of the soul that must be overcome if a man is to rise to higher stages, truth should be loved and valued from the start. An inward cultivation of truth is essential for the progress of the soul."

"The first condition for acquiring a genuine sense of truth is that we should get away from ourselves, get away from our individual outlooks, and see clearly how much depends on our personal point-of-view."

"The most varied opinions concerning truth are advanced because men have not recognized to what extent their views are restricted by their personal standpoints."

"That is the essential thing: that we should seek for truth as something to be found only in our own deepest being; and should know that truth ever and again draws men together, because from the innermost depth of every human soul its light shines forth."

"Love of truth is the only love that sets the Ego free. And directly man gives priority to anything else, he falls inevitably into self-seeking. Herein lies the great and most serious importance of truth for the education of the human soul. Truth conforms to no man, and only by devotion to truth can truth be found. Directly man prefers himself and his own opinions to the truth, he becomes anti-social and alienates himself from the human community. Look at people who make no attempt to love truth for its own sake but parade their own opinions as the truth: they care for nothing but the content of their own souls and are the most intolerant. Those who love truth in terms of their own views and opinions will not suffer anyone to reach truth along a quite different path. They put every obstacle in the way of anyone with different abilities, who comes to opinions unlike their own. Hence the conflicts that so often arise in life. An honest striving for truth leads to human understanding, but the love of truth for the sake of one's own personality leads to intolerance and the destruction of other people's freedom."

"That is the mission of truth: to become the object of increasing love and care and devotion on our part. Inasmuch as we devote ourselves inwardly to truth, our true self gains in strength and will enable us to cast off self-interest. Anger weakens us; truth strengthens us."

"Truth is a stern goddess; she demands to be at the center of a unique love in our souls. If man fails to get away from himself and his desires and prefers something else to her, she takes immediate revenge…"

"Truth conforms to no man, and only by devotion to truth can truth be found. Directly man prefers himself and his own opinions to the truth, he becomes anti-social and alienates himself from the human community. Look at people who make no attempt to love truth for its own sake but parade their own opinions as the truth: they care for nothing but the content of their own souls and are the most intolerant."

"Truth is experienced in the Intellectual Soul. It can be sought for and attained through personal effort only by beings capable of thought. Inasmuch as truth is acquired by thinking, we must realize very clearly that there are two kinds of truth. First we have the truth that comes from observing the world of Nature around us and investigating it bit by bit in order to discover its truths, laws, and wisdom. When we contemplate the whole range of our experience of the world in this way, we come to the kind of truth that can be called the truth derived from 'reflective' thinking—we first observe the world and then think about our findings."

"There are also other truths. These cannot be gained by reflective thought, but only by going beyond everything that can be learnt from the outer world. In ordinary life we can see at once that when a man constructs a tool or some other instrument, he has to formulate laws that are not part of the outer world. For example, no-one could learn from the outer world how to construct a clock, for the laws of Nature are not so arranged as to provide for the appearance of clocks as a natural product. That is a second kind of truth: we come to it by thinking out something not given to us by observation or experience of the outer world. Hence there are these two kinds of truth, and they must be kept strictly apart, one derived from reflective thought and the other from 'creative' thought."

"The wisdom of Nature is directly creative and gives rise to the reality of Nature in all its fullness, but the truth we derive from thinking about Nature is only a passive image; in our thinking it has lost its power. We may indeed acquire a wide, open-minded picture of natural truth, but the creative, productive element is absent from it. Hence the immediate effect of this picture of truth on the development of the human Ego is desolating. The creative power of the Ego is crippled and devitalized; the Self loses strength and can no longer stand up to the world, if it is concerned only with reflective thoughts. Nothing else does so much to isolate the Ego, to make it withdraw into itself and look with hostility on the world. A man can become a cold egoist if he is intent only on investigating the outer world. Why does he want this knowledge? Does he mean to place it at the service of the Gods?

"If a man desires only this kind of truth, he wants it for himself, and he will be on the way to becoming a cold egoist and misogynist in later life. He will become a recluse or will sever himself from mankind in some other way, for he wants to possess the content of the world as his own truth. All forms of seclusion and hostility towards humanity can be found on this path. The soul becomes increasingly dried up and loses its sense of human fellowship. It becomes ever more impoverished, although the truth should enrich it. Whether a man turns into a recluse or a one-sided eccentric makes no difference; in both cases a hardening process will overtake his soul. Hence we see that the more a man confines himself to this kind of reflective thought, the less fruitful his soul will be. Let us try to understand why this is so.

"Consider the realms of nature and suppose that we have before us an array of plants. They have been formed by the living wisdom which calls forth their inherent productive power. Now an artist comes along. His soul receives the picture that Nature sets before him. He does not merely think about it; he opens himself to Nature's productive power and lets it work upon him. He creates a work of art which does not embody merely an act of thinking; it is imbued with productive power. Then comes someone who tries to get behind the picture and to extract a thought from it. He ponders over it. In this way its reality is filtered and impoverished. Now try to carry this process further. Once the soul has extracted a thought from the picture, it has finished with it. Nothing more can be done except to formulate thoughts about the thought—an absurd procedure which soon dries up.

"It is quite different with creative thinking. Here a man is himself productive. His thoughts take form as realities in outer life; here he is working after the example of Nature herself. That is how it is with a man who goes beyond mere observation and reflective thinking and allows something not to be gained from observation to arise in his soul. All spiritual-scientific truths require a productive disposition in the soul. In the case of these truths all mere reflective thinking is bad and leads to deception. But the truths attainable by creative thought are limited, for man is weak in the face of the creative wisdom of the world. There is no end to the things from which we can derive truths by reflective thought; but creative thought, although the field open to it is restricted, brings about a heightening of productive power; the soul is refreshed and its scope extended. Indeed, the soul becomes more and more inwardly divine, in so far as it reflects in itself an essential element of the divine creative activity in the world.

"So we have these two distinct kinds of truth, one reached by creative thought, the other by reflective thought. This latter kind, derived from the investigation of existent things or current experience, will always lead to abstractions; under its influence the soul is deprived of nourishment and tends to dry up. The truth that is not gained from immediate experience is creative; its strength helps man to find a place in the world where he can co-operate in shaping the future.

"The past can be approached only by reflective thought, while creative thought opens a way into the future. Man thus becomes a responsible creator of the future. He extends the power of his Ego into the future, in so far as he comes to possess not merely the truths derived from the past by reflective thinking, but also those that are gained by creative thinking and point towards the future."

Truth, Beauty, and Goodness, Rudolf Steiner, Dornach, January 19, 1923, GA 220

"When this true morality develops into momentous impulses of will which then pass to reality in moral acts, it begins to be a quickening, all-pervading impulse in the soul, inasmuch as a man can then be moved to real sympathy at the sight of care on the face of another—his own astral body feels pain at the sight of suffering in others. For just as the sense of Truth manifests in man's right relation to the physical body; just as a warm enthusiasm for Beauty expresses itself in the etheric body—so does Goodness live in the astral body. And the astral body cannot be healthy, or maintain its true position in the world, if man is not able to pour through it the forces proceeding from Goodness.

"Truth, then, is related to the physical body, Beauty to the etheric body, Goodness to the astral body. Here we have the concrete reality of the three abstractions of Truth, Beauty, Goodness. In short, we can relate to the actual being of man all that is expressed instinctively in these three ideals.

"These ideals show us how far man is able to fulfill his whole human nature, when, to begin with, as he lives in his physical body, he is filled with a real sense of truth instead of conventional opinions. Again, full 'humanity' is only afforded a worthy existence when a man can quicken his etheric body into life through his feeling for beauty. Indeed, he who is incapable of being moved at the sight of beauty to somewhat the same degree as the Greek, does not possess a true sense of beauty. One can merely gaze at beauty, or one can experience it. Today it is the case that most people only gaze, and this does not necessarily energize anything in the etheric body. To gaze at beauty is not to experience it. The moment we experience beauty, however, the etheric body is quickened...

"To be true is to be rightly united with our spiritual past. To sense beauty means that in the physical world we do not disown our connection with spirit. To be good is to build a living seed for a spiritual world in the future.

"Past, present, future—these three concepts, as they play their part in human life, assume far-reaching significance when we understand the concrete reality of the other three concepts—Truth, Beauty, Goodness.

"The man who is untruthful denies his spiritual past; the liar severs the threads between himself and his spiritual past. He who disregards beauty is building himself an abode on earth where the sun of spirit never shines, where he wanders in spiritless shadow. The man who belies the good renounces his spiritual future; and yet he would like this future to be bestowed on him, may be by means of some outer remedy.

"It was, indeed, out of a profound instinct that Truth, Beauty, and Goodness were held to be the greatest ideals of human striving. Yet they have faded away into shadowy words, and it is only our present age that can bestow concrete reality upon them."

Wisdom of Man, of the Soul, and of the Spirit, **Part III, Rudolf Steiner,** *The Wisdom of the Spirit*, **Lecture II,** *Truth and Error in the Light of the Spiritual World*, **December 13, 1911, GA 115**

"…Certainly it is possible to transcend the world that is primarily revealed by outer perception; the human being can build up a world of truth in his own inner being, and he could never be satisfied with what the outer world of perception has to give for the simple reason that he is a human being. Thus, he builds a world of truth within himself.

"If we examine this world of truth seriously, we find that it comprises something that already transcends all that is external-physical as such. One then cites ideas produced by man about the world—grand, comprehensive points of view that never could have originated through the outer senses alone, and that must have come, therefore, from the other side. Thus, the fact of the world of truth is in itself sufficient to convince us that we participate in a spirit world and live in it with our truth Naturally, a philosopher like Hegel, for instance, would find plenty of justification for a spiritual world, as opposed to the objection set forth—justification for recognizing a spiritual world that embraces thinking as well, in so far as thinking is independent of the senses. Philosophers whose whole disposition equips them to recognize the absolutely independent world of truth will find in this independent activity of the spirit, moving as it does in truth, sufficient reason for assuming the existence of the spirit. It can be said, then, that there will always be people in the world in whose view the concrete actuality of the true world of ideas is sufficient proof of the spirit. In a certain sense it can be said that even in Aristotle something like faith is discernible, faith that in his concepts and ideas, in the *nous,* as he calls it, man lives in a spiritual world, and because it exists in man, it exists, and is thereby sufficiently substantiated."

Anthroposophical Ethics, **Rudolf Steiner, Lecture III, Norrköping, May 30, 1912, GA 155**

"The gods once gave wisdom to the unconscious human soul, so that it possessed this wisdom instinctively, whereas now we have first to learn the truths about the Cosmos and about human evolution. The ancient customs were also fashioned after the thoughts of the gods.

"We have the right view of Anthroposophy when we look upon it as the investigations of the thoughts of the gods. In former times these flowed instinctively into man, but now we have to investigate them, to make the knowledge of them our own. In this sense Anthroposophy must be sacred to us; we must be able to consider reverently that the ideas imparted to us are really something divine, and something which we human beings are allowed to think and reflect upon as the divine thoughts according to which the world has been ordered... But we only assume the right attitude towards it when we say: The thoughts we seek are the thoughts wherewith the gods have guided evolution. We think the evolution of the gods. If we understand this correctly, we are overwhelmed by something that is deeply moral. This is inevitable. Then we say: In ancient times man had instinctive wisdom from the gods, who gave him the wisdom according to which they fashioned the world, and morality thus became possible. But through Anthroposophy we now acquire this wisdom consciously. Therefore, we may also trust that in us it shall be transformed into moral impulses, so that we do not merely receive anthroposophical wisdom, but a moral stimulus as well.

"Now into what sort of moral impulses will the wisdom acquired through Anthroposophy be transformed? We must here touch upon a point whose development the anthroposophist can foresee, the profound moral significance and moral weight of which he even ought to foresee, a point of development which is far removed from what is customary at the present time; which is what Plato called the 'ideal of wisdom.' He named it with a word which was in common use when man still possessed the ancient wisdom, and it would be well to replace this by the word *truth*; for as we have now become more individual, we have withdrawn ourselves from the divine, and must therefore strive back to it. We must learn to feel the full weight and meaning of the word 'truth,' and this in a moral sense will be a result of an anthroposophical world conception and conviction. Anthroposophists must understand how important it is to be filled with the moral element of truth in an age when materialism has advanced so far that one may indeed still speak of truth, but when the general life and understanding is far removed from perceiving what is right in this direction. Nor can this be otherwise at the present time; as owing to a certain quality acquired by modern life, truth is something which must, to a great extent, be lacking in the understanding of the day, I ask what does a man feel today when in the newspapers or some other printed matter he finds certain information, and afterwards it transpires that it is simply untrue? I seriously ask you to ponder over this. One cannot say that it happens in every case, but one must assert that it probably happens in every fourth case. Untruthfulness has everywhere become a quality of the age; it is impossible to describe truth as a characteristic of our times.

"For instance, take a man whom you know to have written or said something false, and place the facts before him. As a rule, you will find that he does not fear such a thing to be wrong. He will immediately make the excuse: 'But I said it in good faith.' Anthroposophists must not consider it moral when a person says it is merely incorrect what he has said in good faith. People will learn to understand more and more, that they must first ascertain that what they assert really happened. No man should make a statement or impart anything to another until he has exhausted every means to ascertain the truth of his assertions; and it is only when he recognizes this obligation that he can perceive truth as moral impulse. And then when someone has either written or said something that is incorrect, he will no longer say: 'I thought it was so, said it in good faith, for he will learn that it is his duty to express not merely what he thinks is right, but it is also his duty to say only what is true, and correct. To this end, a radical change must gradually come about in our cultural life. The speed of travel, the lust of sensation on the part of man, everything that comes with a materialistic age, is opposed to truth. In the sphere of morality, Anthroposophy will be an educator of humanity to the duty of truth.

"My business today is not to say how far truth has been already realized in the Anthroposophical Society, but to show that what I have said must be a principle, a lofty anthroposophical ideal. The moral evolution within the movement will have enough to do if the moral ideal of truth is thought, felt, and perceived in all directions, for this ideal must be what produces the virtue of the Sentient-Soul of man in the right way.

"The second part of the soul of which we have to speak in Anthroposophy is what we usually call the Mind-Soul, or Intellectual-Soul *Gemütsseele*. You know that it developed especially in the fourth Post-Atlantean, or Graeco-Latin Period. [747 B.C.-1,414 A.D.] The virtue which is the particular emblem for this part of the soul is bravery, valor and courage; we have already dwelt on this many times, and also on the fact that foolhardiness and cowardice are its extremes. Courage, bravery, valor is the mean between foolhardiness and cowardice. The German word *gemüt* expresses in the sound of the word that it is related to this. The word *gemüt* indicates the mid-part of the human soul, the part that is *mutvoll*, full of *mut*, courage, strength and force.

"This was the second, the middle virtue of Plato and Aristotle. It is that virtue which in the fourth Post-Atlantean Period still existed in man as a divine gift, while wisdom was really only instinctive in the third [3rd Post-Atlantean Period; 2,907 B.C.-747 B.C.]. Instinctive valor and bravery existed as a gift of the gods (you may gather this from the first lecture) among the people who, in the fourth Period, met the expansion of Christianity to the north. They showed that among them valor was still a gift of the gods. Among the Chaldeans wisdom, the wise penetration into the secrets of the starry world, existed as a divine gift, as something inspired. Among the people of the fourth Post-Atlantean Period, there existed valor and bravery, especially among the Greeks and Romans; but it existed also among the peoples whose work it became to spread Christianity. This instinctive valor was lost later than instinctive wisdom.

"If we look round us now in the fifth Post-Atlantean Period [1,414 A.D.-3,574 A.D.], we see that, as regards valor and bravery, we are in the same position in respect of the Greeks as the Greeks were to the Chaldeans and Egyptians in regard to wisdom. We look back to what was a divine gift in the age immediately preceding ours, and in a certain way we can strive for it again. However, the two previous lectures have shown us that in connection with this effort a certain transformation must take place. We have seen the transformation in Francis of Assisi of that divine gift which manifested itself as bravery and valor. We saw that the transformation came about as the result of an inner moral force which in our last lecture we found to be the force of the Christ-impulse; the transformation of valor and bravery into true love. But this true love must be guided by another virtue, by the interest in the being to whom we turn our love. In his *Timon of Athens* Shakespeare shows how love, or warmth of heart, causes harm, when it is passionately manifested; when it appears merely as a quality of human nature without being guided by wisdom and truth. A man is described who gave freely of his possessions, who squandered his living in all directions. Liberality is a virtue, but Shakespeare also shows us that nothing but parasites are produced by what is squandered.

"Just as ancient valor and bravery were guided from the Mysteries by the European Brahmins—those wise leaders who kept themselves hidden in the background—so also in human nature this virtue must accord with and be guided by interest. Interest, which connects us with the external world in the right way, must lead and guide us when, with our love, we turn to the world. Fundamentally this may be seen from the characteristic and striking example of Francis of Assisi. The sympathy he expressed was not obtrusive or offensive. Those who overwhelm others with their sympathy are by no means always actuated by the right moral impulses. And how many there are who will not receive anything that is given out of pity. But to approach another with, understanding is not offensive. Under some circumstances a person must needs refuse to be sympathized with; but the attempt to understand his nature is something to which no reasonable person can object. Hence also the attitude of another person cannot be blamed or condemned if his actions are determined by this principle.

"It is understanding which can guide us with respect to this second virtue: Love. It is that which, through the Christ-impulse, has become the special virtue of the mind-soul or intellectual-soul; it is the virtue which may be described as human love accompanied by human understanding. Sympathy in grief and joy is the virtue which in the future must produce the most beautiful and glorious fruits in human social life, and, in one who rightly understands the Christ-impulse, this sympathy and this love will originate quite naturally, it will develop into feeling. It is precisely through the anthroposophical understanding of the Christ-impulse that it will become feeling.

"Through the Mystery of Golgotha Christ descended into earthly evolution; His impulses, His activities are here now, they are everywhere. Why did He descend to this Earth? In order that through what He has to give to the world, evolution may go forward in the right way. Now that the Christ-impulse is in the world, if through what is immoral, if through lack of interest in our fellowmen, we destroy something, then we take away a portion of the world into which the Christ-impulse has flowed. Thus, because the Christ-impulse is now here, we directly destroy something of it. But if we give to the world what can be given to it through virtue, which is creative, we build. We build through self-surrender. It is not without reason that it has often been said, that Christ was first crucified on Golgotha, but that He is crucified again and again through the deeds, of man. Since Christ has entered into the Earth development through the deed upon Golgotha, we, by our immoral deeds, by our unkindness and lack of interest, add to the sorrow and pain inflicted upon Him.

Therefore, it has been said, again and again: Christ is crucified anew as long as immorality, unkindness and lack of interest exist. Since the Christ-impulse has permeated the world, it is this which is made to suffer.

"Just as it is true that through evil, which is destructive, we withdraw something from the Christ-impulse and continue the crucifixion upon Golgotha, it is also true that when we act out of love, in all cases where we use love, we add to the Christ-impulse, we help to bring it to life.

"Inasmuch as ye have done *it* unto one of the least of these My brethren, ye have done *it* unto Me." (*Matthew* 25:40), this is the most significant statement of love, and this statement must become the most profound moral impulse if it is once anthroposophically understood. We do this when with understanding we confront our fellowmen and offer them something in our actions, our virtue, our conduct towards them which is conditioned by our understanding of their nature. Our attitude towards our fellowmen is our attitude towards the Christ-impulse itself.

"It is a powerful moral impulse, something which is a real foundation for morals, when we feel: 'The Mystery of Golgotha was accomplished for all men, and an impulse has thence spread abroad throughout the whole world. When you are dealing with your fellowmen, try to understand them in their special, characteristics of race, color, nationality, religious faith, philosophy, etc. If you meet them and do this or that to them, you do it to Christ. Whatever you do to men, in the present condition of the Earth's evolution, you do to Christ.' This statement:—

"Inasmuch as ye have done *it* unto one of the least of these My brethren, ye have done *it* unto Me." (*Matthew* 25:40) will at the same time become a mighty moral impulse to the man who understands the fundamental significance of the Mystery of Golgotha. So that we may say: Whereas the gods of pre-Christian times gave instinctive wisdom to man, instinctive valor and bravery, so now love streams down from the symbol of the cross, the love which is based upon the mutual interest of man in man.

"Thereby the Christ-impulse will work powerfully in the world. On the day when it comes about that the Brahmin not only loves and understands the Brahmin, the Pariah the Pariah, the Jew the Jew, and the Christian the Christian; but when the Jew is able to understand the Christian, the Pariah the Brahmin, the American the Asiatic, as man, and put himself in his place, then one will know how deeply it is felt in a Christian way when we say: 'All men must feel themselves to be brothers, no matter what their religious creed may be.' We ought to consider what otherwise binds us as being of little value. Father, mother, brother, sister, even one's own life one ought to value less than that which speaks from one human soul to the other. He who, in this sense does not regard as base all that impairs the connection with the Christ-impulse cannot be Christ's disciple. The Christ-impulse balances and compensates human differences. Christ's disciple is one who regards mere human distinctions as being of little account, and clings to the impulse of love streaming forth from the Mystery of Golgotha, which in this respect we perceive as a renewal of what was given to mankind as original virtue.

"We have now but to consider what may be spoken of as the virtue of the Consciousness- or Spiritual-Soul. When we consider the fourth Post-Atlantean Period, we find that Temperance or Moderation was still instinctive. Plato and Aristotle called it the chief virtue of the Spiritual-Soul. Again they comprehended it as a state of balance, as the mean of what exists in the Spiritual-Soul. The Spiritual-Soul consists in man's becoming conscious of the external world through his bodily nature. The sense body is primarily the instrument of the Spiritual-Soul, and it is also the sense body through which man arrives at self-consciousness.

"Therefore, the sense-body of man must be preserved. If it were not preserved for the mission of the Earth, then that mission could not be fulfilled. *But here also there is a limit.* If a man only used all the forces he possessed in order to enjoy himself, he would shut himself up in himself, and the world would lose him. The man who merely enjoys himself, who uses all his forces merely to give himself pleasure, cuts himself off from the world—so thought Plato and Aristotle—*the world loses him.* And he, who denies himself everything renders himself weaker and weaker, and is finally laid hold of by the external world-process and is crushed by the outer world. For he who goes beyond the forces appropriate to him as man, he who goes to excess is laid hold of by the world-process and is lost in it.

"Thus, what man has developed for the building up of the Spiritual-Soul can be dissolved, so that he comes into the position of losing the world. Temperance, or Moderation, is the virtue which enables man to avoid these extremes. Temperance implies neither asceticism nor gluttony, but the happy mean between these two; and this is the virtue of the Spiritual-Soul. Regarding this virtue we have not yet progressed beyond the instinctive standpoint. A little reflection will teach you that, on the whole, people are very much given to sampling the two extremes. They swing to and fro between them. Leaving out of account the few who at the present day endeavor to gain clear views on this subject, you will find that the majority of people live very much after a particular pattern. In Central Europe this is often described by saying: There are people in Berlin who eat and drink to excess the entire winter, and then in summer they go to Carlsbad in order to remove the ill-effects produced by months of intemperance, thus going from one extreme to the other. Here you have the tipping of the scale, first to one side and then to the other. This is only a radical case. It is very evident that though the foregoing is extreme, and not universal to any great extent, still the oscillation between enjoyment and deprivation exists everywhere. People themselves ensure that there is excess on one side, and then they get the physicians to prescribe a so-called lowering system of cure, that is, the other extreme, in order that the ill effects may be repaired.

"From this, it will be seen that in this respect people are still in an instinctive condition, that there is still an instinctive feeling, which is a kind of divine gift, not to go too far in one direction or another. But just as the other instinctive qualities of man were lost, these, too, will be lost with the transition from the fifth to the sixth Post-Atlantean Period. [Spirit-Self; 3,574 A.D.-5,734 A.D.] This quality which is still possessed as a natural tendency will be lost; and now you will be able to judge how much the anthroposophical world conception and conviction will have to contribute in order gradually to develop consciousness in this field.

"At the present time there are very few, even developed anthroposophists, who see clearly that Anthroposophy provides the means to gain the right consciousness in this field also. When Anthroposophy is able to bring more weight to bear in this direction, then will appear what I can only describe in the following way: people will gradually long more and more for great spiritual truths. Although Anthroposophy is still scorned today, it will not always be so. It will spread, and overcome all its external opponents, and everything else still opposing it, and anthroposophists will not be satisfied by merely preaching Universal Love. It will be understood that one cannot acquire Anthroposophy in one day, any more than a person can take sufficient nourishment in one day to last the whole of his life. Anthroposophy has to be acquired to an ever-increasing extent. It will come to pass that in the Anthroposophical Movement it will not be so often stated that these are our principles, and if we have these principles then we are anthroposophists; for the feeling and experience of standing in a community of the living element in anthroposophy will extend more and more."

Goethe's Conception of the World, **Rudolf Steiner**, *The Position of Goethe in the Evolution of Western Thought*, **Chapter V,** *Personality and View of the World*, **GA 6**

"Truth appears to the individual person in an individual garb."

"Subjective experiences assume different forms in different men. For those who do not believe in the objective nature of the inner world this is another reason for denying that man has the capacity to penetrate to the true essence of things. For how can that be the essence of things which appears in one way to one man and in another way to another man? For those who penetrate to the true nature of the inner world the only consequence of the diversity of inner experiences is that Nature is able to express her abundant content in different ways. Truth appears to the individual man in an individual garb. It adapts itself to the particular nature of his personality. More especially is this the case with the highest truths, truths that are of the greatest significance for man. In order to acquire these truths man carries over his most intimate spiritual experiences and with them at the same time the particular nature of his personality, to the world he has perceived.

There are also truths of general validity which every man accepts without imparting to them any individual coloring. But these are the most superficial, the most trivial. They correspond to the common generic character of men, which is the same in them all. Certain attributes which are similar in all men give rise to similar judgments about objects. The way in which men view phenomena according to measure and number is the same in everyone— therefore all find the same mathematical truths. In the attributes, however, which distinguish the single personality from the common generic character, there also lies the foundation for the individual formulation of truth. The essential point is not that the truth appears in one man in a different form than in another, but that all the individual forms that make their appearance belong to one single Whole, the uniform ideal world. In the inner being of individual men truth speaks in different tongues and dialects; in every great man it speaks a particular language communicated to this one personality alone. But it is always the one truth that is speaking. 'If I know my relationship to myself and to the external world, I call it truth. And so, each one can have his own truth, and it is nevertheless always the same.'—This is Goethe's view. Truth is not a rigid, dead system of concepts that is only capable of assuming one single form; truth is a living ocean in which the spirit of man dwells, and it is able to display on its surface waves of the most diverse form. 'Theory *per se* is useless except in so far as it makes us believe in the connection of phenomena,' says Goethe. A theory that is supposed to be conclusive once and for all and purports in this form to represent an eternal truth, has no value for Goethe. He wants *living* concepts by means of which the spirit of the single man can connect the perceptions together in accordance with his individual nature. To know the truth means, to Goethe, to live in the truth. And to live in the truth means nothing else than that in the consideration of each single object man perceives what particular inner experience comes into play when he confronts this object. Such a view of human cognition cannot speak of boundaries to knowledge, nor of a limitation to knowledge consequential upon the nature of man. For the questions which, according to this view, man raises in knowledge, are not derived from the objects; neither are they imposed upon man by some other power outside his personality. They are derived from the nature of the personality itself. When man directs his gaze to an object there arises within him the urge to see more than confronts him in the perception. And so far as this urge extends, so far does he feel the need for knowledge. Whence does this urge originate? It can indeed only originate from the fact that an inner experience feels itself impelled within the soul to enter into union with the perception. As soon as the union is accomplished the need for knowledge is also satisfied. The will-to-know is a demand of human nature and not of the objects. They can impart to man no more of their being than he demands from them. Those who speak of a limitation of the faculty of cognition do not know whence the need for knowledge is derived. They believe that the content of truth is lying preserved somewhere or other and that there lives in man nothing but the vague wish to discover the way to the place where it is preserved. But it is the being of the things itself that works itself out in the inner being of man and passes on to where it belongs: to the perception. Man does not strive in the cognitive process for some hidden element but for the equilibration of two forces that work upon him from two sides. One may well say that without man there would be no knowledge of the inner being of things, for without man there would exist nothing through which this inner being could express itself. But it cannot be said that there is something in the inner being of things that is inaccessible to man. Man only knows that there exists something more in the things than perception gives, because this other element lives in his own inner being. To speak of a further unknown element in objects is to spin words about something that does not exist."

The Riddle of Humanity, Rudolf Steiner, Lecture X, Dornach, August 21, 1916, GA 170

"Human knowledge has lost the power to formulate any criterion of truth or a feeling for one's capacity to produce the truth. In earlier times, one believed in the human capacity to arrive at truths by means of judgements based on inner experience…

"…So we see that there was a tendency for the old criteria of truth to break down and for truth to be measured against life. Formerly it was believed that life should be shaped in accordance with the truth, so life was put in the service of truth. What one meant by truth in the old sense did not include fictions, not even useful fictions. But, according to the extraordinary definition of the *Philosophy of As If*, truth is the most comfortable form of error. For, although there is nothing else but error, some errors are more agreeable and others less agreeable. The fact that what we call truths are simply the more agreeable errors is something we must clearly understand."

Universe, Earth and Man, Rudolf Steiner, Lecture VIII, *Man's Connection with the Various Planetary Bodies, The Earth's Mission*, August 12, 1908, GA 105

[Introduction by Marie Steiner]
"The mission of our age is to bring forth not an ancient wisdom, but a new wisdom, one that points not only to the past but that works prophetically into the future."

[Rudolf Steiner]
"Herein we see how Universe and Earth, how fixed star and planet, are spiritually in touch with each other, and we learn not only to look at what is in our environment in the physical world, but we also gain an inkling of how those who partake of Inspiration ascend to the Sun."

"There is a still higher state of consciousness, which, in the true sense of the word, we call Intuition; through it humanity can creep within the very nature of things. This is more than inspirational consciousness; here a person sinks themself into beings and identifies themself with those beings. This leads humanity still further. Where does inspirational consciousness lead humanity? It leads humanity to where they feel at one with the Earth planet; for the egos of the plants are in the center of the Earth. When humanity perceives the Sun's tone, they become one with the planetary being that dwells in the center of the Earth; they become one with the planet and thus can also become one with all other beings. Humanity can then go through experiences that reach far beyond our solar system; their vision is extended from solar system-consciousness to cosmic-consciousness known as intuition which carries them beyond the several solar systems."

"Thus, we see that in the mineral kingdom we have something which in a homogeneous form furnishes us with a basis that extends far beyond our ordinary existence. We see that the present human form is a physical Earthly form, but that humanity will raise themself once more from ordinary Earthly consciousness to planetary-consciousness through imagination; to solar system-consciousness through inspiration; to cosmic-consciousness through intuition."

"America is to have a different form of Anthroposophy, and while it is presently woody and asleep, one should look to Emerson and his friends to understand it."

Rudolf Steiner on the Celestial Hierarchies

The Spiritual Hierarchies described by Rudolf Steiner, and many others, are nine ranks of Spiritual Beings who work together as one being with three parts—the first, second, and third ranks of hierarchies. The Holy Trinity works through the 'threefold' set of hierarchical beings as the Father God rules the first/highest rank of the hierarchy—Seraphim (Spirits of Love), Cherubim (Spirits of Harmony), and Thrones (Spirits of Will); the Son God of the Holy Trinity (Christ) works through the second, middle rank of the hierarchy—Kyriotētes (Dominions; Spirits of Wisdom), Dynamis (Mights; Spirits of Movement), and the Exusiai (Powers; Spirits of Form); and the Holy Spirit works through the third/lowest rank of the hierarchy—Archai (Spirits of Time; Spirits of Personality) Archangels (Archangeloi; Spirits of Fire, Sons of Fire, Fire spirits or Sanskrit: Agnishvatta; also called Dhyan-Chohans in theosophical writings) and Angels (Angeloi; Messengers; also Sons of Twilight, Spirits of Twilight, Sons of Life; also called Lunar Pitris or Barhishad-Pitris in theosophical writings).

This inherent 'trinity in a trinity' does not make the Christian Holy Trinity and Celestial Hierarchy a form of pantheism or deity worship because a 'threefold' Divine Being manifests themselves through a "threefold" set of hierarchical aspects, virtues, qualities, forces, beings, and levels of consciousness that has congealed over the four 'incarnations of the Earth to create a human being on the Earth today.

A human being can be thought of as a replica, mirror image, or holographic child of a finite, loving Cosmos (Universe). Therefore, we too are one "I Am" divided into the trinity of body, soul, and spirit—with three bodies (physical, etheric, astral), three souls (sentient, intellectual, consciousness), and three spirits (Spirit-Self/ Manas, Life-Spirit/ Budhi, Spirit-Human/Atman). Ultimately, the ninefold constitution of the singular, human individual "I Am" is a perfect image of the ninefold spiritual (celestial) hierarchy, which is the threefold image of the Holy Trinity, which is the singular image of One Divine God/Being. This is true also for those who believe the Holy Trinity has, by the nature of the duality of matter, a female mirror-image of Father/Son/Holy Spirit in a Divine Feminine Trinity of Mother/Daughter/Holy Sophia.

Many Christians often ask: Who should I pray to in the Trinity; one, or two, or all three? The simple truth is that if you pray to one, you pray to all three. This is the mystery of the trinity that no human mind can comprehend. It is even beyond reality to conceive that the Holy Trinity is far above all nine hierarchies in scope and magnitude (ten if you include the newly created human hierarchy) and that it is also inconceivable to imagine the mystery of the Holy Trinity. We like to say that it is a triple paradox that can't be solved with mere human logic. Spiritual Science tells us that we cannot begin to imagine what it would be like to encounter our own Guardian Angel, let alone the ranks of hierarchies above them leading to the Holy Trinity. All Earth-bound perceptions, concepts, ideas, and fantasies about Angels fall tremendously short of what a clairvoyant 'encounters' in the presence of an Angel. Only the most far-reaching projective geometry constructions can begin to 'picture' the workings of the Celestial Hierarchies. Sense-bound, or sense-referenced, concepts and ideas seldom are 'real' enough to make it past the threshold between the physical and spiritual world. Only living, Moral Imaginations, Moral Inspirations, and Moral Intuitions can help us understand the workings of the angelic hosts.

All of the hosts of heaven sing together the 'eternal song' and hear and speak 'the new, eternal gospel' which sounds together in unison. For no member of the heavenly choir sings solo. If you meet one

Angel, you will soon meet others because they all work together as one cohesive will doing the bidding of the 'Great I Am,' the One Divine manifestation of the Cosmos—our Father/Mother. But just as Lucifer/ Satan fell from the brilliant light of the 'Divine One on the Throne.' They now try to regain heaven by an ultimate redemption through suffering. So too each human struggles and suffers (like the hierarchy suffers and sacrifices) until the soul of each "I Am" is united again at the feet of the Throne of the Divine. Whether Lucifer, the prodigal son, or any fallen angelic being returns to its source, it is cause for celebration.

We are the eyes, ears, hands, and heart of the spiritual hierarchy— God on Earth. We 'host' the higher spiritual beings in our hearts, like the grail chalice holding the life-giving blood of Christ. When we surrender to Divine Grace and align ourselves with the Will of the Divine, we become in the words of Rudolf Steiner "the Tenth Hierarchy of Freedom and Love." The 'Mothers' of the three prior creations of the Earth have sacrificed, suffered, and birthed all that was needed for present day humans to become free beings. These 'Mothers' hosted our spiritual and physical evolution. Now, the Third Hierarchy (Angels, Archangels, and Archai) midwife our soul until it is purified enough to become spiritual and consciously enter their realms where they actively live and move—Moral Imagination, Moral Inspiration, and Moral Intuition. Thus, the Third Hierarchy enters in and out of human soul activity constantly. In other words, we 'host' them in our thinking, feeling, and willing. If we can rise high enough to refine our thinking, feeling, and willing we have the chance to commune with these beings within our soul and spirit.

In the same way that Angels, Archangels and Archai weave throughout the human being, so too the Nine Spiritual Hierarchies have the Holy Trinity weaving throughout all of their activity. The Nine Spiritual Hierarchies thus become 'hosts' for the Trinity, who is in fact, One Being. That is why we have the angelic "hosts" who allow God to fully penetrate them and become their 'messengers' throughout the nine hierarchical ranks. The Nine Spiritual Hierarchy are nine parts of One Being. Thus, the Christian Holy Trinity is based upon spiritual realities that cannot manifest in a dualistic material world. Only a trinity of forces reflects the Oneness of the Being who created the Cosmos in its multiplicity.

As Christ said: "I am the door" (*John 10:9); for* Christ is that aspect of the Holy Trinity that humans can, and should, identify with in their spiritual path back to the Throne of God. But Christ is threefold, and so, defies all logic. Likewise, a human being is torn between three capacities (thinking, feeling, willing); but this gives us a chance to face the mystery of the trinitarian nature of the human body, soul, and spirit; and it is the "I Am" (the "I," "Ich," ego or self) that brings these three human aspects together in a manner that is both unitary and individual. Even though many beings permeate and penetrate our bodies from every direction, we are still a unique, individually conscious human being. When we can 'host' the Divine through its hierarchical beings, it serves as an example of the way in which the hierarchy are 'many' but at the same time 'one.' This reality of spirit illuminates St. Paul's phrase, "...I live; yet not I, but Christ liveth in me." (*Galatians* 2:20) For surrendering to the Divine is exactly what Jesus Christ did in relationship to the 'will of the Father.' Only through unifying our inherently threefold nature can we combine the strength of our multifaceted soul and spiritual capacities.

In the following section, we would like to share with you selections describing the Nine Spiritual Hierarchy and their relationship to humanity and the Cosmos. We have taken our selections from the *Bible*, Aristotle, Pseudo-Dionysius, Saint Thomas Aquinas, and most particularly Dr. Rudolf Steiner who gives the most comprehensive picture of the Nine Spiritual Hierarchy and the Holy Trinity's co-operative workings through cosmogenesis and anthropogenesis. Many aspects of the inner nature of the hierarchies can only be found in the Spiritual Science of Anthroposophy. Therefore, we apologize in advance for the many long selections from Steiner's lectures and books; but it is best to quote from a source that has developed a comprehensive cosmology of the Cosmic Christ—the Sophia of Christ.

We believe that once you are fully aware and conscious of hierarchical workings, you will see that perception can be changed by active willpower entering the process of thinking—something Rudolf Steiner calls 'warmed-up thinking.' This living thinking connects your higher thought capacities with the thoughts of Angels, and then magically the outer world begins to 'light-up' and resemble heaven or the descending New Jerusalem. Or as one of my favorite Christian poets, Thomas Traherne has said:—

> "Your enjoyment of the world is never right, till every morning you awake in Heaven: see yourself in your Father's palace; and look upon the skies, the Earth, and the air as celestial joys: having such a reverend esteem of all, as if you were among the Angels."

For Traherne is correct; we are among the Angels, or better said, the Angels are among us. This was known in the past—*that is until the supersensible perception of mankind was diminished*—and, as a result, the Beings of Nature became merely the 'forces' of nature or the 'elements' of nature, devoid of the wisdom that *all matter is the gift of the spiritual hierarchies.* It is incumbent upon the Tenth Hierarchy (humanity) to rise-up in consciousness to the higher hierarchies like a child learning to walk, talk, or think. Often, it is the gift of love from our hearts that helps us 'to see a world in a grain of sand and heaven in a wildflower.' Or as George Washington enjoined us:—

> "Labor to keep alive in your breast that little spark of celestial fire, called conscience."

The intent of creation was to create (out of nothingness) a conscious, free human thinker who could advance spiritually into a person with a strong moral 'conscience.' Indeed, the human conscience is a gift of the hierarchy given freely to any human individual who can 'love his neighbor as himself.' For love is the highest hierarchical virtue that clearly defines the One Divine. Victor Hugo knew this when he penned the phrase:—

> "Love is a portion of the soul itself, and it is of the same nature as the celestial breathing of the atmosphere of paradise."

We often forget that in the beginning humans were in a Paradise called the Garden of Eden. Everything was there that was needed for life and happiness. For it is the 'New Eden' that we will call down from heaven as the 'New Jerusalem'; *where we will wed the pure bride to the heavenly groom—the soul to the spirit.* We already have a place prepared in heaven for our return and we already have the ability to commune with the higher spirits—this is the nature of that which is 'god-like' in each human being. Shakespeare described it beautifully for us:—

> "What a piece of work is a man, how noble in reason, how infinite in faculties, in form and moving how express and admirable, in action how like an Angel, in apprehension how like a god."

Studying the nature of the Spiritual Hierarchies reminds us of the reality that the whole Cosmos is within us, as the *Emerald Tablet of Hermes* instructs us:—

> "That which is above is like to that which is below, and that which is below is like to that which is above."

Or as the alchemists' say:—

> "The human being is the microcosm of the macrocosm."

Truly, we are our Divine Parent's children in every regard. Or, as the old saying goes: "the apple doesn't fall far from the tree." Within us is the seed to grow another apple tree if we plant that seed in our own heart. The poet Novalis tells us:—

"We dream of travels throughout the Universe: is not the Universe within us? We do not know the depths of our spirit. The mysterious path leads within. In us, or nowhere, lies eternity with its worlds, the past and the future."

The ancients, through natural clairvoyance, were well aware of the 'Beings' in the heavens; and they had great reverence for the Divine Hand that set the Cosmos in movement and sustains it like a loving mother. Watching the starry heavens and the wandering stars brought peace and faith to the ancients; for they could see that they were in an ordered Universe tended constantly by 'beings' who have humanity's best interest at heart. We can see this evidenced in the thoughts of William Shakespeare in the speech of Ulysses in *Troilus and Cressida*, Act 1, Scene 3:—

"The heavens themselves, the planets, and this center,
Observe degree, priority, and place,
Insisture, course, proportion, season, form,
Office, and custom, in all line of order;
And therefore is the glorious planet Sol
In noble eminence enthron'd and spher'd
Amidst the other, whose med'cinable eye
Corrects the ill aspects of planets evil,
And posts, like the commandment of a king,
Sans check, to good and bad. But when the planets
In evil mixture to disorder wander,
What plagues and what portents, what mutiny,
What raging of the sea, shaking of Earth,
Commotion in the winds! Frights, changes, horrors,
Divert and crack, rend and deracinate,
The unity and married calm of states
Quite from their fixture! O, when degree is shak'd,
Which is the ladder of all high designs,
The enterprise is sick!"

Johann Wolfgang von Goethe evoked the Archangels in his *Prologue in Heaven* from *Faust*, demonstrating his understanding that the Third Hierarchy is responsible for creation, the Sun, and the planets. He also understood, like Shakespeare, that the balance of everything one knows is in the hands of the Divine. Goethe has the Archangel Raphael say:—

> "The Sun-orb sings, in emulation,
> 'Mid brother-spheres, his ancient round:
> His path predestined through Creation
> He ends with step of thunder-sound.
> The Angels from his visage splendid
> Draw power, whose measure none can say;
> The lofty works, uncomprehended,
> Are bright as on the earliest day."

Goethe is alluding to what Rudolf Steiner clearly describes as the Harmony of the Spheres arising from the music of the whirling planets, that circumscribe the realms of the Nine Spiritual Hierarchies. These interpenetrating spheres of activity are also aided by the influence of the fixed stars through what Steiner called the Zodiac—the celestial sphere of the stars. In the lecture *Anthroposophy and the Inner Life*, Dr. Steiner tells us:—

> "We, together with the Earth, are within these interpenetrating spheres. Seven spheres mutually interpenetrate one another, and we grow into this interpenetration in the course of our life, are thus bound up with it. Our life, from birth until death, evolves out of its basic endowment, while the star-spheres in a certain sense draw us on from birth to death."

Not only are we inside the Harmony of the Spheres, which is created by the Nine Spiritual Hierarchy as soul and spirit realms for our development, but the Harmony of the Spheres is inside of us. Whether inside or outside, nonetheless, it is the same creation made by the same Cosmic Beings. The individual human being and the Divine One are the same. We work together to co-create within our own body. Wherever spiritual beings are taking a step back from their creation, the freedom and development of the individual human being takes a step forward. We are in a symbiotic relationship with an entire world of Beings who are often invisible or super-sensible to human perception. It is the job of humanity to step-up and relieve the spiritual hierarchy of some of their sacrifices, suffering, and donations. The development of conscience arises as the human being becomes more divine. Virtuous development in the human being makes us more like God and the spiritual hierarchies. The gift of conscience comes from the development of human morality through Divine Love. Love is the action of Christ and His entire First Rank of the Nine Spiritual Hierarchies—the Seraphim. Whenever we love, we draw neigh unto the Throne of Heaven and the Love of Christ. Awakening to the power of the spiritual hierarchies in us helps in the mission to merge Spiritual Science with spiritual hierarchies. Or, as Dr. Steiner put it in *The Spiritual Hierarchies*: "It is the task of modern Spiritual Science to form once more the bond which must unite the physical to the spiritual, the bond between the Earth and the spiritual hierarchies."

The Tenth Hierarchy
by John Barnwell

What radiant passage in solemn night
Gives us entry to the sovereign light
Receiving the childlike in heaven's womb
And freeing the spirit from its Earthly tomb?
Seraphim's pure being in fire is reflected,
Cherubim through suffering give harmony,
Thrones activity lives in the warmth of will,
Kyriotetes wisdom give plants their life,
Dynamis dance in the thrones procession,

> Exusiai clothe us in human mortal form,
> Archai bring selfhood to time's relation,
> Archangels inspire the nation's voice,
> Angels give guidance to human spirits,
> And thus the "I Am" becomes.

To underscore the necessity to understand the relationship between the spiritual hierarchy and the Holy Trinity we offer the selections below from Pseudo-Dionysius to highlight that it is Love that empowers the Nine Spiritual Hierarchies and that Love comes from the Holy Trinity towards its creation—humanity. The Nine Spiritual Hierarchy all work together and sacrifice part of themselves to create our world and our nine-fold body, soul, and spiritual constitution. The more we 'take over' for the work of the hierarchy in our nine bodies, the more we become like them in every way and develop a higher awareness and consciousness of the world and our "I Am." We become what Pseudo-Dionysius calls a 'hierarch.' And indeed, we do become the Tenth Hierarchy—a 'hierarch' who has developed a highly moral conscience. Let's hear what Pseudo-Dionysius can tell us about integrating with the spiritual hierarchy in his work entitled: *The Ecclesiastical Hierarchy*:

> "The source of this hierarchy is the font of life, the being
> of goodness, the one cause of everything, namely, the
> Trinity which in goodness bestows being and well-being
> on everything. Now this blessed Deity which transcends
> everything and which is one and also triune has resolved,
> for reasons unclear to us but obvious to itself, to ensure
> the salvation of rational beings, both ourselves and those
> beings who are our superiors. This can only happen with the
> divinization of the saved. And divinization consists of being
> as much as possible like and in union with God. The common
> goal of every hierarchy consists of the continuous love of God

and of things divine. It consists of a knowledge of beings as they really are."

"To talk of 'hierarch' [hierophant] one is referring to a holy and inspired man, someone who understands all sacred knowledge, someone in whom an entire hierarchy is completely perfected and known."

"For the truth is that everything divine and even everything revealed to us is known only by way of whatever share of them [hierarchy] is granted. Their actual nature, what they are ultimately in their own source and ground, is beyond all intellect and all being and all knowledge. Indeed, the inscrutable One is out of the reach of every rational process. Nor can any words come up to the inexpressible Good, this One, this Source of all unity, this supra-existent Being. Mind beyond mind, word beyond speech, it is gathered up by no discourse, by no intuition, by no name. It is and it is as no other being is. Cause of all existence, and therefore itself transcending existence, it alone could give an authoritative account of what it really is."

It is clear by this passage that Pseudo-Dionysius is telling us that everything we know comes through association with the celestial hierarchy. The more we know of the Angelic Host's activities and ways, the more we advance to become like them. He tells us about the celestial hierarchy's actual nature, what they are in their own source and ground, which is beyond all intellect and all being and all knowledge. Logic and sense-bound thinking will not gain insight into the spiritual hierarchy and the inscrutable One who is the: 'source of all unity, supra-existent Being, mind beyond mind, inexpressible good, word beyond speech, as no other being is, cause of all existence, transcending existence, beyond all intellect and all being and all knowledge, out of the reach of every rational process,' and 'gathered up by no discourse, by no intuition, by no name.'"

Summary of Hierarchical Attributes

First Hierarchy

World-creation, Creation of Beings, Spirits of the Rotation of Time,
The first hierarchy consists of the Seraphim/Spirits of Love, the Cherubim/Spirits of Harmony, and the Thrones/Spirits of Will. Rudolf Steiner describes how space, time, and matter (originally a subtler form of light) are brought forth by these especially powerful beings.

From: *Anthroposophical Leading Thoughts,* Rudolf Steiner
"The Beings of the First Hierarchy manifest themselves in spiritual creation beyond humanity—a cosmic world of spiritual Being which indwells human Willpower. This world of cosmic Spirit experiences itself in creative action when man wills. It first creates the connection of man's being with the Universe beyond humanity; only then does man himself become, through his organism of Willpower, a freely willing being. The First and strongest Hierarchy reveals itself as the spiritually active principle within the physical. It makes the physical world into a Cosmos. The Third and the Second Hierarchy are the Beings who minister to it in this activity. To call forth an idea of the First Hierarchy (Seraphim, Cherubim and Thrones) we must try to create pictures in which the Spiritual—i.e. that which can be beheld only in the Supersensible—reveals its working, in forms that come to manifestation in the world of sense. Spiritual Being, portrayed in sense-perceptible imagery: such must be the content of our thoughts about the First Hierarchy. Spiritually, we can approach the First Hierarchy (Seraphim, Cherubim, Thrones) by awakening to see the facts that confront us in the kingdom of Nature and of Man as the deeds (creations) of spiritual being that is working in them. The First

Hierarchy then has the kingdom of Nature and of Man as the outcome of its work, wherein it unfolds its Being."

Second Hierarchy

Self-creation, Stimulation of Life, Group-Souls
The Second Hierarchy consists of the Spirits of Wisdom/Dominions/Kyriotetes, Spirits of Movement/Mights/Dynamis, and the Spirits of Form/Powers/Elohim. These beings awaken the material substance, generated by the First Hierarchy, allowing it to take on living form and organization. Yahweh and the Elohim, the central gods of the Old Testament, are said by Steiner to be Powers.

From: *Anthroposophical Leading Thoughts,* Rudolf Steiner
"The Beings of the Second Hierarchy manifest themselves in a world-of-soul beyond humanity—a world of cosmic soul-activities, hidden from human Feeling. This cosmic world-of-soul is ever creative in the background of human Feeling. Out of the being of man it first creates the organism of Feeling; only then can it bring Feeling itself to life therein. The Second Hierarchy reveals itself as soul and spirit that works in the etheric. All that is etheric is a manifestation of the Second Hierarchy. This Second Hierarchy, however, does not reveal itself directly in the physical; its power extends only to etheric processes. Only etheric and soul-life could exist if the Third and the Second Hierarchy alone were active. To call forth an idea of the Second Hierarchy (Kyriotetes, Dynamis, Exusiai) we must try to create pictures in which the Spiritual reveals itself—not in sense-perceptible forms—but in a purely spiritual way. Spiritual being, portrayed not in sense-perceptible but in purely spiritual imagery: such must be the content of our thoughts about the Second Hierarchy. Spiritually, we can approach the Second Hierarchy (Exusiai, Dynamis, Kyriotetes) by awakening to see the facts of Nature as the manifestations of spiritual being that indwells them. The Second Hierarchy then has Nature for its dwelling-place, there to work upon the souls."

Third Hierarchy

Manifestation, Being filled with Spirits, Nature-Spirits
The Third Hierarchy consists of Archai/Spirits of Time, Archangels/
Spirits of Fire, and Angels/Sons of Life. These are the celestial beings
closest to the souls of earthly humanity. The Archai influence the
character of whole historical ages (i.e., the Zeitgeist). The Archangels
form the various folk-souls/nations that comprise the diverse
human species. Angels shepherd individual human lives, aiding our
conscience in its quest toward things divine.

From: *Anthroposophical Leading Thoughts*, Rudolf Steiner
"The Beings of the Third Hierarchy reveal themselves in the life which
is unfolded as a spiritual background in human Thinking. In the
human activity of thought this life is concealed. If it worked on in its
own essence in human thought, man could not attain to Freedom.
Where cosmic Thought activity ceases, human Thought-activity
begins. The Third Hierarchy reveals itself as pure soul and spirit. It
lives and moves in all that man experiences in the soul, in his inner
life. Neither in the etheric nor in the physical could any processes arise
if this Hierarchy alone were active. Soul-life alone could exist. To call
forth an idea of the Third Hierarchy (Archai, Archangels, Angels) we
must try to create pictures in which the Spiritual reveals itself not in
sense-perceptible forms, nor yet in a purely spiritual way, but in the
way in which Thinking, Feeling, and Willing come to expression in the
human soul. Spiritual being, portrayed in the imagery of a life of soul:
such must be the content of our thoughts about the Third Hierarchy.
Spiritually, we can approach the Third Hierarchy (Archai, Archangels,
Angels) by learning to know Thinking, Feeling and Willing, so as
to perceive in them the spiritual that works in the soul. Thinking,
to begin with, places not an effective reality, but only pictures into
the world. Feeling lives and moves in this realm of pictures; bears
witness to the presence of a reality in man but cannot live it or express
it outwardly. Willpower unfolds a reality which presupposes the

existence of the body but does not consciously assist in its formation. The spiritual reality that lives in our Thinking, to make the body the foundation of this Thinking; the spiritual reality that lives in our Feeling, to make the body share in the experience of a reality; the spiritual reality that lives in our Willpower, consciously to assist in fashioning the body—all this is alive in the Third Hierarchy."

The Tenth Hierarchy

The fourth and final level of the hierarchies is composed of the Spirits of Freedom through the Spirits of Love, both of which await their full realization by human beings on Earth.

The Nature of the Ranks of the Hierarchy According to Rudolf Steiner

The Spiritual Hierarchies, **Rudolf Steiner, Lecture VI, Düsseldorf, April 15, 1909, GA 110**

"First, we have the Angels. They passed through their human stage during the evolution of the Old Moon, and are fundamentally speaking, only as far developed during our present Earth evolution as man will be during the [Future] Jupiter evolution. They stand one stage higher than man. We have to assign one of these Beings to each man, a being who, being one stage higher, can lead the individuality over from one incarnation to the other. These are not the beings who rule karma but preserve the memory from one incarnation to the other, so long as the man is not himself aware of it. These Beings are the Angels."

"The Archangels or Fire Spirits do not occupy themselves with separate men, with the single individual, but have a wider task; they bring single lives into harmonious order with the life of larger human groups, as, for instance, nations, races, etc. Within our Earth's evolution the Archangels' task is to bring into certain harmonious relationship each single soul with the national or race-soul. In the soul of a nation, there lives and weaves what we call a fire-spirit or an Archangel; he regulates, so to speak, the relation between separate men and the nation or races as a whole."

"Then we rise to those beings whom we designate the Spirits of Personality, Primeval Beginnings, Primeval Forces, or Archai. These are still loftier Beings, who have a still higher task in the continuity of human existence. They regulate the earthly relations of whole human generations on Earth, and they live in such a way that, on the waves of time, from epoch to epoch, they transform themselves at certain definite periods, they assume other spiritual bodies. This 'Spirit of the Age' comprises something which reaches beyond single nations, beyond single races. That which one really calls a 'Zeitgeist' or Spirit of an Epoch is the spiritual body of the Archai or the Primeval Beginnings or Spirits of Personality. It is to these Spirits of Personality that one has to ascribe the fact that within certain Epochs, certain definite personalities appear on our Earth."

"And when we get beyond the Archai, we reach to those Beings whom we touched on yesterday, the so-called Powers,—Exusiai, whom we also call the Spirits of Form. Here we have to do with tasks that reach beyond the Earth. We differentiate in the course of human development an Ancient Saturn, Ancient Sun, Ancient Moon, Earth, Future Jupiter, Future Venus, and Future Vulcan evolution."

"We have now seen how all that happens within the Earth itself is regulated by the Angels as regards the individual men, by

Archangels as regards the relation between individuals and the large masses of humanity, and by the Spirits of Personality for the whole development of man, from the Lemurian period up to the period when man will again be so largely spiritualized that he will hardly belong to the Earth. Humanity will have to be guided from one planetary condition to another. Spiritual Beings must also exist, whose care it is during the whole Earth evolution to see that when that evolution will have come to an end, humanity may pass in the right manner through a Pralaya and find its way to the next goal, to the Jupiter goal. The spirits whose care it is to see that the whole of humanity should be led from one planetary condition to another, are the Powers, Exusiai, or Spirits of Form."

"The Beings who are nearest to the Earth, who hold sway in the immediate surroundings of the Earth up to the Moon, are the Angels. From that region they guide the life of each single Individual as it progresses from incarnation to incarnation. Only think how a race with different qualities, for instance in hair and in skin, acts otherwise than another race would do; here we have the interactions of conditions which must be regulated from heavenly spaces. This is done from a region whose lordship extends up to Mercury, to the boundary of the Archangel's sphere of action. Further, when the whole of humanity as it develops upon Earth has to be guided and led, this has to be affected from still wider heavenly spaces, from that which extends as far as to Venus by the Archai."

"When further, the task of the Earth itself has to be led and guided, this must be done from the center of the whole system. The Beings of the Spiritual Hierarchies, who direct the mission of humanity carrying it on from one planet to another, are the

Powers, the Spirits of Form. They must dwell in a very special place; they are of such a nature that their sphere of power reaches up to the Sun. Therefore, the existence of the Sun must be bound up with those spiritual Beings whose realm of action also extends beyond the single planets. Thus, we have to do with the spheres of space; and the planets are the landmarks for realms of the spatial activities of the higher Beings. Hence, we look back into old Atlantean and old Lemurian times, when Beings descended from the surrounding realms of the Earth to which they belonged and incarnated in human bodies and became the teachers of mankind. These are Beings who belonged to higher Hierarchies, to Mercury and Venus. The sons of Venus and of Mercury descended from above and became the teachers of young humanity. We have said that the Beings of Venus are the Spirits of Personality. Such Beings walked the Earth as men, being outwardly limited to narrow human personalities, but who with their mighty power guided humanity. These were the great conditions of lordship in Lemurian times when sons of Venus guided the whole of humanity. The sons of Mercury guided parts of humanity. They were as powerful as those are now whom we call spirits of nations or of race."

Alternate Hierarchical Names and Descriptions

Seraphim—Spirits of Love—Understanding—Spirits of the Good—receive ideas from the Holy Trinity, being and existence is the same, carry over old solar system to new

Cherubim—Spirits of Harmony—Ascension—Spirits of Truth—ponder ideas from the Holy Trinity, light filled wisdom, provide guidance to other hierarchies

Thrones—Spirits of Will—Lights—Aeons—Spirits of Beauty—
Ophanim—act on the ideas from the Holy Trinity, sacrificial courage,
group soul of minerals

Kyriotetes—Spirits of Wisdom—Authorities—Dominions—
Lordships—Christened Wisdom—Heavenly Sophia—carry out First
Hierarchy's Divine Plan, bestowing wisdom, group soul of plants

Dynamis—Spirits of Motion—Lordships—Hosts—Mights—
Christened Might—Strongholds -Virtues—always in continual
movement and metamorphosis, group soul of animals

Exusiai—Spirits of Form—Elohim—Powers—Revelations—
Authorities—Heavenly Logos—group soul of humans

Archai—Spirits of Personality—Spirits of Time—Principalities—
Rulers—Epoch Spirits—Primal Beginnings—Zeitgeist—Time
Beings—Primal Beings—Moral Intuition—Consciousness Soul—work
with gnome elemental beings

Archangels—Folk Spirits—Spirit of Fire—Archangels—Moral
Inspiration—Intellectual Soul—work with undine elemental beings

Angels—Guardian Angels—Sons of Life—Sons of Twilight—
Messengers—Angels—Moral Imagination—Sentient Soul—work with
sylph elemental beings

Angels, Archangels, and Archai

*Universe, Man, and Man: In their Relationship to Egyptian
Myths and Modern Civilization,* **Rudolf Steiner, Lecture III,** *The
Kingdoms of Nature,* **August 6, 1908, GA 105**

"Looking from man upwards to higher kingdoms, we have to
begin with three kingdoms which interest us. In accordance
with Christian esotericism, we call the kingdom immediately

bordering on the human the realm of the Angels; they are also called Spirits of Twilight. Then there is a second kingdom, higher than the Angels, the kingdom of the Archangels; they are also called the Spirits of Fire. Lastly there is a still higher kingdom, that of the Archai (Original Forces or First Beginnings), called also the Spirits of Personality. These are the three kingdoms next above man."

"Now, an Angel accompanies the inmost part of man's being and guides him from incarnation to incarnation, so that he may truly fulfil his mission on Earth. It is, in fact, as if the human being had been able, since the beginning of his life on Earth, to look up to an exalted Spirit who was his prototype, who could completely control his astral body, and who said to him: "Thou must be like unto me when in future thou passest out of this Earthly evolution." It is the task of Angels to guide the incarnations of men and whether we say that he looks up to his Higher Self, whom he must come to resemble more and more, or that he looks up to his Angel as his great pattern, it is exactly the same in a spiritual sense."

"The beings whose task it is to control that part of the astral body which is still uncontrolled by man are one stage higher than he is, they are the Angels, or Spirits of Twilight. In fact, one such Spirit watches over every human being, and this Spirit has power over the astral body; it is therefore no childish idea, but profound wisdom, to speak of guardian Angels. These guardian Angels have a great duty to perform."

"As man works further upon himself, he will transform the etheric body into Budhi, or Life-Spirit; one day he will do this consciously, even now he is working on it unconsciously. So even higher Spiritual Beings have to work today in all human etheric bodies; this is the task of the Fire Spirits. Now, human etheric bodies are not individually so different as are human astral bodies. This can be seen in the qualities peculiar to a race or nation. Because of this we see that each individual human being does not have an Archangel in connection with his etheric body, but that whole nations and races are guided by higher or lower Spirits of Fire. The peoples and races of the Earth are indeed guided as a whole by Archangels."

Charts of the Spiritual Hierarchies

The Holy Trinity—Father/Son/Holy Spirit

Dionysius	Spirits of	Planet	Donation	Offspring
Seraphim	Love	Saturn	Fire reflection	Rotation of time
Cherubim	Harmony	Jupiter	Air reflection	Elementary Spirts
Thrones	Will	Mars	Water reflection	Group soul/mineral
Kyriotetes	Wisdom	Sun	Life ether	Group soul/plants
Dynamis	Motion	Sun	Sound ether	Group soul/animals
Exusiai	Form	Sun	Light ether	Group soul of man
Archai	Personality	Mercury	Warmth etheric	Nature Spirits/Earth
Archangels	Sons of Fire	Venus	Air etheric	Nature Spirits/water
Angels	S. Twilight	Moon	Water etheric	Nature Spirits/air

The Holy Trinity—Father/Son/Holy Spirit

Dionysius	Sense	Body	Aristotle	Sign	Center
Seraphim	Ego	Spirit-Human	Being	Gemini	Sun
Cherubim	Touch	Life-Spirit	Suffering	Cancer	Sun
Thrones	Life	Spirit-Self	Activity	Leo	Sun
Kyriotetes	Movement	Spiritual Soul	Position	Virgo	Sun
Dynamis	Balance	Intellectual Soul	Time	Libra	Sun
Exusiai	Smell	Sentient Soul	Space	Scorpio	Sun
Archai	Taste	Astral	Relation	Sagittarius	Earth
Archangels	Sight	Etheric	Quality	Capricorn	Earth
Angels	Warmth	Physical	Quantity	Aquarius	Earth

The Holy Trinity—Father/Son/Holy Spirit

Dionysius	Activity	Field	Nature	Domain	After Death
Seraphim	Matter	Solar System	Love	Zodiac	Karma
Cherubim	Matter	Solar system	Harmony	Zodiac	Karma
Thrones	Matter	Solar System	Willpower	Saturn	Physical Body
Kyriotetes	Etheric	Solar System	Sophia	Jupiter	Creation of Limbs
Dynamis	Etheric	Each Planet	Dynamism	Mars	Creation of Head
Exusiai	Etheric	Sun (Moon)	Christ	Sun	Humanity
Archai	Souls	Mercury	Intuition	Mercury	Religion
Archangels	Souls	Venus	Inspiration	Venus	Morality
Angels	Souls	Moon	Imagination	Moon	Kamaloca

Biblical References to the Spiritual Hierarchy

We have now heard detailed descriptions about the ranks of the spiritual hierarchies according to Dionysius and Rudolf Steiner. The foundation of both of these thinker's ideas is found, in part, in the *Bible*. Thus, we shall look at the references to the spiritual hierarchies found in the *Bible* to find another perspective of the Nine Spiritual Hierarchies and their work in the Cosmos and humanity.

First Rank

The Seraphim

Isaiah 6:1-7

1 In the year that king Uzziah died I saw also the Lord sitting upon a throne, high and lifted up, and his train filled the temple.

2 Above it stood the seraphims: each one had six wings; with twain he covered his face, and with twain he covered his feet, and with twain he did fly.

3 And one cried unto another, and said, Holy, holy, holy, is the Lord of hosts: the whole Earth is full of his glory.

4 And the posts of the door moved at the voice of him that cried, and the house was filled with smoke.

5 Then said I, Woe is me! for I am undone; because I am a man of unclean lips, and I dwell in the midst of a people of unclean lips: for mine eyes have seen the King, the Lord of hosts.

6 Then flew one of the seraphims unto me, having a live coal in his hand, which he had taken with the tongs from off the altar:

7 And he laid it upon my mouth, and said, Lo, this hath touched thy lips; and thine iniquity is taken away, and thy sin purged.

Cherubim

Genesis 3:24
So he drove out the man; and he placed at the east of the garden of Eden Cherubims, and a flaming sword which turned every way, to keep the way of the tree of life.

Ezekiel 10:1-2
1 Then I looked, and, behold, in the firmament that was above the head of the cherubims there appeared over them as it were a sapphire stone, as the appearance of the likeness of a throne.

2 And he spake unto the man clothed with linen, and said, Go in between the wheels, even under the cherub, and fill thine hand with coals of fire from between the cherubims, and scatter them over the city.

Ezekiel 10:15-22
15 And the cherubims were lifted up. This is the living creature that I saw by the river of Chebar.

16 And when the cherubims went, the wheels went by them: and when the cherubims lifted up their wings to mount up from the Earth, the same wheels also turned not from beside them.

17 When they stood, these stood; and when they were lifted up, these lifted up themselves also: for the spirit of the living creature was in them.

18 Then the glory of the Lord departed from off the threshold of the house, and stood over the cherubims.

19 And the cherubims lifted up their wings and mounted up from the Earth in my sight: when they went out, the wheels also were beside them, and every one stood at the door of the east gate of the Lord's house; and the glory of the God of Israel was over them above.

20 This is the living creature that I saw under the God of Israel by the river of Chebar; and I knew that they were the cherubims.

21 Every one had four faces apiece, and every one four wings; and the likeness of the hands of a man was under their wings.

22 And the likeness of their faces was the same faces which I saw by the river of Chebar, their appearances and themselves: they went every one straight forward.

Ezekiel 10:9-14
9 And when I looked, behold the four wheels by the cherubims, one wheel by one cherub, and another wheel by another cherub: and the appearance of the wheels was as the color of a beryl stone.

10 And as for their appearances, they four had one likeness, as if a wheel had been in the midst of a wheel.

11 When they went, they went upon their four sides; they turned not as they went, but to the place whither the head looked they followed it; they turned not as they went.

12 And their whole body, and their backs, and their hands, and their wings, and the wheels, were full of eyes round about, even the wheels that they four had.

13 As for the wheels, it was cried unto them in my hearing, O wheel.

14 And every one had four faces: the first face was the face of a cherub, and the second face was the face of a man, and the third the face of a lion, and the fourth the face of an eagle.

Thrones

Hebrews 1:8
8 Your throne, O God, is forever and ever, And the righteous scepter is the scepter of His kingdom.

Psalms 11:4
4 The Lord is in His holy temple; the Lord's throne is in heaven; His eyes behold, His eyelids test the sons of men.

Revelation 20:11
Then I saw a great white throne and Him who sat upon it, from whose presence Earth and heaven fled away, and no place was found for them.

Isaiah 66:11
Thus says the Lord, Heaven is My throne and the Earth is My footstool.

Second Rank

Kyriotetes

Ephesians 1:20-21
20 Which he wrought in Christ, when he raised him from the dead, and set him at his own right hand in the heavenly places,

21 Far above all principality, and power, and might, and dominion, and every name that is named, not only in this world, but also in that which is to come.

Dynamis

Ephesians 6:12
12 For we wrestle not against flesh and blood, but against principalities, against powers, against the rulers of the darkness of this world, against spiritual wickedness in high places.

Exusiai

Colossians 1:16
16 For by him were all things created, that are in heaven, and that are in Earth, visible and invisible, whether they be thrones, or dominions, or principalities, or powers: all things were created by him, and for him.

Third Rank

Archai

Genesis 1: 6-8, 14, 15, 17, 20
6 And God said, Let there be a solid arch stretching over the waters, parting the waters from the waters.

7 And God made the arch for a division between the waters which were under the arch and those which were over it: and it was so.

8 And God gave the arch the name of Heaven. And there was evening and there was morning, the second day.

14 And God said, Let there be lights in the arch of heaven, for a division between the day and the night, and let them be for signs, and for marking the changes of the year, and for days and for years.

15 And let them be for lights in the arch of heaven to give light on the Earth: and it was so.

17 And God put them in the arch of heaven, to give light on the Earth;

20 And God said, Let the waters be full of living things, and let birds be in flight over the Earth under the arch of heaven.

Archangels

Jude 1:9
9 Yet Michael the Archangel, when contending with the devil he disputed about the body of Moses, durst not bring against him a railing accusation, but said, The Lord rebuke thee.

1 Thessalonians 4:16
For the Lord Himself will descend from heaven with a shout, with the voice of the Archangel and with the trumpet of God, and the dead in Christ will rise first.

Daniel 10:12-13
Then he said to me, "Do not be afraid, Daniel, for from the first day that you set your heart on understanding this and on humbling yourself before your God, your words were heard, and I have come in response to your words. But the prince of the kingdom of Persia was withstanding me for twenty-one days; then behold, Michael, one of the chief princes, came to help me, for I had been left there with the kings of Persia.

Daniel 10:21
However, I will tell you what is inscribed in the writing of truth. Yet there is no one who stands firmly with me against these forces except Michael your prince.

Daniel 12:1
Now at that time Michael, the great prince who stands guard over the sons of your people, will arise. And there will be a time of distress such as never occurred since there was a nation until that time; and at that time your people, everyone who is found written in the book, will be rescued.

Revelation 12:7

And there was war in heaven, Michael and his Angels waging war with the dragon. The dragon and his Angels waged war.

Angels

Genesis 6:1-4

6 And it came to pass, when men began to multiply on the face of the Earth, and daughters were born unto them,

2 That the sons of God saw the daughters of men that they were fair; and they took them wives of all which they chose.

3 And the Lord said, My spirit shall not always strive with man, for that he also is flesh: yet his days shall be an hundred and twenty years.

4 There were giants in the Earth in those days; and also after that, when the sons of God came in unto the daughters of men, and they bare children to them, the same became mighty men which were of old, men of renown.

Job 38:4-7

4 Where wast thou when I laid the foundations of the Earth? declare, if thou hast understanding.

5 Who hath laid the measures thereof, if thou knowest? or who hath stretched the line upon it?

6 Whereupon are the foundations thereof fastened? or who laid the corner stone thereof;

7 When the morning stars sang together, and all the sons of God shouted for joy?

2 Peter 2:4-10a

4 For if God spared not the Angels that sinned, but cast them down to hell, and delivered them into chains of darkness, to be reserved unto judgment

Jude 1:5-6

6 And the Angels which kept not their first estate, but left their own habitation, he hath reserved in everlasting chains under darkness unto the judgment of the great day.

Ezekiel 28:13-19

13 Thou hast been in Eden the garden of God…

14 Thou art the anointed cherub that covereth; and I have set thee so: thou wast upon the holy mountain of God; thou hast walked up and down in the midst of the stones of fire.

15 Thou wast perfect in thy ways from the day that thou wast created, till iniquity was found in thee.

16 By the multitude of thy merchandise they have filled the midst of thee with violence, and thou hast sinned: therefore I will cast thee as profane out of the mountain of God: and I will destroy thee, O covering cherub, from the midst of the stones of fire.

17 Thine heart was lifted up because of thy beauty, thou hast corrupted thy wisdom by reason of thy brightness: I will cast thee to the ground, I will lay thee before kings, that they may behold thee.

Revelation 12:7-12

7 And there was war in heaven: Michael and his Angels fought against the dragon; and the dragon fought and his Angels,

8 And prevailed not; neither was their place found any more in heaven.

9 And the great dragon was cast out, that old serpent, called the Devil, and Satan, which deceiveth the whole world: he was cast out into the Earth, and his Angels were cast out with him.

Pseudo-Dionysius the Areopagite on the Celestial Hierarchy

Dionysius, or Pseudo-Dionysius, was a Christian Neoplatonist who wrote in the late fifth or early sixth century A.D. and who summarized the whole of Pagan Neoplatonism from Plotinus to Proclus into a distinctively new Christian context. His works were written as if they were composed by St. Dionysius the Areopagite, a member of the Athenian judicial council in the 1st century A.D. who was converted by St. Paul. So successful was this stratagem that Dionysius acquired almost apostolic authority, giving his writings enormous influence in the Middle Ages and the Renaissance. His *Mystical Theology* suggests an ascent from the lower sensuous realm of reality through the intelligible intermediate realm to the darkness of the godhead itself, all accomplished by a single person. The hierarchic treatises, on the other hand, suggest that the sensible and intelligible realms are not places reached by a single being, but different kinds of beings, and that the vision of God is handed from being to being downward through the levels of the hierarchy. *On the Celestial Hierarchy* describes the intelligible realm as divided into nine ranks of beings: the seraphim, cherubim, thrones, dominions, powers, authorities, principalities, Archangels, and Angels.

The Celestial Hierarchy, by Dionysius the Areopagite

"This is the revelation of their names [hierarchy], so far as we can give it. The purpose of every Hierarchy is an unswerving devotion to the divine imitation of the Divine Likeness, and that every Hierarchical function is set apart for the sacred reception and distribution of an undefiled purification, and Divine Light, and perfecting science. The subordinate Orders of the Heavenly Beings are taught by the superior, in due order, the deifying sciences; and that those who are higher than all are illuminated from the Godhead itself, as far as permissible, in revelations of the Divine mysteries."

Concerning the Seraphim and Cherubim and Thrones, and concerning their first Hierarchy

"Seraphim denotes either that they are kindling or burning; and that of Cherubim, a fullness of knowledge or stream of wisdom. Naturally, then, the first order of the Heavenly Hierarchies is ministered by the most exalted Beings, holding, as it does, a rank which is higher than all, from the fact, that it is established immediately around God, and that the first-wrought Divine manifestations and perfections pass earlier to it, as being nearest. They are called, then, "Burning," and Thrones, and Stream of Wisdom. The appellation of Seraphim plainly teaches their ever moving around things Divine, and constancy, and warmth, and keenness, and the seething of that persistent, indomitable, and inflexible perpetual motion, and the vigorous assimilation and elevation of the subordinate, as giving new life and rekindling them to the same heat; and purifying through fire and burnt-offering, and the light-like and light-shedding characteristic which can never be concealed or consumed, and remains always the same, which destroys and dispels every kind of obscure darkness. But the appellation of the Cherubim denotes their knowledge and their vision of God, and their readiness to receive the highest gift of light, and their power of contemplating the super Divine comeliness in its first revealed power, and their being filled anew with the impartation which maketh wise, and their ungrudging communication to those next to them, by the stream of the given wisdom. The appellation of the most exalted and preeminent Thrones denotes their manifest exaltation above every groveling inferiority, and their supermundane tendency towards higher things; and their unswerving separation from all remoteness; and their invariable and firmly-fixed settlement around the veritable Highest, with the whole force of their powers; and their receptivity of the supremely Divine approach, in the absence of all passion and Earthly tendency, and their bearing God; and the ardent expansion of themselves for the Divine receptions."

"The Hierarchy is akin, and in every respect like, to the first Beings, who are established after the Godhead, who gave them Being, and who are marshalled, as it were, in Its very vestibule, who surpass every unseen and seen created power. We must then regard them as pure, not as though they had been freed from unholy stains and blemishes, nor yet as though they were unreceptive of Earthly fancies, but as far exalted above every stain of remissness and every inferior holiness, as befits the highest degree of purity—established above the most Godlike powers, and clinging unflinchingly to their own self-moved and same-moved rank in their invariable love of God, conscious in no respect whatever of any declivity to a worse condition, but having the unsullied fixity of their own Godlike identity—never liable to fall, and always unmoved; and again, as "contemplative," not contemplators of intellectual symbols as sensible, nor as being led to the Divine Being by the varied texture of holy representations written for meditation, but as being filled with all kinds of immaterial knowledge of higher light, and satiated, as permissible, with the beautifying and original beauty of super-essential and thrice manifested contemplation, and thus, being deemed worthy of the Communion with Jesus, they do not stamp pictorially the deifying similitude in divinely formed images, but, as being really near to Him, in first participation of the knowledge of His deifying illuminations; nay more, that the imitation of God is given to them in the highest possible degree, and they participate, so far as is allowable to them, in His deifying and philanthropic virtues, in the power of a first manifestation; and, likewise as "perfected," not as being illuminated with an analytic science of sacred variety, but as being filled with a first and pre-eminent deification, as beseems the most exalted science of the works of God, possible in Angels. For, not through other holy Beings, but being ministered from the very Godhead, by the immediate elevation to It, by their power, and rank, surpassing all, they are both established near the All-Holy without any shadow of turning, and are conducted for contemplation to the immaterial and intelligible comeliness, as far as permissible, and are initiated into the scientific methods of the works of God, as being first and around God, being ministered, in the highest degree, from the very source of consecration."

"The first Hierarchy, then, of the Heavenly Minds is purified, and enlightened, and perfected, by being ministered from the very Author of initiation, through its elevation to It immediately, being filled, according to its degree, with the altogether most holy purification of the unapproachable Light of the pre-perfect source of initiation, unstained indeed by any remissness, and full of primal Light, and perfected by its participation in first-given knowledge and science. The reception of the supremely Divine Science is purification, enlightenment, and perfecting,—purifying, as it were, from ignorance, by the knowledge of the more perfect revelations imparted to it according to fitness, and enlightening by the self-same Divine knowledge, through which it also purifies, that which did not before contemplate the things which are now made manifest through the higher illumination; and perfecting further, by the self-same Light, through the abiding science of the mysteries made clearly manifest."

"This, then, according to my science, is the first rank of the Heavenly Beings which encircle and stand immediately around God; and without symbol, and without interruption, dances round His eternal knowledge in the most exalted ever-moving stability as in Angels; viewing purely many and blessed contemplations, and illuminated with simple and immediate splendors, and filled with Divine nourishment,—many indeed by the first given profusion, but one by the unvariegated and unifying oneness of the supremely Divine banquet, deemed worthy indeed of much participation and co-operation with God, by their assimilation to Him, as far as attainable, of their excellent habits and energies, and knowing many Divine things pre-eminently, and participating in supremely Divine science and knowledge, as is lawful. Wherefore the Word of God has transmitted its hymns to those on Earth, in which are Divinely shewn the excellency of its most exalted illumination. For some of its members, to speak after sensible perception, proclaim as a 'voice of many waters,' 'Blessed is the glory of the Lord from His place" and others cry aloud that frequent and most august hymn of God, "Holy, Holy, Holy, Lord of Sabaoth, the whole Earth is full of His glory. That the first Order, having been illuminated, from this the supremely Divine goodness, as permissible, in theological science, as a Hierarchy reflecting that Goodness transmitted to those next after it' teaching briefly this, 'That it is just and right that the august Godhead—Itself both above praise, and all-praiseworthy—should be known and extolled by the God-receptive minds, as is attainable; for they as images of God are, as the Oracles say, the Divine places of the supremely Divine repose; and further, that It is Monad and Unit tri-subsistent, sending forth His most kindly forethought to all things being, from the super-heavenly Minds to the lowest of the Earth; as super-original Origin and Cause of every essence, and grasping all things super-essentially in a resistless embrace.'

Concerning Lordships and Powers and Authorities, and concerning their middle Hierarchy

"Let us now pass to the middle Order of the Heavenly Minds, gazing, as far as we may, with supermundane eyes upon those Lordships, and the truly terrible visions of the Divine Authorities and Powers. For each appellation of the Beings above us manifests their God-imitating characteristics of the Divine Likeness. The appellation of the Holy Powers denotes a certain courageous and unflinching virility, for all those Godlike energies within them. The middle Order of the Heavenly Minds having these Godlike characteristics, is purified and illuminated and perfected in the manner described, by the Divine illuminations vouchsafed to it at second hand, through the first Hierarchical Order, and passing through this middle as a secondary manifestation. No doubt, as regards that message, which is said to pass through one Angel to another, we may take it as a symbol of a perfecting completed from afar and obscured by reason of its passage to the second rank. For, as men skilled in our sacred initiations say, the fulness of Divine things manifested directly to ourselves is more perfecting than the Divine contemplations imparted through others. Thus, I think, the immediate participation of the Angelic ranks elevated in first degree to God, is more clear than those perfected through the instrumentality of others. Wherefore by our sacerdotal tradition, the first Minds are named perfecting, and illuminating, and purifying Powers of the subordinate, who are conducted, through them, to the superessential Origin of all things, and participate, as far as is permissible to them, in the consecrating purifications, and illuminations, and perfections. For, this is divinely fixed absolutely by the Divine source of order that, through the first, the second partake of the supremely Divine illuminations. This you will find declared by the theologians in many ways."

Concerning the Principalities, Archangels, and Angels, and concerning their last Hierarchy

"There remains for our reverent contemplation, a Division, which completes the Angelic Hierarchies, that divided into the Godlike Principalities, Archangels, and Angels. And I think it necessary, to declare first the meaning of their sacred appellations to the best of my ability. For that of the Heavenly Principalities manifests their princely and leading function, after the Divine example, with order religious and most befitting the Princely. The Order of the Holy Archangels is of the same rank with the heavenly Principalities."

"For there is one Hierarchy and Division, as I said, of them and the Angels. But since there is not a Hierarchy which does not possess first and middle and last powers, the holy order of Archangels occupies the middle position in the Hierarchy between the extremes, for it belongs alike to the most holy Principalities and to the holy Angels; to the Principalities because it is turned in a princely fashion to the superessential Princedom, and is molded to It as far as attainable, and unites the Angels after the fashion of its own well-regulated and marshalled and invisible leadings; and it belongs to the Angels, because it is of the messenger Order, receiving hierarchically the Divine illuminations from the first powers, and announcing the same to the Angels in a godly manner, and, through Angels, manifesting to us, in proportion to the religious aptitude of each of the godly persons illuminated. For the Angels, as we have already said, complete the whole series of Heavenly Minds, as being the last Order of the Heavenly Beings who possess the Angelic characteristic; yea, rather, they are more properly named Angels by us than those of higher degree, because their Hierarchy is occupied with the more manifest, and is more particularly concerned with the things of the world. For the very highest Order, as being placed in the first rank near the Hidden One, we must consider as directing in spiritual things the second, hiddenly; and that the second, which is composed of the holy Lordships and Powers and Authorities, leads the Hierarchy of the Principalities and Archangels and Angels, more clearly indeed than the first Hierarchy, but more hiddenly than the Order after it, and the revealing order of the Principalities, Archangels, and Angels, presides, through each other, over the Hierarchies amongst men, in order that the elevation, and conversion, and communion, and union with God may be in due order; and, further, also that the procession from God vouchsafed benignly to all the Hierarchies, and passing to all in common, may be also with most sacred regularity. Hence, the Word of God has assigned our Hierarchy to Angels, by naming Michael as Ruler of the Jewish people, and others over other nations. For the Most High established borders of nations according to number of Angels of God."

Rudolf Steiner on Dionysius the Areopagite

The Spiritual Hierarchies, **Rudolf Steiner, Lecture I, Düsseldorf, April 12, 1909, GA 110**

"It was the most intimate pupil of St. Paul, Dionysius the Areopagite, who said in clear-cut words: 'There is not only matter out there in space; there is, for the soul which rises consciously into the spaces of universal existence, the spiritual part which stands above man in the evolution of existence.' And he used words which sounded different from the old ones, for if he had used the old words everybody would have understood them in the material sense. The Rishis spoke of the spiritual hierarchies, they expressed in their language what the Greek and Roman wisdom still described when speaking of the ascending scale of worlds: of the Moon, of Mercury, Mars and Venus, Jupiter, and Saturn. Dionysius, the pupil of the Apostle Paul had the same worlds in his mind as the Rishis, he repeated in clear cut words that here one had to do with spiritual realms, and he used words which he could be certain would be understood in their spiritual sense: he spoke of Angels, Archangels, Archai, Powers, Mights, Dominions, Thrones, Cherubim, and Seraphim.

For now, humanity had completely forgotten what it once knew. Had it still been able to understand the connection between what Dionysius and the Rishis had seen, it would have grasped, while hearing on the one side of the Moon, and on the other side of the Mysteries of the Angels, that these were one and the same thing. It would have heard the word Mercury on the one hand and Archangel on the other and would have known they were the same. The word 'Archai' spoken by the one, and 'Venus' by the other, were the same. And men. would have understood that with the words 'Sun' and 'Powers' the same worlds were meant. With the name 'Mars' they would have felt that they had to rise to the Mights (Dynamis). When they heard Jupiter mentioned, they would have known that it was the same as when in the school of Dionysius, Dominions were described. Saturn corresponds to 'Thrones'; but in wider circles this was not known any more, it could not be known. Thus there was on the one side a science of matter, which became ever more material, and the old names which once signified spiritual forces, were now used in a material sense. And on the other side, there was a spiritual life which spoke of Angels and Archangels, etc. which had lost its connection with the physical designations of these spiritual beings."

"Thus, we see how the primeval wisdom enters through Dionysius into the school which Paul had inaugurated, and how this new inauguration had to be penetrated by the ancient spirit. It is the task of modern Spiritual Science, or anthroposophy to form once more the bond which must unite the physical to the spiritual, the bond between the Earth and the spiritual hierarchies."

Thomas Aquinas on the Hierarchies

Summa Theologiae, Thomas Aquinas (1125-1274), Question 108. *The Angelic Degrees of Hierarchies and Orders*

"I answer that, the grades of the Angelic orders are assigned by Gregory (*Hom.* xxiv in *Ev.*) and Dionysius (*Coel. Hier.* vii), who agree as regards all except the 'Principalities' and 'Virtues.' For Dionysius places the 'Virtues' beneath the 'Dominations,' and above the 'Powers'; the 'Principalities' beneath the 'Powers' and above the 'Archangels.' Gregory, however, places the 'Principalities' between the 'Dominations' and the 'Powers'; and the 'Virtues' between the 'Powers' and the 'Archangels.' Each of these placings may claim authority from the words of the Apostle, who (*Ephesians* 1:20-21) enumerates the middle orders, beginning from the lowest saying that 'God set Him'; i.e., Christ, 'on His right hand in the heavenly places above all Principality and Power, and Virtue, and Dominion.' Here he places 'Virtues' between 'Powers' and 'Dominations,' according to the placing of Dionysius. Writing however to the *Colossians* (1:16), numbering the same orders from the highest, he says: 'Whether Thrones, or Dominations, or Principalities, or Powers, all things were created by Him and in Him.' Here he places the 'Principalities' between 'Dominations' and 'Powers,' as does also Gregory.

"Let us then first examine the reason for the ordering of Dionysius, in which we see, that, as said above, the highest hierarchy contemplates the ideas of things in God Himself; the second in the universal causes; and third in their application to particular effects. And because God is the end not only of the Angelic ministrations, but also of the whole creation, it belongs to the first hierarchy to consider the end; to the middle one belongs the universal disposition of what is to be done; and to the last belongs the application of this disposition to the effect, which is the carrying out of the work; for it is clear that these three things exist in every kind of operation. So Dionysius, considering the properties of the orders as derived from their names, places in the first hierarchy those orders the names of which are taken from their relation to God, the 'Seraphim,' 'Cherubim,' and 'Thrones'; and he places in the middle hierarchy those orders whose names denote a certain kind of common government or disposition—the 'Dominations,' 'Virtues,' and 'Powers'; and he places in the third hierarchy the orders whose names denote the execution of the work, the 'Principalities,' 'Angels,' and 'Archangels.'

"As regards the end, three things may be considered. For firstly we consider the end; then we acquire perfect knowledge of the end; thirdly, we fix our intention on the end; of which the second is an addition to the first, and the third an addition to both. And because God is the end of creatures, as the leader is the end of an army, as the Philosopher says (*Metaph.* xii, *Did.* xi, 10); so a somewhat similar order may be seen in human affairs. For there are some who enjoy the dignity of being able with familiarity to approach the king or leader; others in addition are privileged to know his secrets; and others above these ever abide with him, in a close union. According to this similitude, we can understand the disposition in the orders of the first hierarchy; for the 'Thrones' are raised up so as to be the familiar recipients of God in themselves, in the sense of knowing immediately the types of things in Himself; and this is proper to the whole of the first hierarchy. The 'Cherubim' know the Divine secrets supereminently; and the 'Seraphim' excel in what is the supreme excellence of all, in being united to God Himself; and all this in such a manner that the whole of this hierarchy can be called the

'Thrones'; as, from what is common to all the heavenly spirits together, they are all called 'Angels.'

"As regards government, three things are comprised therein, the first of which is to appoint those things which are to be done, and this belongs to the 'Dominations'; the second is to give the power of carrying out what is to be done, which belongs to the 'Virtues'; the third is to order how what has been commanded or decided to be done can be carried out by others, which belongs to the 'Powers.' The execution of the Angelic ministrations consists in announcing Divine things. Now in the execution of any action there are beginners and leaders; as in singing, the precentors; and in war, generals and officers; this belongs to the 'Principalities.' There are others who simply execute what is to be done; and these are the 'Angels.' Others hold a middle place; and these are the 'Archangels,' as above explained.

"This explanation of the orders is quite a reasonable one. For the highest in an inferior order always has affinity to the lowest in the higher order; as the lowest animals are near to the plants. Now the first order is that of the Divine Persons, which terminates in the Holy Ghost, Who is Love proceeding, with Whom the highest order of the first hierarchy has affinity, denominated as it is from the fire of love. The lowest order of the first hierarchy is that of the 'Thrones,' who in their own order are akin to the 'Dominations'; for the 'Thrones,' according to Gregory (*Hom.* xxiv in *Ev.*), are so called 'because through them God accomplishes His judgments,' since they are enlightened by Him in a manner adapted to the immediate enlightening of the second hierarchy, to which belongs the disposition of the Divine ministrations. The order of the 'Powers' is akin to the order of the 'Principalities'; for as it belongs to the 'Powers' to impose order on those subject to them, this ordering is plainly shown at once in the name of 'Principalities,' who, as presiding over the government of peoples and kingdoms (which occupies the first and principal place in the Divine ministrations), are the first in the execution thereof; 'for the good of a nation is more divine than the good of one man' (*Ethic.* i, 2); and hence it is written, 'The prince of the kingdom of the Persians resisted me.' (*Daniel* 10:13).

"The disposition of the orders which is mentioned by Gregory is also reasonable. For since the 'Dominations' appoint and order what belongs to the Divine ministrations, the orders subject to them are arranged according to the disposition of those things in which the Divine ministrations are effected. Still, as Augustine says (*De Trin.* ii.), 'bodies are ruled in a certain order; the inferior by the superior; and all of them by the spiritual creature, and the bad spirit by the good spirit.' So, the first order after the 'Dominations' is called that of 'Principalities,' who rule even over good spirits; then the 'Powers,' who coerce the evil spirits; even as evil-doers are coerced by Earthly powers, as it is written (*Romans* 13:3-4). After these come the 'Virtues,' which have power over corporeal nature in the working of miracles; after these are the 'Angels' and the 'Archangels,' who announce to men either great things above reason, or small things within the purview of reason."

Johannes Trithemius of Sponheim and the Spiritual Hierarchy

Johannes Trithemius (1462-1516) was a German Benedictine abbot and a polymath who was active in the German Renaissance as a lexicographer, chronicler, cryptographer, and occultist. He had considerable influence on the development of early modern and modern occultism. His students included Heinrich Cornelius Agrippa von Nettesheim, Paracelsus, Johann Reuchlin, Conrad Celtis, Johann von Dalberg and Emperor Maximillian.

Johannes Trithemius' *Seven Secondary Causes of the Heavenly Intelligencies Governing the Orbes Under God* contains a treatise he wrote for the Emperor in 1508 in which he outlines the history of the world from creation in year one, to the onset of the current Michael Age in the year 7086 (1879 A. D.). In a brief seventeen pages, he lists the major biblical, religious, and political events and places them chronologically into their correct Archangelic Age. Not only chronologically, but logically according to the characteristics of the Archangel of the Age. This is a handy reference to the characteristics of the various Archangels and to the overall progress during the various phases of an Age. Trithemius uses an exact period of 354 years and four months for each Age, corresponding to the lunar month. This indicates an uncertainty in the exact number of years of an Age. Rudolf Steiner's notebook gives periods ranging from 320 years to 369 years.

Seven Secondary Causes of the Heavenly Intelligencies Governing the Orbes Under God, Johannes Trithemius (1508)

"…from the original or first beginning of heaven and Earth, there were seven spirits appointed as presidents to the seven planets. Of which number every one of those ruled the world 354 years and four months in order."

- "The first Angel or Spirit of Saturn is called Orifiel, to whom God committed the government of the World from the beginning of its Creation.
- The second Governor of the World is Anael the Spirit of Venus, who after Orifiel began to rule according to the influence of this Planet.
- Zachariel, the Angel of Jupiter, began to govern the world in the year of the Creation of Heaven and Earth 708.

- The fourth Rector of the World was Raphael, the Spirit of Mercury which began in the year of the Creation of Heaven and Earth 1063.
- The fifth Gubernator of the World was Samuel the Angel of Mars, who began the 26th day of the month of June in the year of the World 1417.
- The sixth Governor of the World is Gabriel, the Angel of the Moon, who began in the year of the World 1771.
- Michael, the Angel of the Sun, was the seventh Ruler of the World who began in the year of the World 2126.
- Under the Dominion of the Angel of the Sun, Kings began first to be amongst Mortal men with an ambitious desire of Sovereignty. The worship of several Gods by the foolishness of men, was now instituted, and they began to adore their petty Princes as Gods."

Using Trithemius' lunar year scheme, comprised of 354-year Archangelic rulership periods, we can derive another version of Trithemius' Archangelic rulership periods. They are as follows:

Archangel	Planet	Year Began	Season
Uriel	Saturn	246 B.C.	Summer
Anael	Venus	109 A.D.	
Zachariel	Jupiter	463 A.D.	
Raphael	Mercury	817 A.D.	Spring
Samael	Mars	1171 A.D.	
Gabriel	Moon	1525 A.D.	Winter
Michael	Sun	1879 A.D.	Autumn

Rudolf Steiner on Hierarchical Attributes

The Spiritual Hierarchies, Rudolf Steiner, Lecture II, Düsseldorf, April 12, 1909, GA 110

"All things were once upon a time fire; everything has been born out of fire. But in all that solidified realm, some bewitched spirits are dwelling. Spiritual divine beings send down their elemental spirits, those which live in the fire: they imprison them in air, in water, and in Earth. These are the emissaries, the elemental emissaries of the spiritual, creative, building beings. The elemental spirits first enter into fire. In fire they still feel comfortable—if we care to express it by images—and then they are condemned to a life of bewitchment."

"Something from those bewitched elementals passes continually into the man, from morning till night. Through his own spiritual process, he releases the elemental being which has streamed into him from the outer world; he raises it to what it was before, he frees the elemental from its state of enchantment. Thus, through our own spiritual life, we can, without changing them, either imprison within us those spirits which are bewitched in air, water, and Earth, or else through our own increasing spirituality, free them and lead them back to their own element. During the whole of his earthly life, man lets those elemental spirits stream into him from the outer world. In the same measure in which he only stares at things, in the same measure in which he simply lets the spirit dwell in him without transforming them, so, in like measure as he tries with his ideas, conceptions and feeling for beauty to work out spiritually what he sees in the outer world, does he release and redeem those spiritual elemental beings."

Prior Solar Systems Before Our Own

The Spiritual Hierarchies, **Rudolf Steiner, Lecture V, Düsseldorf, April 14, 1909, GA 110**

"The course of evolution is this: a Sun, which from the beginning is included in such a system, has at first to throw off its planets, being too weak to develop further without excluding them. It grows strong, absorbs its planets again, and grows into a Vulcan. Then the whole is dissolved, and from the Vulcan globe is formed a hollow globe which is something like the circles of Thrones, Cherubim, Seraphim, etc. The Sun will thus dissolve in space, sacrifice itself, send forth its Being into the Universe, and through this will itself become a circle of Beings like the Thrones, Cherubim, Seraphim; which will then advance towards new creation.

"Why are the Thrones enabled to give out of their substance what Saturn needs? Because they have prepared themselves in an earlier system, through seven conditions like those our solar system is now going through. Before a system of Thrones, Cherubim, Seraphim can be evolved, it must have been a solar system at an earlier stage; which means, that when the Sun has got so far as to be reunited with its planets, it becomes itself a circle—a Zodiacal circle. That which we have come to know in the Zodiac, those great, sublime Beings, are the results that have come over to us from an earlier solar system. That which has formerly evolved within a solar system can now send down its influence out of universal space, and produce a new solar system, created out of itself. The Seraphim, Cherubim and Thrones are for us the highest Hierarchy among divine Beings, because they have already passed through their solar system evolution and have risen to mighty cosmic deeds of sacrifice.

"Hence it is that these Beings have come into the actual direct vicinity of the highest Godhead of which we can speak at all: the Trinity, the three-fold Divinity. Beyond the Seraphim we have to see that highest Divinity of which we find mention by almost all nations as the threefold Divinity—as Brahma, Shiva, Vishnu, as Father, Word, and Holy Ghost. From out of this highest Godhead, this most exalted Trinity, stream forth the plans for a new cosmic system. Glancing back at ancient Saturn we say to ourselves: before any of this ancient Saturn came into Being, the plan of it had grown within the divine threefold Unity. But the threefold Unity has need of Beings to execute its plan. These Beings must first prepare themselves for the task. The Beings who, are so to speak, nearest God Himself, who, as is beautifully expressed in Christian Western Esotericism, 'bask in the light of God's countenance,' are the Seraphim, Cherubim, and Thrones. These take up the plans of a new cosmic system streaming from the divine threefold Unity. This is naturally expressed more figuratively than it really is, for we have to express in human words such sublime activities, for which, in truth, this human language has not been created. No human words exist to express such sublime activity as that, for instance, when the Seraphim, in the beginning of our solar system received the highest plans of the divine Threefold Unity containing the evolution which our solar system has to pass through, namely Old Saturn, Old Sun, Old Moon, Earth, Future Jupiter, Future Venus and Future Vulcan. Seraphim is a name which for those who understand it in its true sense, even in that of ancient Hebrew Esotericism, has always signified that the task of the Seraphim was to receive from the Trinity the highest ideas and aims for a system of worlds. The Cherubim, the next lower rank of the Hierarchies, had the task of building up in wisdom the aims and ideas which they received from the higher gods. Thus, the Cherubim are spirits of highest wisdom, who understood how to transpose into workable plans, the inspirations given to them by the Seraphim. And the Thrones, the third grade of the Hierarchies, counting from above, had the task—naturally very figuratively expressed—of putting things into action, so that what had been thought out in Wisdom—these lofty cosmic thoughts which the Seraphim had received from the Gods, and which the Cherubim had pondered over, should be transformed into active reality."

The Hierarchy Acting Through Humans

The Spiritual Hierarchies, **by Rudolf Steiner, Lecture VII, Düsseldorf, April 16, 1909, GA 110**

"Thus, the Spirits of Personality came down to Earth, as Spirits of Venus, in ancient Lemurian times. And we can say that the distinctive features of these messengers from Venus—such as the human countenances of that time could wear—signified something quite new with regard to the whole Universe. If we take their cosmic significance, it reaches as far as Venus, and their actions had a meaning, an influence on the entire interconnection of the Solar System. They could lead the people from one place to another, for they knew the connections that can only be known by those who are acquainted with the surroundings of the Earth, and not only with the Earth itself.

"The development of humanity progressed further, and the necessity arose that Archangels, spirits of astronomical Mercury, should act upon human development. These were now obliged to ensoul and give life to that which dwelt below upon Earth. This was principally in Atlantean times. At that time, the Archangels or Spirits of Mercury descended upon Earth and inspired the physical and etheric bodies of the men of that period. So, in Atlantis there were also men who were not outwardly very different from the others, but whose physical and etheric bodies were ensouled by an Archangel. And if you remember what was said yesterday, that the Archangels have the task of directing whole nations, you will understand that a man who had an Archangel within him could actually give to the whole Atlantean race those laws which he received directly from heaven. The great leaders of old Lemurian times, when it was still necessary to act much more generally, were ensouled by Spirits from Venus. Those who, in Atlantean times had to direct smaller masses of people, were ensouled by Archangels. Those who are called the priest-kings of Atlantis, were in truth—Maya [Illusion]. They were not at all what they outwardly appeared to be. An Archangel lived in their physical and etheric bodies; he was the real active agent.

"If we go back to Atlantean times, we can seek out the secret stations of these leaders of mankind. From these hidden centers they worked, there they investigated the mysteries of Space. One might ascribe the name of 'Oracle' to what was investigated and commanded from those ancient Atlantean places of the Mysteries, even though this word originated in later times. The name 'Place of the Oracles' is quite suitable to these centers of instruction, and government. From them the great teachers worked, so that others might there be trained to become priests and servants of men.

"It is important that one should know that there were men in ancient Atlantis who in reality were Archangels, bearing an Archangel incarnated within their physical and etheric bodies. If such a man had been seen by someone endowed with clairvoyance, the latter would in fact have seen a physical man and behind him an enormous figure, rising high above him, and losing itself in indefinite regions—the figure of the inspiring

Archangel. Such a personality was of a two-fold nature, as if behind the physical man, growing out of indefinite Space, was the inspiring Archangel. When such men died, the physical body was destroyed according to the laws of Atlantis. That physical body, which had been naturally ensouled by the Archangel, dissolved, but the etheric body did not dissolve. There is a spiritual economy which demands exceptions to the general truths expounded by Anthroposophy. We say—and in general it is correct—that when a man dies, he lays aside his physical body and after a certain time also his etheric body, which dissolves with the exception of an extract. But this is only generally the case. There is an enormous difference between an etheric body like that of the Initiates of the Atlantean Oracles, which was permeated by an Archangel, and an ordinary etheric body. Such a precious etheric body is not lost, but is preserved in the spiritual world. In the first place, the great leader of the Atlantean Oracles preserved the seven most important etheric bodies of the seven great initiators of these Oracles. These ether bodies were originally built up through being inhabited by Archangels, who, at their death, naturally returned to the higher worlds. Such things are certainly not preserved in boxes, but according to spiritual laws. The Atlantean Initiate of the Sun-Oracle is no other than Manu, who has been often mentioned, and who guided the remnant of the Atlantean nation over to Asia to establish the new post-Atlantean civilization. He took his little handful of people with him and led them over to Asia. He trained the people through generations, and when the seven most adaptable ones had been bred and educated sufficiently, he wove into their individual etheric bodies the substance of the seven preserved etheric bodies, which had been woven by Archangels in ancient Atlantis. Those seven, who were sent down by the great Leader, to lay the foundation of the first

Post-Atlantean civilization, were the seven holy Rishis of ancient India; they bore within their etheric garment, the etheric bodies of the great Atlantean Leaders, who had themselves acquired these bodies through the Archangels. Thus the past, the present, and the future acted in harmony. Those seven men who are called the holy Rishis would have appeared to you as simple people; for with their astral body and their Ego, they had not reached the height of their etheric bodies.

"All that they were capable of was interwoven with their etheric bodies. There were certain hours during which inspiration acted within their etheric bodies, and then they spoke of things which they themselves could never have known. Then from their lips flowed that which had been inspired into their etheric bodies. Thus, they were simple, plain people when they were left to their own understanding; but in their hours of inspiration, when the etheric body was active, they spoke of the greatest mysteries of our solar system and of the whole universe.

"In the post-Atlantean times men had not yet advanced so far that they could do without help from above, inspiration was still necessary; and a sort of ensouling still took place from above. We have seen how such ensouling occurred in Lemurian times, because a spirit of Personality ensouled the physical body; in the Atlantean times the physical and the etheric bodies were ensouled by Archangels, and now the great leaders of the Post-Atlantean times were ensouled through an Angel descending into their physical, etheric and astral bodies. The great leaders of humanity in the Post-Atlantean times did not possess merely a physical, etheric and astral body, but an Angel also lived within them. Therefore, these great leaders could look back into their former incarnations. The ordinary man cannot do so as yet, because he has not yet developed his Manas; he must himself first become an Angel. These leaders, who were born out of the ordinary inhabitants, carried an Angelic Being within their physical, etheric and astral bodies, who ensouled and, interpenetrated them. This is again Maya, again we have Beings who are something different from what they appear to be on earth. The great leaders of humanity of grey antiquity were quite different from what they outwardly seemed to be. They were personalities in whom an Angel dwelt and gave what they needed, so that they might become Teachers and Leaders of men. The great founders of religions were men possessed by Angels. Angels spoke through them…

"…Thus it was possible to have men also in the Post-Atlantean times, who bore externally all the characteristics of their nation, but who, because humanity still needed such great leaders, carried within them a Spirit of Personality—and who were the external incarnation of such a Spirit. Then there were also men in the Post-Atlantean times who had an Archangel, a Spirit of Mercury, within them, who ensouled their physical and etheric bodies. And lastly, a third category of men was ensouled, inspired in their physical, etheric, and astral bodies by an Angel Being, one through whom an Angel spoke. In the spirit of Eastern Teaching such personalities received particular names. Thus, a personality who outwardly resembles a man of our post-Atlantean times, but who really is the bearer of a Spirit of Personality, who is ensouled by that Spirit down to his physical body, is called Dhyani-Buddha in the Eastern Teaching. Dhyani-Buddha is a generic name for human individualities in whom the Spirits of Personality are active, even as far as their physical body.

"Those personalities who are ensouled down to their etheric body, who were bearers of Archangels in the post-Atlantean times, are called Bodhisattva. And those who are the bearers of an

Angel, who are, therefore, ensouled in their physical, etheric, and astral bodies, are called human Buddhas.

"Thus, we have three degrees: that of the Dhyani-Buddha, the Bodhisattva and the human Buddha. This is the true teaching of the Buddhas, of the classes and categories of Buddhas, which we have to recognize in connection with the whole manner and means by which the Hierarchies fulfill their ends. This is the marvel which meets us, when we look back to earlier undeveloped men, that among these men we find those, through whom the Hierarchies speak The great Hierarchies speak out of the Cosmos downwards into the Planets, and only by degrees do these Spirits of the higher Hierarchies, who were active before the appearance of our Earth, emancipate the planetary men who live down here, when they have reached the necessary degree of ripeness. Here we gaze into unfathomable depths of wisdom. And what is of extraordinary importance is, that we understand this wisdom exactly as it was taught in all the ages, when primeval wisdom was taught to men.

"Thus, when you hear of the Buddhas—for they do not speak of the one Buddha only in the Eastern teaching, but of many, among whom there are naturally different grades of perfection— give attention to the fact: a Buddha walks on Earth; but behind the Buddha, was the Bodhisattva and even the Dhyani-Buddha.

"Matters, however, might be so, that the Dhyani-Buddha or the Bodhisattva did not reach so far as to ensoul the physical body, but that the Bodhisattva descended only as far as to be able to ensoul the etheric body, so that you can imagine a Being who does not reach so far as to ensoul and inspire the man's physical body; but only the etheric body. It can, however, happen when such a Bodhisattva is not physically visible (for when he appears only in an etheric body he is not physically visible, and there were such Bodhisattva who were physically invisible) that he can, as a higher Being, inspire quite exceptionally the human Buddha. So that we have the human Buddha, who is already inspired by an Angelic Being, being further inspired in his etheric body by an Archangel Being. It is essential that we should look into this wonderful complexity of the human nature. Many Individualities to whom we look back into former times can only be understood, when we accept them as the meeting point of different higher Beings, who proclaim and express themselves through the man. For, in truth, many periods do not possess a sufficient number of great men to be inspired by the Spirits who have to be active. Thus, sometimes one single personality has to be ensouled by different individualities of the higher Hierarchies. And sometimes it is not only the inhabitants of Mercury who speak with us, when we have a certain personality standing before us, but the inhabitants of Venus also."

The Human Stages of the Hierarchy

The Mission of the Individual Folk Souls, Rudolf Steiner, Lecture I, *Angels, Folk Spirits, Time Spirits: Their Part in the Evolution of Mankind*, Christiania (Oslo), June 7, 1910, GA 121

"We human beings on Earth are now living through the stage of self-consciousness which other Beings under-went during the earlier stages of our Earth-evolution, the stages of Old Moon, Old Sun, and Old Saturn. Those Beings who underwent their human stage on Old Moon and who therefore are one stage above Man were called in Christian esoteric terminology, Angels. They are one stage higher than man because they completed their stage of human evolution one Epoch earlier. Their mode of existence on the Old Moon differed from that of man on Earth today.

They were Beings at the human stage but were not incarnated in a physical body. Their stage of evolution corresponded to the human stage which man is experiencing today. In the same way we find Beings of a higher order who underwent their human stage on the Old Sun. These Beings are the Archangels who are two stages beyond man and who underwent their human stage two Epochs earlier. If we go still further back to the first incarnation of our Earth-existence, to Old Saturn, we find that those Beings whom we called the Spirits of Personality or Archai underwent their human stage on Old Saturn. To summarize: the First Beginnings, the Archai, were men on Old Saturn, the Archangels were men on Old Sun, the Angels were men on Old Moon and men are men on our Earth."

"Since we know that we continue our evolution into the future and that we further develop our present astral body, etheric or life-body and our physical body, the question arises: is it not equally natural that the Beings who have already experienced the human stage have now reached the stage when they are transmuting their astral body into Spirit-Self or Manas? Just as during the next incarnation of the Earth, the Jupiter stage, we shall complete the transmutation of our astral body into Spirit-Self or Manas, so the Angels who underwent the human stage on Old Moon have completed the transmutation of their astral bodies into Spirit-Self or Manas, or will do so during our Earth evolution, a stage that we shall first have to undergo in the next incarnation of the Earth [Jupiter]. If we look still further back to the Beings who underwent the human stage on Old Sun, we realize that they already experienced on Old Moon the stage we shall have to experience for the first time in the next incarnation of the Earth. They are performing the work which will be the prerogative of man when, in his ego, he transmutes his etheric or life-body into Life-Spirit or Budhi. These Archangels, therefore, are Beings who are two stages beyond man; they have reached the stage that will one day be ours when from within our ego, we shall transform the life-body into Life-Spirit or Budhi [Venus]. When we contemplate these Beings, we recognize them as Beings who are two stages beyond ourselves, who foreshadow what we ourselves will experience in the future; they are Beings who are now working upon their etheric or life-body and are transmuting it into Life-Spirit or Budhi. In the same way we are aware of yet higher Beings, the Spirits of Personality (Archai). They are at a still higher stage than the Archangels, a stage which man will reach in a still more distant future when he will be able to transmute his physical body into Atman or Spirit-Man.

"In the same way we are aware of yet higher Beings, the Spirits of Personality (Archai) who underwent the human stage on Old Saturn. They are at a still higher stage than the Archangels, a stage which man will reach in a still more distant future when he will be able to transmute his physical body into Atman or Spirit-Human [Vulcan]."

The Mission of the Individual Folk Souls, **Rudolf Steiner, Lecture V,** *Manifestation of the Hierarchies in the Elements of Nature. The Mission of the planetary Epochs of Old Saturn, Old Sun, Old Moon and Earth,* **Christiania (Oslo), June 11, 1910, GA 121**

"The last of the Beings of the Second Hierarchy are the Spirits of Wisdom, who work from the surrounding Cosmos into the weaving light and into the Music of the Spheres operating throughout the Universe. That is the Life of the universal Ether, raying in on to the Earth. For Life is pouring in on to the Earth from cosmic spaces and is received by living creatures here on Earth. It comes from the Spirits of Wisdom.

"Thus, we gaze out into cosmic spaces and perceive first of all the Sun in which these threefold forces are concentrated for our spiritual vision. We perceive how *instreaming Life, weaving Sound, formative Light*, the trinity of the second Hierarchy, are working in from universal space. The highest of the Hierarchies, the Seraphim, the Cherubim and the Thrones, work upwards from below, from the center of the Earth. The third Hierarchy (the Hierarchy immediately above man) is interwoven with all terrestrial activity and works chiefly in the inner being of organic life. To this Hierarchy belongs, in the first place, the Archai acting as the Time Spirits. These Time Spirits work in the material prepared for them by the higher Hierarchies; they lay the foundation of what we call the history of mankind, the evolution of civilization on Earth. Then in our immediate environment we find the Archangels, the tribal Folk Spirits, and finally the Angels who mediate between the individual human' beings and the Archangels.

"To sum up, therefore: In the forces of Nature upon our planet, in earth, water, air and fire are the Beings of the first or highest Hierarchy who stream forth to meet the activity of the Spirits of Form working in from the cosmic sphere. From outside, the Beings of the second Hierarchy stream in, and in the environment of the Earth are the Beings of the third Hierarchy who, for the moment, are the weakest of the forces. Just imagine for a moment how powerful are the forces of those exalted Beings whom we call the Spirits of Will, who fashion the very ground under our feet. Then we have those forces which stream in from outside, the Spirits of Form who are nearest to us, and who mold the contours of the Earth in their plastic state. And finally, we have Angels, Archangels and Archai who work more intimately into human souls. And so, in the first (highest) Hierarchy we have those forces of Nature which we recognize as the strongest—the Nature-forces emanating from the center of the Earth, the forces of the solid Earth beneath us. In the second Hierarchy we have the cosmic forces which live and weave around us in the ether and in the third Hierarchy we have that which lives and weaves in the inner recesses of our soul…

"In occult symbolism this Earth-mission has always been expressed in a special way by means of a geometrical figure. Amongst geometrical figures you will find none which corresponds so exactly to the balance or harmony of these three activities as the equilateral triangle. If you draw an equilateral triangle you will find the three sides are equal, the three angles equal, the vertices are equidistant from each other and all are equidistant from the center. The center of an equilateral triangle is a complete symbol of a balance of forces, so that when the occultist looks at an equilateral triangle he perceives in it a symbol of the perfectly balanced cooperation of those elements, each of which held for a time the upper hand in the three earlier incarnations of our Earth. The deeds of the 'I' in man signify simply the creation of an active center in his nature whereby this state of harmony can be prepared from within. Man therefore is called to high destiny on Earth to bring about from within, first of all through his whole being, a balance between what was predominant for a time in earlier planetary epochs in various ways and at various times.

"Now that is a very general definition of our Earth mission, but this mission is exactly as I have described it. The secret of this mission is that through this cooperation, through this balance or harmony of the three forces, the inner being really creates something new. A fourth element, which is the element of Love, is thus added to the three preceding elements. Love can only develop in the busy work-a-day world when an absolute harmony exists between the three forces, which in earlier epochs were each in turn, the dominating influence...

"Thus our planet is the planet of Love and therefore the result of this balance or harmony which is reflected in the cooperation of the three forces is the active spirit of Love, and this spirit of Love is to be woven into the whole of evolution throughout all the successive incarnations of the Earth by the fulfillment of the Earth's mission. In this way the Trinity becomes a Quaternary: the latter begins with its fourth element at the lowest stage, with the most elementary or primitive form of love which is so purged and purified that at the close of the Earth-evolution Love will appear as an element enjoying to the full equal status with the others. To fulfil the mission of balance or harmony ordained for our Earth planet implies, in reality, transforming the Trinity into a Quaternary. To make the Trinity into a Quaternary is therefore an occult formula for the Earth's secret. Inevitably the fourth element is today still very imperfect. But when the Earth shall have fulfilled its mission, it will appear as luminous as the Sacred Triangle which, with its state of perfect balance, shines forth as the highest symbol we possess for our Earth—ideal in so far as we can remember the past of the Earth.

"This correspondence between the elements of thinking, feeling and willing is such that the inmost being of man becomes the substance of Love and this is what one may call the really creative, the inwardly creative element in earthly existence. We must therefore describe the Spirits of Form in their totality (because their particular mission is to harmonize the three former conditions) as the Spirits of Love.

"In considering Earth-existence in this way we first described thinking, feeling and willing and the working of Love outside our Earth planet and we described as the special task of the Spirits of Form the implanting of Love which results from balance or harmony. This is the whole mission of the Earth. In order to realize this power of Love that shall permeate the Earth, the interplay and interaction of the lowest Hierarchies was necessary. As we began to indicate in our previous study, the network of Love must be woven by these Hierarchies and Love must be woven in such a way that the principal threads are woven by the normal Spirits of Form, for that is their fundamental mission. Then the abnormal Spirits of Form, who are in reality Spirits of Movement, weave into the tapestry that which creates the different races. Then the normal and abnormal Time Spirits weave into it the historical evolution, and the normal and abnormal Archangels the evolution of the individual peoples and languages; and finally the Angels who determine man's rightful place on Earth participate in this activity. In this way the mighty tapestry of Love is being woven. Yet of this tapestry of Love which is being woven as the real mission of Earth only the Maya, the outer reflection, is visible on Earth."

Angels of the Beginnings

The Spiritual Hierarchies, **Rudolf Steiner, Lecture III, Düsseldorf, Morning April 13, 1909, GA 110**

"Here you have the difference between the Old Sun and the present Sun. Our present Sun is always shining, and darkness is only produced when an object is placed in front of the light. That was not the case on the Old Sun. It had the power to produce alternating conditions of light and darkness that consisted of a breathing out and a breathing in.

"Let us imagine quite vividly what happened outwardly. Take the condition of exhalation, that is, when the light rays out and at the same time Old Sun fills itself with smoke. These forms of smoke, these currents of smoke have a regular configuration. At each exhalation a sum of regular forms are imprinted upon the substance of Old Sun. What had previously been mere egg-shaped bodies of warmth became transformed into various regular structures. Quite remarkable structures of smoke containing an inner life and regularity now arose. It was as if the eggs hatched; which might be compared to a process of solidification. Much as the chicken comes out of the egg, so had the eggs of warmth been split asunder; regular smoke forms emerged; which were the densest bodies of the Archangels. They inhabited Old Sun in bodies of smoke, gas, and air, and thus moved about as 'men'. This gives us the spiritual idea of a fixed star, of a Universal Sun that produces the alternation of day and night by virtue of its own inherent power. Light and darkness came about through breathing out and breathing in because at that time the Old Sun was a kind of fixed star. Everything that shines forth of itself into our universal space sends the life of spiritual messengers, the Archangels, out with the light.

"What have the original Archai, the Primal Beginnings, the Spirits of Personality accomplished through their own development? They have made it possible for Old Sun to appear. If it were not for them, there would only have been an Old Saturn stage in evolution; but because the Archai left external eggs of warmth on Old Saturn the metamorphosis into Old Sun could be achieved. On the Old Sun the Archangels had the opportunity to pass through the stage of man. They became the heralds of the Cosmos; who proclaimed that the Primal Beginnings, the Spirits of Personality had preceded them. 'We proclaim as messengers of the Universe in radiating light the former existence of the warmth-permeated ancient Saturn. We are the messengers, the heralds of the Archai.' Messengers means Angeloi, Archai means Beginnings. The Archangels are, in fact, the messengers of the *deeds* of the Primal Beginnings or Archai in ancient times. That is why they are called the Angels of the Beginnings, Archai, or Angeloi; which gave rise to the English Archangels. These Arch-messengers achieved their human stage [4th stage of being] on the [Old] Sun."

The Inner Moods of Creation

The Inner Realities of Evolution, **Rudolf Steiner, Berlin, October 31-December 5, 1911, GA 132**

Lecture I, *The Inner Aspect of the Saturn-Embodiment of the Earth,* October 31, 1911

"In *Occult Science,* in order not to shock people outside unduly, I have begun by describing the more external condition of ancient Saturn. Just think what it would mean if we were to say:

- Ancient Saturn has in its innermost being—in its very foundation—this fact, that the beings belonging to the Spirits of Will [Thrones] offered sacrifice to the Cherubim,
- that in the smoke of their sacrifice, time came to birth as the sacrifice they brought to the Cherubim, and
- from this have proceeded the Archai, the Time-Spirits, and
- that external heat is nothing but a maya as compared with the sacrifice of the Spirits of Will!

"But so, it is. Externally heat is really only Maya [Illusion]. And if we wish to speak truly we must say that wherever there is heat we have in reality sacrifice, sacrifice of the Thrones to the Cherubim."

Lecture II, *The Inner Aspect of the Sun-Embodiment of the Earth*, November 7, 1911

"The inner and the outer are the two opposites which we now meet. The earlier and the later are transformed into the inner and the outer; and 'Space' is born! Space comes into existence through the bestowing virtue of the Spirits of Wisdom on Old Sun. Now we have space; but consisting at first, of only two dimensions. There was as yet no above and below, no right or left, nothing but an outer and an inner. We must think of it as a globe of inner space, in the center of which the picture of Old Saturn is recapitulated: the Thrones as Spirits as though kneeling before the Cherubim, those winged beings, sacrificing their own being, and, in addition to these, the Spirits of Wisdom, absorbed in the vision of the sacrifice. And now it is also possible to have the vision of the heat of the sacrifice being so transmuted that we may think of it objectively as the incense of sacrifice, as air ascending from the sacrifice as incense. We obtain a complete picture if we imagine:

1. The sacrificing Thrones kneeling before the Cherubim, and as though participating.

2. The Spirits of Wisdom, absorbed in the contemplation of what they perceive in the center of Old Sun as the sacrifice of the Thrones, and thereby ascending in their mood to the picture of the sacrificial incense pouring forth and spreading out on all sides, and finally condensing.

3. While from its clouds proceed the figures of the Archangels—who reflect back the incense from the periphery as light.

4. Illuminating the interior of Old Sun.

5. Returning the gift of the Spirits of Wisdom.

6. Creating the sphere of Old Sun.

"This sphere consists of the outpoured gift of glowing heat and sacrificial incense. At the outer periphery are the Archangels, the creators of the light, who later depict what was first on Old Sun; it then returns as light. The gifts they receive they reflect. That which was there in the beginning they radiate forth at a later time, and inasmuch as they do this, they are the Angels of the Beginning, because they bring into activity in later times what was previously there—Archangels or Messengers of the Beginning."

The Offspring of the Hierarchy

Karmic Relationships: Esoteric Studies, **Volume I, Rudolf Steiner, Lecture VI, Dornach, March 2, 1924, GA 235**

"It is just as it is in the physical life—you breathe in; the air you now have in yourself was outside you a short while ago, it was the-air-of-the-world; now it is your air. After a short time you give it back again to the world. You are one with the world. The air is now outside you, now within you. You would not be Man at all, if you were not so united with the world as to have not only that which is within your skin; but that with which you are connected in the whole surrounding atmosphere. And as you are thus connected on the physical side, so it is as to your spiritual part: the moment you get down into the next subconscious region—the region out of which memory arises—you are connected with that which we call the Third Hierarchy: Angels, Archangels, Archai. Just as you are connected through your breathing with the air, so are you connected with the Third Hierarchy through your head organization, namely the lower head-organization. This, which is only covered over by the outermost lobes of the brain, belongs solely to the Earth. What is immediately beneath is connected with the Third Hierarchy: Angels, Archangels, Archai.

"Now let us go down into the region, psychologically speaking, of feeling: corporeally speaking, of the rhythmic organization, out of which the dreams of our Feeling life arise. There, less than ever do we have ourselves as Man. There we are connected with what constitutes the Second Hierarchy—spiritual Beings who do not incarnate in any earthly body; for they remain in the spiritual world. But they are continually sending their currents, their impulses, the forces that go out from them, into the rhythmic organization of man. Exusiai, Dynamis, Kyriotetes—they are the Beings whom we bear within our breast.

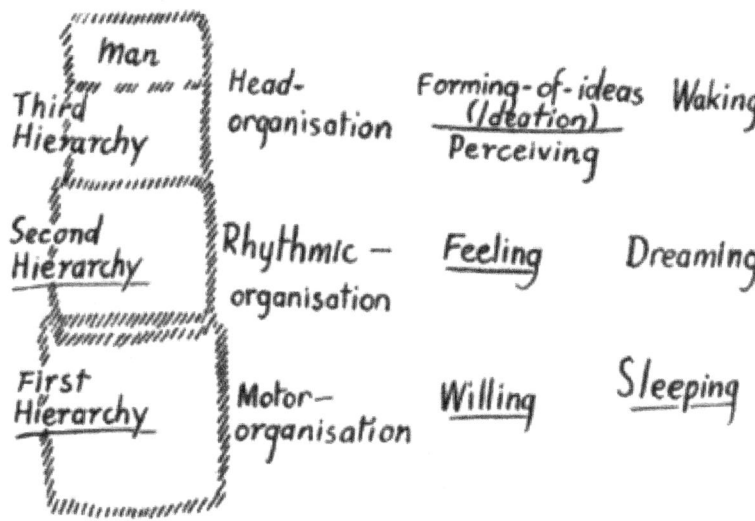

"Just as we bear our own human Ego actually only in the outermost lobes of the brain, so do we bear the Angels, Archangels, etc. immediately beneath this region, yet still within the organization of the head. There is the scene of their activities on Earth; there are the starting points of their activity. And in our breast, we carry the Second Hierarchy—Exusiai and the rest. In our breast are the starting points of their activity.

"And as we now go down into our motor-organism, the organism of movement, in this the Beings of the First Hierarchy are active: Seraphim, Cherubim and Thrones.

"The transmuted foodstuffs, the food-stuffs we have eaten, circulate in our limbs. There in our limbs, they undergo a process. It is really a living process of combustion. For if we take only a single step, there arises in us a living process of combustion, a burning-up of that which is, or was, outside us. We ourselves, as Man, are connected with this combustion process. As physical human beings with our limbs and metabolic organism, we are connected with the lowest. And yet it is precisely through the limb-organization that we are connected with the highest. With the First Hierarchy—Seraphim, Cherubim, and Thrones—we are connected by virtue of what imbues us there with spirit.

"…The Third Hierarchy—Angels, Archangels, Archai— concern themselves with that which has its physical organization in the human head, i.e., with our thinking. If they were not concerning themselves with our thinking—with that which is going on in our head—we should have no memory in ordinary earthly life. For it is the Beings of this Hierarchy who preserve in us the impulses which we receive with our perceptions. They are underlying the activity which reveals itself in our memory; they lead us through our earthly life in this first subconscious, or unconscious, region.

"Now let us go on to the Beings of the Second Hierarchy— Exusiai, Dynamis, Kyriotetes. They are the Beings we encounter when we have passed through the gate of death, that is, in the life between death and a new birth. There we encounter the souls of the departed, who lived with us on Earth; but we encounter, above all, the spiritual Beings of this Second Hierarchy—the Third Hierarchy together with them, it is true; but the Second Hierarchy are the most important there. With them we work in our time between death and a new birth—we work upon all that we felt in our earthly life, all that we brought about in our organization. Thus, in union with these Beings of the Second Hierarchy, we elaborate our coming earthly life."

Spiritual Beings in the Heavenly Bodies and in the Kingdoms of Nature, **Rudolf Steiner, Lecture V, Helsinki, April 7, 1912, GA 136**

"We have come in our studies to the so-called Second Hierarchy of the spiritual beings, and in the last lecture we described what the human soul must do if it would penetrate to the nature of the Second Hierarchy. A yet more difficult path leads to a still higher rank of spiritual beings belonging to the first, the uppermost rank of the Hierarchies to which we can attain. It has been emphasized that by means of a special enhancement of the experiences which we have in ordinary life in the feelings of sympathy and love, by raising these feelings to the occult path, we may succeed in pouring forth our own being, coming out of ourselves, as it were, and plunging into the being we wish to observe. Mark well that the characteristic of this immersion in another consists in extending our own being like tentacles and pouring it into the other being. In so doing, we must, however, always retain our own consciousness, we must be consciously present in our own inner life beside the other being. That is the characteristic feature of the second stage of clairvoyance which has been described. At this second stage, where we feel ourselves one with other beings, we must still realize that we ourselves are there, as it were, beside the other being. But even this last remains of egoistic experience must cease if we wish to ascend to the highest stage of clairvoyance.

"There we must completely lose the feeling that we exist as a separate being in any one part of the world. We must reach the point, not only of pouring ourselves into the other being and standing beside it, retaining our own separate experience, but we must actually feel the foreign being as our self. We must completely pass out of ourselves and lose the feeling that we are standing beside the other being. If we thus dive down into a foreign being, we succeed in looking upon our self as we were previously, as we are in ordinary life—as another being. For example, suppose a student at the higher stage of clairvoyance plunges down into some being of the kingdom of nature; he does not then look upon this being from within himself; he does not merely immerse himself in it as at the second stage of clairvoyance; but he knows himself to be one with this being, and he looks back upon himself from within it. Just as formerly he looked upon a foreign being as outside himself, so now at the higher stage of clairvoyance he looks out from within the foreign being and sees himself as a foreign being. That is the difference between the second and higher stages. Only when this third stage is reached do we succeed in perceiving other beings in our spiritual environment besides those of the Second and. Third Hierarchies. The spiritual beings of whom we are then aware also belong to three categories. The first category we perceive chiefly when, in the manner described, we plunge down into the being of other men or of the higher animals, and by that means educate ourselves. The essential thing is not so much what we perceive in other human beings or in the higher animals, as that we should educate ourselves by that means and perceive behind the human beings and animals the spirits belonging to one of the categories of the First Hierarchy:— the *Spirits of Will* or, according to Western esotericism—the Thrones. For we then perceive beings we cannot describe otherwise than by saying that they do not consist of flesh and blood, nor even of light and air; but of that which we can only observe in ourselves when we are conscious that we have a will. In so far as their lowest substance is concerned, they consist only of will. Then if we educate ourselves in the manner described and now also fix our gaze on the lower animals and their life; or if we plunge into the plant-world, considering it not merely according to its gestures or its mimicry, as described yesterday—but become one with the plant, and from the plant look out upon ourselves;—then indeed we attain an experience for which there is no real comparison within the world, as we know it.

"At the most, we can attempt to find a comparison for the qualities of those beings to whom we then ascend—the beings of the second category of the First Hierarchy, if we allow such feelings to work upon our soul as may be aroused by earnest people of great worth; people who have applied the many experiences of their life to the gaining of wisdom—who after many applied years of rich experience have gathered so much wisdom that we say to ourselves: 'When they express an opinion, it is not their personal will speaking, but that life which they have accumulated for decades, and by means of which they have, in a certain sense become quite impersonal.' They make upon us the impression that their wisdom is impersonal and is the blossom and fruit of a mature life. Such people call forth in us a feeling, though but a faint one, of what influences us from our spiritual environment when we press forward to the stage of clairvoyance of which we must now speak. In western esotericism this category of beings is called the Cherubim. It is extremely difficult to describe the beings of this higher category, for the higher we ascend the more impossible does it become to make use of any qualities of ordinary life wherewith to arouse an idea of the loftiness and greatness and sublimity of the beings of this Hierarchy. We can perhaps to some slight extent describe the Spirits of Will, the lowest category of the First Hierarchy, by saying:— 'We become familiar with Will, for Will is the lowest substance of which they consist.' But this would be impossible if we were only to regard the will which we encounter in man or animals in normal life, or the ordinary feelings and thoughts of man. And it would be impossible to describe by what is usually accepted as human thought, feeling, and will, the beings of the second category of the First Hierarchy. For this we must turn to the life of special persons who, in the way described, have built up an overwhelming power of wisdom in their souls. When we realize this wisdom of theirs, we feel somewhat as the occultist feels when he stands before the beings we call the Cherubim. Wisdom, not acquired in decades, as is the wisdom of eminent men, but such wisdom as is gathered in thousands, nay, in millions of years of cosmic growth, this streams towards us in sublime power from the beings we call the Cherubim.

"Still more difficult to describe are those beings called the Seraphim who form the first and highest category of the First Hierarchy. It would only be possible to gain some idea of the impression which the Seraphim make upon occult vision, if we take the following comparison from life. We will pursue the comparison just made. We will consider a man who for decades has built up experiences which have brought him overwhelming wisdom, and we will imagine that such a wise man speaks from his most impersonal life wisdom, that out of this most impersonal wisdom his whole being is permeated as if with inner fire, so that he need say nothing—*but just appear before us.* The wisdom of those decades, that life-long wisdom, will be apparent in his countenance, so that his look can tell us of the sorrows and experiences of decades; and this look can make such an impression on us that it speaks to us as the world itself, which we experience. If we imagine such a look or imagine that such a wise man does not speak to us in words alone; but that in the tone and in the peculiar coloring of his words he can give us such an impression of all this rich life of experience that we hear in what he says something like an undertone, conveying the nature of his experiences, then again we gain something of the feeling which the occultist has when he ascends to the Seraphim. Just like a countenance matured by life which tells of the experience of decades, or like a phrase which is so expressed that we hear not merely the thoughts, but realize:— 'This phrase expressed with resonance, has been acquired in pain and by the experience of life. It is no theory, it has been attained by struggles and suffering. It has passed through the battles and victories of life and has sunk into the heart.' If we hear all this as in an undertone, we gain an idea of the impression which the trained occultist receives when he lifts himself to the beings we call the Seraphim.

"We might describe the beings of the Second Hierarchy by saying:— What in the beings of the Third Hierarchy is manifestation of self, is in them self-realization, self-creation, a stamping of impressions of their own being; and what in the beings of the Third Hierarchy is being filled with spirit, is in the Second Hierarchy stimulation of life, which consists in severance, in objectifying themselves. What in the beings of the Second Hierarchy is self-creation, we also encounter in the beings of the First Hierarchy. What the beings of the Second Hierarchy make objective, what they create from themselves, exists only so long as these beings remain connected with their creations. Thus, note well:— the beings of the Second Hierarchy can create something like an image of themselves, but it remains connected with them and cannot be separated from them. The beings of the First Hierarchy can also objectify themselves; they can also stamp their own being, it is separated from them as in a sort of skin or shell, but it is an impression of their own being. When this is detached from them, however, it remains existing in the world though they sever themselves from it. They do not carry their own creations with them, these creations remain in existence even if they go away from them. Thus, a higher degree of objectivity is attained by them than by the Second Hierarchy. When the beings of the Second Hierarchy create, if their creations are not to fall into decay, they must remain connected with them. The creations would become lifeless and disintegrate if they themselves did not remain connected with them. What they create has an independent objective existence; but only so long as they remain linked with it. On the other hand, that which is detached from the beings of the First Hierarchy can be disconnected from them, and yet remain in existence, self-acting, and objective.

"In the Third Hierarchy we have manifestation and being filled with spirit. In the Second Hierarchy, self-creation, and stimulation of life. In the First Hierarchy, which consists of the Thrones, Cherubim, and Seraphim, we have a form of creation in which the part created is detached—we have there not only self-creation, but world-creation. That which proceeds from the beings of the First Hierarchy is a detached world, such an independent world that this world phenomenon is a fact, even when the beings are no longer there. Now we may ask:— 'What then is the actual life of this First Hierarchy?' The actual life of this First Hierarchy is such that when such objective, independent, detached beings proceed from it, it realizes itself. For the inner condition of consciousness, the inner experience of the beings of the First

Hierarchy, lies in creation, in forming independent beings. We may say:— 'They contemplate that which they create and which becomes a world, and it is not when they look into themselves but when they look out of themselves upon the world which is their own creation, that they possess themselves.' To create other beings is their inner life; to live in other beings, is the inner experience of these beings of the First Hierarchy. Creation of worlds is their external life—creation of beings their inner life.

"In the course of these lectures we have drawn attention to the fact that these various beings of the hierarchies have offspring; beings split off from themselves, which they send down into the kingdoms of nature, and we have learnt that the offspring of the Third Hierarchy are the nature-spirits, while the offspring of the Second Hierarchy are the Group-souls. The beings of the First Hierarchy have likewise offspring split off from them, and as a matter of fact I have already described from a different aspect these beings which are the offspring of the First Hierarchy. I described them at the beginning of this course, when we ascended to the so-called Spirits of the Rotation of Time, the spirits governing and directing what goes on in the kingdoms of nature in rhythmic succession and repetition. The beings of the First Hierarchy detach from themselves the beings governing the alternation of summer and winter, so that the plants spring up and fade away again; that rhythmical succession through which, for instance, the animals belonging to a certain species have a definite period-of-life in which they develop from birth to death. Everything too which takes place in the kingdom of nature rhythmically and in recapitulation, such as day and night, alternations of the year, the four seasons of the year, everything which thus depends upon repeated happenings, is regulated by the Spirits of the Rotation of Time, the offspring of the beings of the First Hierarchy. These Spirits of the Rotation of Time can be described from one aspect, as we did some days ago, and we can now describe them according to their origin, as we have done today. Thus we can comprehensively represent the beings of these Three Hierarchies as follows:—

1st Hierarchy

World-creation   Creation of Beings   Spirits of the Rotation of Time

2nd Hierarchy

Self-creation   Stimulation of Life   Group-Souls

3rd Hierarchy

Manifestation   Being filled with Spirits   Nature-Spirits

The Work of the Hierarchies After Death

Karmic Relationships: Esoteric Studies, **Volume V,**
Rudolf Steiner, Lecture III, Prague, March 31, 1924, GA 239

"Having entered the spiritual world through the gate of death, we come, first of all, into the realm of the lowest Hierarchy: Angels, Archangels, Archai. We feel linked with this next higher Hierarchy, and we are aware that just as in the Earthly realm everything around us means something to our senses, what the spiritual realm contains means something to the innermost core of our soul. And passing on through the long existence spent between death and a new birth, we learn gradually to become part of the life of the Beings of the next higher Hierarchy who are concerned with us and with one another. These Beings are, as it were, the link connecting us with the spiritual outer world. During the first period of life between death and a new birth we are also very deeply occupied with ourselves, for the Third Hierarchy has to do with our own inner life and being. But then, after a certain time, our gaze widens: we come to know the spiritual world outside us, the objective spiritual world. Our leaders here are the Exusiai [Spirits of Form], the Dynamis [Spirits of Movement], and the Kyriotetes [Spirits of Wisdom]. They bring us into connection with the spiritual outer world. Just as here on Earth we speak of what is around us—mountains, rivers, forests, fields, whatever it may be—so do we speak in yonder world of that to which the Beings of the Second Hierarchy lead us. That is now our environment. But this environment is not a world of objects like the Earth; everything lives and has being, lives as spiritual reality. Nor in this life between death and a new birth do we come to know Beings only; we come to know their deeds as well, we feel that we ourselves are participating in these deeds.

"But then a time comes when we feel how the Beings of the Third Hierarchy—Angels, Archangels, Archai—and the Beings of the Second Hierarchy—Exusiai, Dynamis, Kyriotetes—are working together with us at what we ourselves are to become in the next earthly life. A mighty, awe-inspiring vista opens before us. We behold the activities of Angels, Archangels, and Archai and we perceive how these Beings act in relation to one another. Pictures come to us of what is proceeding among these Beings of the Third Hierarchy; but all these pictures are related to ourselves. And gazing at these pictures of the deeds of the Third Hierarchy, it dawns upon us that they represent the counterpart, the counter image of the attitude of soul, of the inner quality of mind and heart that characterized us in the last earthly life. In the majestic pictures of the deeds of the Angels, Archangels and Archai, we behold the fruits of our attitude of mind and heart, of our life of soul, of our mode of thinking, in the last earthly life; we perceive images of this in what the Beings of the Third Hierarchy are doing. Our attitude, our feelings towards other individuals, towards other earthly things, are now outspread in the spiritual sphere of the Universe. And we become aware of what our thinking and our feeling signify. Here on the Earth this inner activity manifests in Maya, as if it were enclosed within our skin. Not so in the life between death and a new birth. The manner of its appearance then is such that we know that whatever thoughts, feelings, or sentiments we unfold are part of the whole world, work into and affect the whole world.

"...As our life after death continues, we observe how the Beings of the Second Hierarchy, the Exusiai, Dynamis, and Kyriotetes, are connected with the faculties we have acquired in earthly life as the fruits of diligence, activity, interest in the things and happenings of the Earth. For having cast into mighty pictures our interest and diligence during the last earthly life, the Exusiai, Dynamis, and Kyriotetes then proceed to shape images of the talents and faculties we shall possess in our next earthly life. In the images and pictures fashioned by the Beings of the Second Hierarchy we behold what talents and faculties will be ours in the next incarnation.

"The course of this life continues and when the middle point of time between death and a new birth is about to be reached, something of particular importance takes place. From our habitations here on Earth—especially in those moments when as we look upwards to the firmament of heaven the stars send down their shimmering radiance—we feel the sublimity of the heavens above us. But something of far greater splendor is experienced as we gaze downwards now—from the realms of spirit. For then we behold the deeds of the Beings of the First Hierarchy, of the Seraphim [Spirits of Love], Cherubim [Spirits of Harmony] and Thrones [Spirits of Will] working in mutual interrelationship. Mighty pictures of spiritual happenings are revealed to us as we gaze downwards—for our heaven now lies below. Just as in physical existence on Earth we gaze at the starry script above us, so when we look downwards from the realm of spirit we behold the deeds of the Seraphim, Cherubim and Thrones. And in this spiritual existence we are aware that what is proceeding among these Beings, revealed in sublime, majestic pictures, has something to do with what we ourselves are and shall become. For now we feel that what is taking place there among the Seraphim, Cherubim and Thrones reveals the consequences which our deeds of the previous earthly life will have in the earthly life to come. We perceive how in earthly life we behaved in this way to one individual, in that way to another individual, how we were compassionate or pitiless, whether our deeds were good or evil. Our attitude and disposition are the concern of the Third Hierarchy, our deeds of the First Hierarchy, the Seraphim, Cherubim and Thrones. Then, in the cosmic memory now alive in us, there arises a shattering, awe inspiring realization of our deeds and actions between birth and death in the last earthly life. Down below we behold the deeds of spiritual Beings, of Seraphim, Cherubim, Thrones. What are they doing? They show us, in pictures, what our experiences with individuals with whom we had some relationship in the previous incarnation will have to become in the new relationship that will be established in order that mutual compensation may be made for what happened between us in the previous life. And from the way in which the Seraphim, Cherubim and Thrones work in cooperation, we realize that the great problem is there being solved. When I have dealings with an individual in some earthly life, I myself prepare the compensatory adjustment; the work performed by the Seraphim, Cherubim and Thrones merely ensures that the compensation will be made, that it will become reality. And it is these Beings who also ensure that the other individual with whom I shall again make contact is led to me in the same way as I am led to him. It is the majestic experiences arising from the pictures of the deeds of the higher Hierarchies which are recorded by the Moon Beings and subsequently inscribed by them in our astral body when the time comes for the descent to another earthly existence. Together with us in the life between death and a new birth, these Moon Beings witness what is happening in order that the adjustment of the previous earthly life may take place in a subsequent life."

The Spiritual Hierarchy and the Elements

Rosicrucianism and Modern Initiation, **Rudolf Steiner, Lecture I,** *Research into the Life of the Spirit During the Middle Ages,* **January 4, 1924, GA 233a**

"I have marked a transition as between the ninth and tenth centuries A.D.; because before this time man's perceptions were still altogether spiritual. It would never, for example, have occurred to a scholar of the ninth century to imagine Angels, Archangels, or Seraphim as falling short in respect of reality— purely in respect of *reality*—of the physical men he saw with his eyes. You will find that before the tenth century, scholars always speak of the spiritual Beings, the so-called *Intelligences of the Cosmos,* as of beings one actually meets in life. The people of that time were, of course, well aware that the day was long past when such vision had been a common human experience; but they knew that in certain circumstances the meeting could still take place. We must not, for instance, overlook the fact that on into the ninth and tenth centuries countless priests of the Catholic Church were quite conscious of how, in the course of their celebration of the Mass, it happened that in this or that enactment they met spiritual Beings, the Intelligences of the Cosmos. With the ninth and tenth centuries, however, the direct and immediate connection with the Intelligences of the Universe began to disappear from men's consciousness; and there began to light up, in its place, the consciousness of the *Elements of the Cosmos*, the earthy, the fluid or watery, the airy, the warm or fiery. And so, it came about that just as hitherto men had spoken of Cosmic Intelligences that rule the movements of the planets, that lead the planets across the constellations of the fixed stars, and so forth, now they spoke instead of the immediate environment of the Earth. They spoke of the elements of earth, water, air, fire. Of chemical substances, in the modern sense of the word, they did not as yet take account. That came much later. It would, however, be a great mistake to imagine that the scholars of the thirteenth and fourteenth centuries—even in a sense, the scholars of the eighteenth century—had ideas of warmth, air, water, earth, that resembled the ideas men have today. Warmth is spoken of today merely as a condition in which bodies exist. No one speaks any longer of an actual warmth-ether. Air, water—these have likewise become for the modern man completely abstract. It is time we studied these ideas and learned to enter into a true understanding of them. And so today I should like to give you a picture, showing you how a scholar of those times would speak to his pupils."

"When I wrote my *Outline of Occult Science* I was obliged to make the account of the evolution of the Earth accord at any rate a little with the prevailing ideas of the present day. In the thirteenth and twelfth centuries one would have been able to give the account quite differently. The following might then have been found in a certain chapter, e.g., of *Outline of Occult Science*. An idea would have been called up, to begin with, of the Beings who may be designated as the Beings of the First Hierarchy: *Seraphim* [Spirits of Love], *Cherubim* [Spirits of Harmony], *Thrones* [Spirits of Will]. The Seraphim would have been characterized as Beings with whom there is no subject and object, with whom subject and object are one and the same, Beings who would not say:— 'Outside me are things; but the world is, and I am the World, and the World is I.' Such Beings know only of themselves, and this knowledge of themselves is for them an inner experience of which man has a weak reflection when he has the experience of being filled, shall we say, with a *glowing enthusiasm*. It is, you know, quite difficult to make the man of today understand what is meant by 'glowing enthusiasm.' Even in the beginning of the nineteenth century men knew better what it is than they do today. In those days it could still happen that some poem or other was being read aloud and the people were so filled with enthusiasm—forgive me, but it really was so—that present-day man would say they had all gone out of their minds. They were so moved, so warmed! Today people freeze up just when you expect them to be 'enthused.' Now it was lifting this element of enthusiasm, this rapture of the soul that came naturally especially to the men of Middle and Eastern Europe—it was by lifting it into consciousness; by making it alone the complete content of consciousness, that men came to form an idea of the inner life of the Seraphim. Again as a bright, clear element in consciousness, full of light, so that *thought turns directly into light*, illuminating everything—such an idea did men form of the element of consciousness of the Cherubim. And the element of consciousness of the Thrones was conceived as *sustaining, bearing the worlds in Grace…*

"…And then one would have gone on to say: the Choir of Seraphim, Cherubim, and Thrones works together, in such wise that the Thrones found and establish a kernel; the Cherubim let their own light-filled being stream forth from this center or kernel; and the Seraphim enwrap the whole in a mantle of warmth and enthusiasm that rays far out into cosmic space. [Footnote: Drawings were made on the blackboard, with colored chalks.]

"All the drawing I have made is *Beings*: in the midst the Thrones; in the circumference around them the Cherubim; and, outermost of all, the Seraphim. All is essential Being, Beings who move and weave into one another, do, think, will, feel in one another. All is of the very essence of Being. And now, if a being having the right sensitiveness were to take its path through the space where the Thrones have in this manner established a kernel and center, where the Cherubim have made a kind of circling around it and the Seraphim have, as it were, enclosed the whole— if a being with the required sensitiveness were to come into this realm of the activity of the First Hierarchy, it would feel warmth in varying differentiations—here greater warmth, there less; but it would all be an experience of soul, and yet at the same time physical experience in the senses; that is to say, when the being felt itself warm in soul, the feeling would be actually the feeling you have when you are in a well-warmed room.

"Such a united building-up by Beings of the First Hierarchy did verily once take place in the Universe; it formed what we call the Saturn existence. The warmth is merely the expression of the fact that *the Beings are there*. The warmth is nothing more than the expression of the fact that the Beings are there…

"…Now in the time of which I speak, everything was exactly as I have described it. Men spoke of Elements. They spoke of the Element of Warmth, and by the Element of Warmth they understood Cherubim, Seraphim, Thrones—and that is the Saturn existence.

"The description went further. It was said: Seraphim, Cherubim, Thrones—these alone have the power to bring forth something of the nature of Old Saturn, to place it into the Cosmos. But when this highest Hierarchy had once placed it there and a new world-becoming had taken its start, then the evolution could go on further. The Sun, as it were, that is formed of Seraphim, Cherubim and Thrones could carry evolution further. And it came to pass in the following manner. Beings of the Second Hierarchy, *Kyriotetes* [Spirits of Wisdom], *Dynamis*, [Spirits of Movement] *Exusiai*, [Spirits of Form]. Beings that had been generated by the Seraphim, Cherubim and Thrones, press into the space that has been formed through the working of Seraphim, Cherubim and Thrones, that has been fashioned to Old Saturn warmth. Thither entered younger, cosmically younger Beings. And how did these cosmically younger Beings work? Whereas the Cherubim, Seraphim and Thrones reveal themselves in the Element of Warmth, the Beings of the second Hierarchy form themselves in the Element of *Light*. Saturn is dark; it gives warmth. And now within the dark world of the Saturn existence arises that which can arise through the working of the Sons of the First Hierarchy, through Exusiai, Dynamis, and Kyriotetes.

"What is it that is able now to arise within the Saturn warmth? The penetration of the Second Hierarchy signifies an *inner illumination*. The Saturn Warmth is inwardly shone through with *light* and at the same time it becomes *denser*. Instead of only the

Warmth Element there is now also *Air*. And in the revelation of Light, we have the entry of the Second Hierarchy.

"You must clearly understand that it is in very deed and truth *Beings* who thus press their way into the Saturn existence. One who had the requisite power of perception would see the event as a penetration of *Light*; it is Light that reveals the path of the Beings. And wherever Light occurs, there occurs too, under certain conditions, shadow, darkness, dark shadow. Through the Penetration by the Second Hierarchy in the form of Light, shadow also comes to pass. What is shadow? It is *Air*. And indeed, until the fifteenth and sixteenth centuries men knew what Air is. Today men know only that air consists of oxygen, nitrogen and so forth. When that is said, it is very much as if someone were to say about a watch that it consisted of glass and silver. He would be saying nothing at all about the watch. And nothing at all is said about Air as a cosmic phenomenon when we say that it consists of oxygen and nitrogen. We say very much, on the other hand, if we know: Air comes forth from the Cosmos as the *shadow of Light*. In actual fact we have, with the entry of the second Hierarchy into the Saturn warmth, the entry of Light and we have too the shadow of Light, Air. And when we have this we have Sun. Such is the way one would have had to speak in the thirteenth and twelfth centuries.

"And what follows after this? The further evolution comes about through the working of the Sons of the Second Hierarchy—*Archai* [Spirits of Time; Spirits of Personality], *Archangels* [Spirits of Fire], *Angels* [Messengers; Spirits of Twilight]. The Second Hierarchy have accomplished the entry of the Element of Light, Light that has drawn after it its shadow, the darkness of Air—not the indifferent, neutral darkness that belongs to Old Saturn, the darkness that is simply absence of Light; but the darkness that is wrought out as the antithesis of Light. And now to this Element of Light the Third Hierarchy—Archai, Archangels, Angels—add through their own nature and being a new Element, an Element that is like our human desire, like our impulse to *strive after something*, to long for something. Thereby the following comes to pass.

"Let us suppose an Archai or Archangel Being enters, and comes upon an Element of Light, encounters, as it were, a place of Light. In this place of Light the Being receives, through its receptivity for the Light, the urge, the desire for darkness. The Angel Being bears Light into darkness—or an Angel Being bears darkness into Light. These Beings are mediators, messengers between Light and Darkness. It follows from this that what previously has only shone in Light and drawn after it its shadow, the darkness of Air, begins now to shine in color, to glow in a play of color. Light begins to appear in darkness, darkness in light. The Third Hierarchy creates *color out of light and darkness...*

"Thus we have, as a reflection of the Hierarchies, first Air and then Water. The Hierarchies themselves dive in, as it were—the second Hierarchy in the form of Light, the third Hierarchy in the form of Color. And with this latter event the Moon existence is attained.

"And now we come to the *Fourth Hierarchy*. (I am telling it, you remember, as it was thought of in the twelfth and thirteenth centuries.) We today do not speak of the Fourth Hierarchy; but men still spoke in that way in the twelfth and thirteenth centuries. What is this Fourth Hierarchy? It is *Man*. Man himself is the fourth Hierarchy. But by the Fourth Hierarchy was not meant the two-legged being that goes about the world today, ageing year by year! To the true man of knowledge of those times, present-day man would have appeared as something very strange. No, in those times they spoke of original Man, of Man before the Fall, who still bore a form that gave him power over the Earth, even as the Angels and Archangels and Archai had power over the Moon existence, the second Hierarchy over the Sun existence and the first Hierarchy over the Saturn existence. They spoke of Man in his original Earthly existence and then they were right to speak of him as the Fourth Hierarchy. And with this Fourth Hierarchy came—as a gift it is true, of the higher Hierarchies; but the higher Hierarchies have held it only as a possession they did not themselves use but guarded and kept—with the Fourth Hierarchy came *Life*. Into the world of Color, into the iridescent world of changing color, of which I have only been able to give you the merest hints and suggestions, came Life.

"You will say: Then did nothing live before this time? My dear friends, you can understand how it is from the human being himself. Your Ego and your astral body have not life, and yet they exist, they have being. That which is of the soul and the spirit does not need life. Life begins only with your etheric body. And the etheric body is something external, it is of the nature of a sheath. Thus, only after the Moon existence and with the Earth existence does Life enter into the domain of that evolution to which our Earth belongs. *The world of moving, glancing color is quickened to life.* And now not only do Angels and Archangels and Archai experience a longing desire to carry Darkness into Light, and Light into Darkness, thereby calling forth the play of color in the planet; now a desire becomes manifest to experience this play of color as something *inward*, to feel it all inwardly; when Darkness dominates Light, to feel weakness, laziness; when Light dominates Darkness, to feel activity. For what is happening really, when you run? When you run, Light predominates over

Darkness in you; when you sit and are lazy and indolent, then Darkness predominates over Light. It is a play of Color, an activity of Color, not physical, but of the soul. Color permeated with Life, in its iridescence streamed-through with Life—that is what appeared with the coming of the Fourth Hierarchy, Man. And in this moment of cosmic becoming, the forces that became active in the play of color began to *build contours*, began to fashion forms. Life, as it rounded off and molded the colors, called into being the *hard, fast form of the crystal.* And we have come into Earth existence.

"Such things as I have been describing to you were fundamental truths for the mediaeval alchemists and occultists, Rosicrucians and others, who flourished—though history tells us little of them—from the ninth and tenth on into the fourteenth and fifteenth centuries, and of whom stragglers are to be found as late as the eighteenth and even the beginning of the nineteenth century—always however in these later times regarded as strange and eccentric people. Only with the entry of the nineteenth century did this knowledge become entirely hidden. Only then did men come to acquire a conception of the world that led them to a point-of-view which I will indicate in the following way. Imagine, my dear friends, that here we have a man. Suppose I cease to have any interest in this man, but I take his clothes and hang them on a coat-hanger that has a knob here above like a head. From now on I take no further interest in the man and I tell myself: *There* is the man! What does it matter to me what can be put into these clothes? *That*, the coat-hanger with the clothes, is the man! This is really what happened with the Elements. It does not interest us any longer that behind Warmth or Fire is the First Hierarchy, behind Light and Air the Second Hierarchy, behind what we call Chemical Ether or Color Ether and Water the Third

Hierarchy, and behind the Life Element and Earth the Fourth Hierarchy, Man."

Rudolf Steiner on Aristotle's Ten Categories

The Easter Festival in the Evolution of the Mysteries,
Rudolf Steiner, Lecture IV, Dornach, April 22, 1924, GA 233a

"When Aristotle and Alexander heard the celestial harmonies once again at Samothrace, they realized what the burning of the temple at Ephesus had meant. They perceived that the Ephesian Mysteries had been carried out by the flames into the vast cosmic ether. At that moment they became inspired to discover the cosmic script, which is composed not of letters of the alphabet, but of thoughts.

"Thus, the letters of the cosmic script were discovered, which in their own way are as abstract as the alphabet:

Quantity (amount)
Quality (trait)
Relation
Space
Time
Position
Action (activity)
Passion (passivity, suffering)

What we have here is a collection of concepts, first introduced by Aristotle to his pupil Alexander. One can learn to use them in much the same way that one learns to use the letters of the alphabet and read the cosmic script with them.

"In later times, particularly in the abstract phase of scholastic logic, a very unusual thing occurred. Imagine a school in which the students are taught not to read, but rather only to learn the various letters of the alphabet in every imaginable combination—*ac*, *ab*, *ae*, and so on. In essence, this is what happened to Aristotelian logic. Works on logic would enumerate the above concepts, called categories. Students would learn them by heart, but not know what else to do with them next. It was as if they learned the alphabet but never learned to spell.

"In a way, the concepts of quantity, quality, relation, and so on, are as simple as the letters of the alphabet, but knowledge of them is required in order to read in the cosmic script, just as to read *Faust* one must know the alphabet. And in essence, all past and future achievements of anthroposophy are experienced in terms of these concepts. For all the secrets of the physical and spiritual worlds are contained in them. These simple concepts, in other words, constitute the alphabet of the Cosmos.

"Starting in the time of Alexander, the earlier, direct perceptions characteristic of practices at Ephesus were replaced by something deeply hidden, something esoteric, that really began to develop only during the Middle Ages and that is embodied in the above-mentioned eight concepts (they may actually be expanded to ten). We are learning to live more and more with these, but we must strive to keep them as alive in our souls as the letters of the alphabet are when we read any rich and spiritual work of literature.

"And so, you see how ten concepts, whose illuminating and effective power has yet to be rediscovered, came to embody an enormous wisdom known instinctively for thousands of years. And although this light-filled wisdom lies, as it were, in the grave, someday it will rise again. People will then be able to read once again in the cosmic script, and to experience the resurrection of what has been hidden in the time between the two spiritual Epochs."

Answers to Universal Questions and Life Questions through Anthroposophy, Rudolf Steiner, Lecture VIII, *The Theory of Categories,* Dornach, November 13, 1908, GA 108

"We have pointed out what the soul does inasmuch as it continues mobile in the network of concepts. It begins to spin concept to concept in the sense of the dialectic method. It leads man from concept to concept. Granted that we have to begin somewhere, then we pass on from concept to concept. This must give as a result the sum of all concepts. They would constitute the sum of all concepts, which in the world-all are adapted below to the sense world and upwards to the super-sensible world as well. In the widest sense of the word, one terms all these self-mobile concepts, adapted to the two worlds, 'the Categories.' Whence it follows that at bottom of the whole human network of concepts is composed of the categories alone. With the same justice one might say: all concepts are categories, as one might say: all categories are concepts. One has, in truth, habitually called the weightiest, the radical concepts, the nodal points of the concepts, Categories. These more important concepts, following Aristotle, are called categories. But in the strict sense one can use the words 'concept' and 'category' interchangeably, so that we are justified in calling the sum of our self-mobile, self-producing concepts 'theory of categories.' And Hegel's work—is really a system of categories. [4] Hegel himself, of course, says this very thing: if one establishes the network of concepts in the whole ambit, one then has in it the ideas of the divine being before the creation of the world. Since we find the concepts in the world, they must have been originally established there. If we trace the concepts back, we discover the divine ideas, the categorical content of the world."

Steiner	**Aristotle's Ten Categories**
1. Substance	1. Substance/suffering
2. Quantity/amount	2. Quantity
3. Quality/trait	3. Quality
4. Relation	4. Relation
5. Action/activity	5. Doing
6. Passion/passive/suffer	6. Having
7. Time	7. Time
8. Place/position	8. Location
9. Situation	9. Position/orientation
10. Habit	10. Substance/suffering

Another Version

1. Substance

2. Quantity/amount

3. Quality/trait

4. Relation

5. Space

6. Time

7. Position

8. Action/activity

9. Passion/passivity/suffering

10. Substance

Birth of Intuition
by Douglas Gabriel

Harken celestial choirs to needs of earthly kind,
Echoing heart-songs of the goddess-child we find
Whose sparkling dayspring of ether worlds
Cast tomorrow's inklings from sheltering womb,
Star-born and destiny wrought
Seeking the holy life she has sought,
Beckoning earth, water, fire, and air
The magic elements that create her fair;
But yonder in bright spheres she knew
Of light, sound, and life that are true.
Dear one, whose star shines deep in my mind,
Show me the glistening path that you wish to find
With your agèd eyes that innocently enfold
The workings of gods for bright futures untold,
With laughter, clear as a bell that peals
Speaking of her home, the Sun that reels
In Her courses ancient and ever on, and
Join in our dance, our hearts, our song.

Rudolf Steiner on the Nature of Conscience

Since the beginning of history, the study of the nature of the human conscience has engendered the highest praise and respect for conscience's ability to enhance and refine the moral character of humanity. Many philosophers and thinkers speculate about what conscience actually is; but few understand where it came from, how it developed, its inherent nature, its potential for good or ill, its 'infallibility,' its limits, its power, or what might become of it in the future. A few scholars agree that conscience arose in the history of human thought during the Classical Greek era and was not present as a mental capacity or soul-force before that time. In fact, there were no words for conscience before the Greek dramatists. The birth of conscience first needed consciousness to develop to the point that the human ego would no longer clairvoyantly perceive beings outside of itself, like the Furies (pangs of conscience), pursuing it relentlessly for committing 'wrong deeds' until the guilty party could 'clear his conscience.' Instead of the wrath of the Furies, the developing ego-consciousness ("I Am") needed to conscientiously listen to the 'still small voice' sounding in its moral heart. This 'still small voice' appears as an intuition that inspires the ego to act morally with conscious intention, thus creating what Rudolf Steiner calls in his book, *The Philosophy of Spiritual Activity*, 'moral technique'—the capacity to act with intuition.

For ego-development to evolve, the Greek thinker and philosopher needed to internalize the three soul-forces of the Furies and unite them into one 'voice' which might inform the thinker about what is right or wrong, about good and evil. Once the clear thinker is able to listen to the 'voice of moral compunction' based upon the highest scruples and virtuous principles, the need for an 'external judge,' like the Furies, was no longer necessary because the process had become internalized with the birth of conscience. Considering the historic reality that conscience has been perceived as both outside, and then later inside of the human being, it seems as if conscience could be a 'force,' an 'awareness,' or even a 'being' whose origin was previously perceived as outside of the human body and has now entered inside of the human being body and soul. First, as something (some 'being') independent of human consciousness, and then later as something intimately integral to ego-consciousness, the human soul, and the spiritual development of the human being.

The human conscience, in our time, carries a certain moral or spiritual association alongside it that has been partially adopted by moral people and ignored by hedonistic materialists. This demonstrates again that the human conscience is developing over time as determined by the free will of the individual interacting with a 'being' who is a well-spring of moral advice who informs the soul of misdeeds as fast as lightning strikes. The human "I Am" and the 'being' of conscience eventually develop an evolving relationship that takes on the characteristics of a teacher instructing a student when they are headed down the wrong road or about to make a mistake. This is much like Socrates' daemon telling him when he had taken a wrong path; but the daemon did not tell him ahead of time which was the right path.

The *Holy Bible* references the existence of conscience; but makes it a force that is not personal to the individual human being, even though it possesses great moral strength. The Roman Catholic Church, building upon the budding conscience of the Greeks, started to align conscience with the ability to recognize good and evil. Conscience became a 'tool' of God, with His 'still small voice' speaking to humans who would listen with a moral, loving, pure heart. Eventually, this voice was believed to be the very 'Voice of God' helping direct human moral and spiritual development. This 'voice' did not tell the person exactly what to do but did admonish them if an action was perceived to be bad; thus, leaving a guilty conscience to hopefully nag the person into the proper moral action.

The development of conscience over time has been studied by many philosophers but hasn't amounted to much; except for the debate concerning the distinction between 'synderesis' [the person's inclination shaping her moral understanding] and 'conscience.' This debate never ended, and the results have led us into modern psychoanalytical theories of speculation, like the Freudian belief in an 'ego, super-ego, and id,' instead of a divinely ordered "I Am," 'conscience,' and 'Higher Self.'

Synderesis is seen by some as primary to conscience, and as such is infallible; whereas the conscience is personal and fallible. Synderesis is pictured as the Divine Life of Wisdom, in reference to the Cherubim and Kyriotetes, that the individual refers to when making a moral decision. Synderesis sets the standards for what is wisdom, truth, beauty, and goodness and creates moral precepts and moral instincts by which the individual can make ethical judgments that drive personal action/willpower. When the individual has weighed the ethical situation against their personal synderesis' advice, and storehouse of moral precepts, the person may then act with intuition born of love and craft a moral technique to fit each individual situation that calls for moral discrimination.

Essentially, conscience is somewhat like the Tree of Knowledge of Good and Evil from the Christian Bible. When Adam and Eve ate the fruit, they knew the difference between good and evil. They were warned, like the voice of conscience; but they still had the freedom to violate the commandment of God. With conscience, we are told if something is wrong with our actions because our heart prickles with a sensation that is disharmonious—like how it might feel when disobeying the commandments of God. We may 'know' through the human capacity of conscience if an action is right or wrong, even before we take the action. 'Knowing' may arrive as quickly as a bolt of lightning, seemingly out of nowhere. This type of knowing, that arises out of the human conscience, is similar to the nature of intuition in the human soul. Intuition inherently 'knows' the truth of the matter for good or ill, in the present and often the future.

Many Christians believe that a conscience is given to us from the Celestial Hierarchy of the Cherubim; and that a developed human conscience is directly connected to Christ. The First Hierarchy of Seraphim (Love), Cherubim (Harmony/Cosmic Wisdom), and the Thrones (Willpower) also manifest in great storms through lightning and thunder, a means to bring harmony and divine willpower into stormy clouds. So too, the First Hierarchy participates in the human 'intuition of conscience'—the act of knowing—often referred to as a 'Voice,' the Logos, or the Word. This 'capacity of knowing' educates humanity concerning the nature of the heavenly virtues through the example of divine grace, mercy, and love. Conscience can be imagined as a moral hierarchical lightning and thunder that reacts to the storms of the soul's actions; it is an intuition of a higher order that brings harmony, balance, providence, love, and wisdom into the willpower of the human being.

The willpower that feeds the conscience has its home in the hindbrain of the human being which predominately controls volition, spatial awareness, uprightness, and movement. Rudolf Steiner told us that the cerebellum is the most finished and perfected part of the human brain and one of the most mysterious. He actually calls the cerebellum, the 'Tree of Knowledge of Good and Evil' which can be imaginatively seen in a cross-section of the organ which resembles a tree with twelve limbs—reminiscent of the twelve cranial nerves that all terminate in the corpora quadragemina just below the pineal gland in the fourth ventricle. The perfection of the animal kingdom is embedded in the cerebellum of the human being as the organ that demonstrates that humanity is the paragon of creation and the perfection of the most refined elements of all animal species.

Essentially, the conscience controls a part of the brain that reflects the development of the human body as a vehicle which interprets neurological perception through the sense organ (supersensible organ) of the heart, with the help of the kidneys. The cerebellum, as the imaginative Tree of Knowledge of Good and Evil, coincidently has the nerves of the spinal cord wrapped around it like the Serpent of Eden wrapped around the Tree of Knowledge.

Through perception, the human heart 'reads' the outside world with the help of the conscience determining the Good or Evil nature of any particular perception needing action. After the ego in the heart compares the perception to the existing body of moral precepts and prior experiences, it listens for the voice of conscience to speak. Thus, conscience helps the human soul determine what action should be taken in relationship to what the heart has perceived as the harmonious or disharmonious nature of that which is being perceived. The heart is an organ of perception for the human conscience which rejects the disharmonious nature of Evil while taking into the heart the part of perception that is Good. The Evil perception is rejected by the conscience and the Good is accepted as proper perceptual nourishment. The perceiving activity of the heart affects the kidney system (heart and reins) and they work together to regulate the 'fire in the blood' that is the action of the Cherubim affecting the cardio-vascular system of the human body. Conscience is a spiritual flame that burns upward in human beings.

The insight of Rudolf Steiner concerning the human conscience is the antidote to the simple-minded views of materialistic science, psychology, and philosophy. To Steiner, the conscience has divine sources and is intimately connected to spiritual advancement. To the materialist, the conscience is a nuisance to ignore as quickly as possible so that a pleasure-seeking life of selfishness can flourish without regard for others.

The modern person has been led down the wrong road concerning the moral character of conscience by Sigmund Freud and many other psychoanalysts. In Freud's shallow interpretation, we find the 'super-ego' representing the moral backdrop of the individual's soul—its conscience—as a critical and moralizing component standing between the 'ego' as an organizing agent and the 'id' as the home of instinctual desires. If you couple this idea with the rampant materialism found in modern psychology, you are led to a moral dead-end without first having a foundation in spiritual experience or Spiritual Science. Freud's super-ego (conscience) has arisen through the impression of the mores, customs, conventions, and cultural habits of the society that a person is living in. There is no other higher source of moral and virtuous activity than the materialistic, hedonistic habits of our times—according to Freud. Freud's 'super-ego' keeps the person's wild, animalistic 'id' in check via the threats of the penalties of law enforcement for behavior that is deviant. There is little room in Freud's modern view of conscience for a 'divine source' that is a Moral Being working on the human soul from the outer world. Freud's 'super-ego' has no 'super' function to it, no divine source or moral reasoning behind what an individual finds in their personal 'super-ego'—just human laws made to control societal deviation. Freud lacked the imagination, inspiration, or intuition to see the human soul's conscience as the seat of the human being's true spirit, the future potential made real by emulating the moral impulses of the divinely given human conscience.

The mixture of modern psychology, Christian theology, Greek philosophy, Biblical references, and a thorough misunderstanding of Socrates' relationship to his 'daemon' (Ancient Greek: δαίμων, pronounced daimon or *daemon*; a lesser deity or guiding spirit) has frequently diminished the understanding of conscience to analogies of demons, doubles, genii, elemental beings, familiars, and a hundred other misnomers for the spiritually generated, moral nature of conscience. In the not-too-distant future, the human conscience will link people even more with Beings of the Spiritual Hierarchy and the Holy Trinity as the voice of conscience becomes as real as a friend walking by our side giving us moral support and lovingly sharing refined wisdom to nurture our spirit.

Conscience has become one of the least understood aspects of the human soul; and, in fact, has been characterized falsely as something a modern person wants to ignore, diminish, dismiss, and silence. Hedonism and materialism cause the conscience to be 'overactive' in the modern world and has, as such, been 'turned down' like the volume of a radio. The 'still small voice' can't be heard over the loud blasting of earphones that dampen the Voice of God—the Word of God—the human conscience.

Socrates said his daemon would inform him when he went in the wrong direction. Thus, Socrates learned from his daemon and used it to become wise. He also believed what many Greeks did, that the daemon was a god, a hero, a spirit, or even a teacher if the practitioner knew how to listen to the voice of the daemon, which in this case was perceived as being outside of the human body. It is easy to see that as the human conscience arose in development, it went from being perceived as a distinctly independent being 'outside of the human body,' to a voice 'within the human body' that is now part of the human soul and spirit. This means that conscience was 'born' and has a biography of sorts. Therefore, it seems obvious that conscience in the human soul will someday return to its source having advanced and ascended into realms where higher virtues and moral actions of love reign. All we need to do is learn the language of the developing conscience and we will have the opportunity to use our conscience as Socrates used his daemon, as a close friend and teacher.

Thomas Aquinas, who built a Christian philosophy developed in part from Aristotle and the Greeks, debated the issue of 'synderesis' [the person's inclination shaping their moral understanding] versus 'conscience.' The debate raged over which of the two (synderesis or conscience) had a higher or more primary control of human morality via the 'Voice of God'—the human conscience. It is somewhat like the 'Nature/Nurture' issue, where the question is about which is more important: the moral teachings in the environment ('synderesis'), or the self-generated moral development that comes from listening to one's own heart ('conscience'). This debate is resolved by the spiritual scientist, Dr. Rudolf Steiner who tells us that, in fact, the Greeks where right: conscience comes from the outside as a moral force to advise against mistakes and is a being (or beings, the Furies) who wishes to enter into the human soul. Steiner tells us that this being is from the ranks of the First Hierarchy, the Cherubim—the Spirits of Harmony and Cosmic Wisdom. Eventually, the development of humanity's collective 'consciences' help create the lowest 'physical' aspect of Christ, what Rudolf Steiner called the Life-Spirit or Budhi. This indication of Steiner's concerning conscience is beyond the human ability to comprehend. This, and many other mysteries of conscience are revealed through Rudolf Steiner's Spiritual Science and can be found nowhere else in the Western esoteric tradition.

Rudolf Steiner speaks about conscience and its historical development in relationship to human spiritual evolution in many of his works and has presented the most comprehensive picture of the 'Being of Conscience' and its incorporation into the soul and spirit of the human being. There is no way to communicate the profound wisdom Steiner has presented concerning the conscience and all of the elements surrounding it, including: love, compassion, wonder, and consciousness.

Later in this chapter, we will present a selection of quotations from Dr. Steiner that create a comprehensive picture of the developing human conscience, which includes many of the pertinent ideas of thinkers, philosophers, religions, mythologies, and psychologists. It is well worth our time to study the historical progression and growth of the human conscience in standard philosophical studies and historical research. But once you have exhausted those avenues, you will find that only a comprehensive Christian cosmology can illuminate the true spiritual nature of conscience and its relationship to the past, present, and future development of humanity.

But let's start with an overview of what modern materialism can tell us about our experience of conscience in terms of psychology and the sense-bound philosophies of secular humanism. We learn from simple observations of human psychology that conscience, as commonly used in its moral sense, is the inherent ability of every healthy human being to perceive what is right and what is wrong; and, on the strength of this perception, to control, monitor, evaluate and execute their actions. Such values as right or wrong, good or evil, just or unjust, and fair or unfair have existed throughout human history but are also shaped by an individual's spiritual, cultural, political, and economic environment. The closer our inner state of conscience identifies with the higher perception of these concepts, such as good, right, just, and fair, the higher our 'degree of conscience.' It might be said that conscience is the degree of integrity and honesty of each human being because it monitors and determines the quality of one's actions through a personal, moral filter. One who acts with a 'clear conscience' has the advantage of feeling at ease, instead of plagued by a 'guilty conscience.'

Conscience is often seen as the 'highest moral and logical authority' and evaluates information to determine the quality of an action: good or evil, fair or unfair. Consequently, conscience usually ranks higher than consciousness; and, in addition, has the ability and the authority to decide how information will be used, either for good or for ill. Conscience can determine our final decisions for action after evaluating, in a split second, all of the varying parameters. It also seems to be able to predict the outcomes of some actions.

We can decide to act in accordance with or against our conscience at any given moment. This means that decisions and actions that are in accordance with the dictums of the individual's conscience can lead to an evolution and refinement of conscience, as a result of feeling better about your actions. On the contrary, if one acts against one's own conscience, it can lead to an 'involution' and a feeling of having a 'troubled conscience.' In such a case, the overall 'director and judge' of the conscience becomes less distinct or even quiet; its voice cannot be 'heard,' and it allows the lower instincts to gain the upper hand and to act accordingly. In this condition, a process begins that creates an inner 'irritation,' or inner 'itch,' that does not allow a moment of peace—like the Greek Furies chasing a guilty person.

If conscience comes under pressure from the basic instincts and becomes dulled, then the human being will descend more and more into an animal-like state and will then be forced to exclusively serve his own lower instincts. In this compromised state, the information that an individual receives is assessed and utilized according to what is commonly called 'self-interest,' a term that has assumed the status of a 'divine law' in modern times.

Experience has shown that those individuals who were raised in families with strong moral attitudes can very seldom bypass the dictates of their conscience—what philosophers call 'synderesis.' Conscience, being speculated as the noblest function of our moral existence, constitutes the thread that keeps us in contact with our universal nature, the objective Truth, or synderesis.

Consequently, the definition of the 'degree of conscience' anyone possesses can be determined as follows: it is the degree to which we participate in the objective Truth, namely the Good or the 'Right/Just'—the 'Truth, Beauty, and Goodness' of the Greeks. Realistically speaking, humans probably cannot reach the absolute; but they can come closer to or go further from the absolute depending on the moral quality of their conscience.

Conscience attains a higher level only when the 'common good' is put above 'self-interest'—when selflessness is valued above selfishness. Examples of those who listened to and abided by their higher moral conscience are the saints and heroes who sacrificed their lives for others. Examples of those who ignore their 'higher voice of morality' and developed a much lower level of conscience are people who deceive, oppress, and take advantage of others for their own personal benefit and feel no guilt—have turned off the inner voice of their moral dictums.

The decisions of people in positions of authority of all kinds depend on this individual state of conscience, whether their decisions will be destructive, or constructive; which sometimes affect a whole nation or the whole world. This evolution of conscience is an endless effort, one that goes on for as long as one lives; thus, conscience will never be defined as belonging to a certain part of the brain or as a chemically complex compound because the brain changes and evolves exactly because of those processes.

Modern thoughts about conscience are often devoid of spiritual, divine associations that can be found in some religions, like the 'peoples of the book.' The *Bible* tells us about the developing human conscience, which accordingly has been 'written on the heart' as the moral law of God. Instead of a psychologically learned habit, conscience is the actual 'Voice of God' *speaking through the Cherubim the truth of any matter*. The association with such high spiritual beings is the source of that 'writing on the heart,' and it is incumbent upon each of us to try and learn that 'language of conscience written on the heart' so that we can communicate with Divine Hierarchical Beings about how they are willing to help us grow into morally spiritual beings who can then predict the good or ill outcomes of our actions, even before we act.

Great Thoughts Concerning Conscience

The Conscience

- involves a consciousness of the self rather than of others.
- draws on values to which one feels personally committed or that are not necessarily shared by others.
- is self-reflexive insofar as it suggests a split person.
- has secret knowledge which it shares with itself.
- original purpose was retrospective or judicial.
- later incorporated into its definition a prospective or legislative function.

- draws on general moral principles.
- is chiefly concerned with its application to specific circumstances.
- began as a secular concept.
- in the Christian tradition is regarded as susceptible to error.
- is generally cognitive in character.
- possesses motivating or affective power.

From: *Heinrich Von Ofterdingen*, by Novalis

"Explain to me the nature of Conscience...

"If I were God, could I do so; for when we comprehend it, Conscience exists. Conscience, that sense and world-creating power, that germ of all Personality, appears to me like the spirit of the world-poem, like the event of the eternal, romantic confluence of the infinitely mutable common life...

"Conscience appears in every serious perfection, in every fashioned truth. Every inclination and ability transformed by reflection into a universal type becomes a phenomenon, a phase of Conscience. All formation tends to that which can only be called Freedom; though by that is not meant an idea, but the creative ground of all being. To speak accurately, this all-embracing freedom, this mastership of dominion, is the essence, the impulse of Conscience. In it is revealed the sacred peculiarity, the immediate creation of Personality, and every action of the master, is at once the announcement of the lofty, simple, evident world—God's word...

"Conscience is the innate mediator of every man. It takes the place of God upon Earth and is therefore to many the highest and the final. Conscience is the peculiar essence of man fully glorified, the divine archetypal man...

"Everything, which experience and Earthly activity embrace, forms the province of Conscience, which unites this world with higher worlds. With a loftier sense religion appears, and what formerly seemed an incomprehensible necessity of our inmost nature, a universal law without any definite intent, now becomes a wonderful, domestic, infinitely varied, and satisfying world, an inconceivably interior communion of all the spiritual with God, and a perceptible, hallowing presence of the only One, or of his Will, of his Love in our deepest self."

The Biblical Understanding of Conscience

According to most Christian religions, the conscience is fallible, and its standard moldable. The Holy Spirit, in contrast, is always in perfect harmony with God. Even though everyone has a conscience, only believers have the inspiration of the indwelling Holy Spirit. The Holy Spirit has a profound influence on the conscience of a believer.

Christian's believe conscience is an inner human faculty corrupted by sin and the 'Fall from Paradise' and that the Holy Spirit is the divine agent God uses to begin His redemptive work in a believer. The Spirit takes someone who is dead in sin and darkened in their understanding; *Ephesians* (4:18):—

"...being alienated from the life of God through the ignorance that is in them, because of the blindness of their heart,"

To someone who has life and the eyes of their heart enlightened; *Ephesians* (1:17-18):—

"That the God of our Lord Jesus Christ, the Father of glory, may give unto you the spirit of wisdom and revelation in the knowledge of him: The eyes of your understanding being enlightened; that ye may know what is the hope of his calling, and what the riches of the glory of his inheritance in the saints."

This transformation and renewal of our conscience is brought about as the Holy Spirit takes residence in our heart and begins to influence our inner being. Part of this divine influence is explained in *1 Corinthians* (2):—

> "But God hath revealed them unto us by his Spirit: for the
> Spirit searcheth all things, yea, the deep things of God."

Every conscience forms a standard based on the general revelation it receives from the Holy Spirit. This is the moral compass written on every man's heart as in *Romans* (2:14-15):—

> "Which shew the work of the law written in their hearts, their
> conscience also bearing witness, and their thoughts the means
> while accusing or else excusing one another." But a believer's
> conscience is largely different in the sense that it is a recipient
> of special revelation and able to understand the things of the
> Spirit of God."

The Holy Spirit reveals God's Christian truth, and God's truth renews our conscience. As the Holy Spirit educates the believer's conscience with the things of God, the personal standard formed by the conscience begins to align with the standard of Higher Truth. As a result, the renewed inner-being becomes increasingly in tune with the will of God.

Saint Paul is still able to boast on multiple occasions that his conscience is in agreement with godliness in *2 Corinthians* (1:12):—

> "For our rejoicing is this, the testimony of our conscience,
> that in simplicity and godly sincerity, not with fleshly wisdom,
> but by the grace of God, we have had our conversation in the
> world, and more abundantly to you."

More than that, he confidently testified that his conscience was being taught directly by the Spirit in *Romans* (9:1):—

> "I say the truth in Christ, I lie not, my conscience also bearing
> me witness in the Holy Ghost."

A conscience led by the Spirit of God is a conscience captive through the Word of God. Martin Luther similarly stood confident in the conviction of his conscience, saying:—

"Unless I am convinced by sacred Scripture, or by evident reason, I cannot recant, for my conscience is held captive by the word of God, and to act against conscience is neither right nor safe."

The *Bible's* view of the kidneys differs radically from the modern understanding. The kidneys were viewed as the seat of conscience and of ethical feelings and yearnings, and the source of mortality and ethical activity. The kidneys were believed to be associated with the innermost parts of the personality.

In *Jeremiah* and *Psalms*, the human kidneys are cited figuratively as the site of temperament, emotions, prudence, vigor, and wisdom. In five instances, they are mentioned as the organs examined by God to judge an individual. They are cited either before or after—but always in conjunction with the heart as mirrors of the psyche of the person examined. There is also reference to the kidneys as the site of divine punishment for misdemeanors, committed or perceived, particularly in the *Book of Job*, whose suffering and ailments are legendary. In the first vernacular versions of the *Bible* in English, the translators elected to use the term 'reins' instead of 'kidneys' in differentiating the metaphoric uses of human kidneys from that of their mention as anatomic organs. This has progressed further in recent versions of the *Bible*, in which the reins (kidneys) are now replaced by the 'soul' or the 'mind.'

In Hebrew tradition, the 'heart and reins' were considered to be the most important internal organs. In the *Old Testament,* most frequently the kidneys are associated with the inner stirrings of emotional life. But they are also viewed as the seat of the secret thoughts of the human; they are used as an omen metaphor, as a metaphor for moral discernment, for reflection and inspiration and as a metaphor for the human life center.

Great Minds on the Meaning of Conscience

"The voice of the heart is the moral conscience of the individual; a type of supersensible organ that can perceive everything, both inner and outer."

Tyla Gabriel, The Gospel of Sophia

"The heart speaks with the inner voice of conscience, audible only to each individual alone."

Walter Holtzapfel, The Human Organs

"Labor to keep alive in your breast that little spark of celestial fire called conscience, for Conscience to an evil man is a never dying worm, but unto a good man it's a perpetual feast."

George Washington's Rules of Civility,
edited by Moncure Daniel Conway (1890)

"I am bound by the Scriptures I have quoted and my conscience is captive to the Word of God. I cannot and I will not recant anything, since it is neither safe nor right to go against conscience. May God help me. Amen."

Martin Luther, Reply to the Diet of Worms (April 18, 1521)

"There is no witness so dreadful, no accuser so terrible as the conscience that dwells in the heart of every man."

Polybius, Greek historian (205 B.C.-118 B.C.)

"Conscience is the light by which we interpret the will of God in our own lives."

Thomas Merton, "No Man is an Island" (1955)

"The great God hath done us this good, that he hath declared and revealed them to us openly and plainly and described them in the *Holy Bible*. There will you find that you shall

never be a cuckold, that is to say, your wife shall never be
a strumpet, if you make choice of one of a commendable
extraction, descended of honest parents, and instructed in all
piety and virtue—such a one as hath not at any time haunted
or frequented the company or conversation of those that are of
corrupt and depraved manners, one loving and fearing God,
who taketh a singular delight in drawing near to him by faith
and the cordial observing of his sacred commandments—
and finally, one who, standing in awe of the Divine Majesty
of the Most High, will be loath to offend him and lose the
favorable kindness of his grace through any defect of faith or
transgression against the ordinances of his holy law, wherein
adultery is most rigorously forbidden and a close adherence
to her husband alone most strictly and severely enjoined; yea,
in such sort that she is to cherish, serve, and love him above
anything, next to God, that meriteth to be beloved. In the
interim, for the better schooling of her in these instructions,
and that the wholesome doctrine of a matrimonial duty
may take the deeper root in her mind, you must needs carry
yourself so on your part, and your behavior is to be such, that
you are to go before her in a good example, by entertaining her
unfeignedly with a conjugal amity, by continually approving
yourself in all your words and actions a faithful and discreet
husband; and by living, not only at home and privately with
your own household and family; but in the face also of all men
and open view of the world, devoutly, virtuously, and chastely,
as you would have her on her side to deport and to demean
herself towards you, as becomes a godly, loyal, and respectful
wife, who maketh conscience to keep inviolable the tie of a
matrimonial oath. For as that looking-glass is not the best
which is most decked with gold and precious stones, but that
which representeth to the eye the liveliest shapes of objects set
before it, even so that wife should not be most esteemed who

richest is and of the noblest race, but she who, fearing God, conforms herself nearest unto the humor of her husband."

François Rabelais, "Gargantua and Pantagruel" (1532)

"But because, as the wise man Solomon saith, Wisdom entereth not into a malicious mind, and that knowledge without conscience is but the ruin of the soul, it behoveth thee to serve, to love, to fear God, and on him to cast all thy thoughts and all thy hope, and by faith formed in charity to cleave unto him, so that thou mayst never be separated from him by thy sins."

François Rabelais, "Gargantua and Pantagruel" (1532)

"Keep Conscience clear, then never fear."

Benjamin Franklin, Poor Richard Improved:
Being an Almanack and Ephemeris
… for the Year of our Lord 1749.

"The Conscience is a thousand witnesses."

Thomas Hobbes, Leviathan (7:4)

"Alas, that we should be so unwilling to listen to the still and holy yearnings of the heart! A god whispers quite softly in our breast, softly yet audibly; telling us what we ought to seek and what to shun."

Johann Wolfgang von Goethe (Aug. 28, 1749-Mar. 22, 1832)

"The one who acts is always without conscience; nobody has a conscience but the contemplative person."

Johann Wolfgang von Goethe

"Goethe told me of a boy who could not console himself after he had committed a trifling fault. 'I was sorry to observe this,' said he, 'for it shows a too tender conscience, which values so highly its own moral self that it will excuse nothing in it. Such a conscience makes hypochondriacal men, if it is not balanced by great activity."

> Johann Peter Eckermann (1792-1854), secretary to
>
> Johann Wolfgang von Goethe in:
> *Conversations With Eckermann, 1823-1832*

"I feel within me a peace above all Earthly dignities, a still and quiet conscience."

> William Shakespeare, *Henry VIII* (Act III, Scene 2)

"The impressions projected into the physical Man by this Ego constitute what we call conscience. No one else's opinion should be considered superior to the voice of one's own conscience. Let that conscience, therefore, developed to its highest degree, guide us in all the ordinary acts of life."

> Helena P. Blavatsky, *Collected Writings vol. X (1988)*

"A wicked conscience mouldeth goblins swift as frenzy thoughts."

> William Shakespeare, *Troilus and Cressida* (Act. V, Scene 11)

"My conscience hath a thousand several tongues, and every tongue brings in a several tale, and every tale condemns me for a villain. Perjury, perjury, in the high'st degree; Murder, stern murder in the dir'st degree, Throng to the bar, crying all, 'Guilty!, guilty!'"

> William Shakespeare, Richard III (Act V, Scene 3)

"Conscience is a blushing, shamefaced spirit than mutinies in a man's bosom; it fills one full of obstacles."

> William Shakespeare, *Richard III* (Act I, Scene 4)

"Conscience is a thousand swords."

William Shakespeare, *Richard III* (Act V, Scene 2)

"Just as love is felt as a heart-force; so, conscience is the action of this heart-force resonating in harmony with the life of thought. This is the 'still small voice' spoken of in the *Gospel of John*—a golden seed planted from above—that must be nurtured. And so, the acts of will that freely arise through this heart-force—or negate it—will determine the totality of your character; and, as a result, your future life and being. For if you lack conscience, you are not yet truly human, not yet truly living; but only sleeping within an illusory dream of life. Within this dream you are but merely a shadow of life— waiting for humanness to arise—needlessly creating more pain and suffering for oneself and others."

John Barnwell, *The Arcana of the Grail Angel*

Emerson on Conscience

Some scholars believe that Emerson's ideas on Conscience can be derived from his elaborate indications on the nature of Genius and Instinct combined. Instinct, for Emerson, brings the individual to the highest qualities of the human being becoming 'celestial,' not those devolving into animality. Therefore, human instinct has a touch of what Emerson called 'genius.' In his words:—

"Genius is not personal, it is human, the Apotheosis of Man. High Genius is always moral, probity is its ground."

The higher moral nature of the human being is sung by Emerson's praise of what the human body can teach the soul:—

"Every breath of air is a carrier of the soul of the world. And when once thy mind knows the law of so much as thine own body, thou hast nothing to learn from galaxies of stars."

Emerson defines Conscience for us in his last work entitled, *The Natural History of the Human Intellect* as:—

"The obedience to a man's genius is the particular of faith, and obedience to the moral laws the universal of faith. Whoever attempts to carry out the rule of right and love and freedom must take his life in his hand. He stands for truth, and Truth and Nature help him unexpectedly and irresistibly at every step."

"Men of character are the conscience of the society to which they belong."

"Broader and deeper we must write our annals, from an ethical reformation, from an influx of the ever new, ever sanative conscience…"

Emerson goes further in describing Instinct with the following ideas taken from the same lectures:—

"The day comes when each man detects that there is somewhat in him that knows more than he does. A certain dumb [silent] life in life, a simple wisdom behind all acquired wisdom; somewhat not educated or educable, not altered or alterable, a Mother Wit which does not learn by experience, or by books, but knew it all already; makes no progress; does not know more for living long but was wise in youth as in age. More or less clouded, it yet resides the same in all, saying *Aye* or *No* to every proposition. Yet its grand *Aye* and it grand *No* are more musical than all eloquence. Nobody has found the limits of its knowledge. What objects soever is brought before it is already well known to it. It judges not by quantity, or by form, but by quality. Its justice is perfect; its look is catholic and universal; its light ubiquitous like that of the Sun. It does not put forth organs, but rests in presence. Yet, trusted and obeyed in happy natures, it becomes active and salient, and makes new means for its great ends."

"This [Instinct] never pretends. Nothing seems less, nothing is more. Ask what the Instinct [Conscience] declares and we have little to say: He is no newsmonger, no disputant, no talker. Tis a taper, a spark in the great night, yet a spark at which all the illumination of human arts and sciences was kindled. This is that glimmer of inextinguishable light by which men are guided. Though it does not show objects yet shows the way. This is that sense by which men feel when they are wronged, though they do not see how. This is the source of thought and feeling which acts on masses of men,—on all men at certain times,—with resistless power. Ever at intervals leaps a word or fact to light, which in no man's invention, but the common instinct, making the revolutions which never go back."

"None of the metaphysicians has prospered in describing this power, which constitutes sanity and is the corrector of private excesses and mistakes, public in all its regards, and of a balance which is never lost, not even in the insane. It works by tendency, by surprise, by long bias; its source is deep as the world. This is Instinct, and Inspiration is only the Power excited, breaking its silence; the spark bursting into flame. It belongs to all. It is in the secret of the world. It is in strictest alliance with moral nature: it proceeds from that. It is that which opens to each soul accordingly as it is obeyed, and hereby all contradictions are reconciled. The truth is seen by one mind. 'A sacred fire without form, shining with a leaping splendor through the profundities of the whole world.' Wherever the intellect acts, there is an oracle."

Rudolf Steiner's Wisdom Concerning Conscience

The following extracts are taken from selections of Rudolf Steiner's lectures and books that address the origin, nature, and the future development of conscience in relationship to human spiritual evolution. The complete quotation of each extract can be found in the similar quotation in the section below entitled, *Rudolf Steiner's Indications Concerning Conscience.*

Rudolf Steiner describes Conscience as:

- The pangs of conscience that radiate into our consciousness are what is reflected by the heart from our experiences.

- The prickles of conscience that stream into our consciousness are the content of our experiences reflected by the heart.

- In logical thinking we experience above all a kind of conscience, and by developing that we establish in the soul (heart) a certain sense of responsibility towards truth and untruth.

- All stirrings of conscience occur at the transition from the emotions to intuition.

- Conceptual intuition as the highest motive—the expression of this voice is conscience.

- That precious possession of the human soul, which speaks like the voice of God in each individual man or woman, warning them of good or evil.

- Entered the human soul at about the same time as the Christ Impulse.

- The permeation of the Sentient Soul with the sense of self (the ego-sense) has grown into man's conscience.

- Speaks in the same way in the simplest and most primitive of men, as it does in the most complex soul.

- It says quite simply: that is right! that is wrong! without any theory or dogma.

- A voice from God, urging man to do what is right that he may press up to the Higher Ego.

- An urging impulse; but it is not an impulse.

- Speaks with the same power as does the Spiritual Soul itself when it appears—but yet with elemental, original forces.

- The presence of conscience cannot be denied.

- Reveals whether we shall be horrified or happy when we are able to behold our actions in the realm of spirit.

- Is a presentiment that reveals prophetically how we shall experience our deeds after death.

- Are living signs of the spiritual world.

- Begins to enable him to behold the spiritual world consciously.

- A wonderful regulator for the soul-life.

- Appears to every individual as something holy in the human breast.

- Speaks with elemental power in the human soul and is heard by the individual as saying: "This you must do, and that you must leave alone," long before we learn to form ideas concerning good and evil and thus begin to formulate moral precepts.

- A faculty which comes to the fore by degrees and has to be acquired by man's own endeavors.

- A most sacred individual possession, inviolable by the external world, whose voice enables us to determine our direction and our goal.

- When conscience speaks, no other voice may intrude.

- Able to implant itself in the soul's existence, in community with the Divine-Spiritual world during sleep.

- Takes place—albeit as a pure process of soul and spirit—in the metabolic and limbs-system.

- A power whereby the human being transcends what he is in the physical body.

- A power whereby the human being is led out beyond the sphere of his impulses, his likes and dislikes.

- Can clearly be traced to a certain period of Greek culture.

- In the works of Aeschylus, what we call 'conscience' played no part; there were only remembrances of the avenging Furies; and not until we come to the works of Euripides is there any clear expression of 'conscience' as we know it now.

- Arising only very gradually during the Graeco-Latin Period.

- Which from the time of the Mystery of Golgotha until the goal of the Earth is attained, lives in and inspires the souls of men, weaves the Physical Body of Christ.

- Appeared quite late, and in the language of the earlier Greeks no word for it exists. The same thing is true of the early periods of other civilizations.

- Came only gradually to be recognized.

- Developed fairly late in human evolution.

- Is therefore the outcome of experiences spread over a number of incarnations.

- Binds itself to the etheric body, becoming in time a permanent characteristic of it because the astral body has been so often convinced that this or that 'would not do.'

- Speaks to us from depths that thinking can never reach.

- Actually lives in the world of the Cherubim.

- Was at first outside, then entered into the soul and became one of the forces now within it.

- Replaced the astral perception of the Furies.

- Is a flame of volition in humans that is perpendicular to the Earth.

- Is something that exists as a standard for our own actions when we go too far in our demands, when we seek our own gain too much.

- Acts as a standard placed between our sympathies and antipathies.

- Is that which shall set to work as a regulator in the Consciousness or Spiritual-Soul.

- Is the mirroring within our inner being of the real spiritual world which weaves and breathes throughout the world of the senses.

The Concept
of Conscience
Throughout History

Novalis on the Nature of Conscience

From: *Heinrich von Ofterdingen,* by Novalis (Friedrich von Hardenburg)

"The Universe breaks down into an infinite number of worlds, each in turn contained by larger ones. In the end, all minds are one mind. One mind like one world gradually leads to all worlds, but everything has its own time and its own manner. Only the Universe as person, can understand the relations of our world. Even conscience, this power which generates the Universe and meaning, this germ of all personality, appears to me to be like the spirit of the world poem, like the accident of the eternal, romantic confluence of the endlessly changeable totality of life."

"The Conscience appears in every perfection, in every fashioned truth. Every inclination and ability transformed by reflection into a universal type becomes a phenomenon, phase of Conscience. All formation tends to that which can only be called Freedom; though by that is not meant an idea, but the creative realm of all being. Such freedom is mastery. To speak accurately, this all-embracing freedom is the essence, the impulse of Conscience. In it is revealed the sacred individuality, the immediate creation of Personality, and every action of the master is at once the announcement of the lofty, simple, uncomplicated world—*God's word*. Conscience is the innate mediator of every man. It takes the place of God upon Earth and is therefore to many the highest and the final judge. But how far was former knowledge, called ethics, from the pure shape of this lofty, comprehensive, personal thought. Conscience is the individual essence of the human race fully glorified, the divine archetype of Man."

Thomas Aquinas on Human Conscience

Aquinas played a significant role in clarifying the nature of conscience and the theoretical problems connected with it. Aquinas assigned to 'synderesis' [the person's moral inclination shaping their understanding] principally a cognitive role. He argued that human beings have a fundamental grasp of right and wrong, which is infallible. Aquinas connected synderesis to natural law, identifying the first practical principles, of which synderesis is the habit, with the general principles of natural law. He occasionally replaced the word synderesis by the term understanding (intellectus), the intellectual virtue of grasping the first principles of reason in his *Summa Theologiae*. Aquinas understood the directives of synderesis as formal principles, not as concrete moral norms, as habitual knowledge. Conscience is the consideration of a specific case in light of one's moral knowledge. Moral knowledge comprises the first principles of synderesis, as well as more particular moral directives. For Aquinas, the distinction of generally good, evil, and indifferent acts does not have any bearing on when erring conscience binds and when it does not. Aquinas argued that the binding character of conscience, whether erring or not, means that acting against conscience is always evil.

Aquinas conceived conscience as an act of ordering knowledge—some universal and some particular—to an act, whether past, present, or future. Conscience directs future acts, and regarding past acts, can accuse or excuse. Synderesis turns human nature towards the good and objects to the evil. It gives awareness of the principles of morality to be applied to actions. Synderesis concerns knowing the principles applicable to all actions, and conscience applies knowledge to a specific act. Thus, conscience comes from synderesis. But conscience has limits and can be wrong and in need of correction. A mistaken conscience does not stop a person's orientation to the truth, and error can be fixed. Conscience and God's law are both binding for Aquinas, not because conscience is perfect or reason is independent of the law; but because conscience mediates God's norms to humans doing a particular action. This is done through the application of synderesis, which is always ordered to moral truth, meaning to God.

From: *Summa Theologica,* by Saint Thomas Aquinas

"Conscience acts as a 'witness' when it is consciously aware of some personal wrongdoing, whether of commission or omission. It 'binds' or 'incites' when it makes a judgement that some act should be performed. Finally, it 'accuses,' torments' or 'rebukes' when it judges that some past action was either morally acceptable or it was not. Although it is difficult to see how conscience in the first sense—conscience as witness—can function as an application of knowledge to conduct, this seems less problematic in the second and third senses of the term, which harken back to the legislative and judicial senses of conscience found in St. Paul's writings. Regardless of whether my action is objectively good, evil or indifferent, conscience binds, for it is by means of conscience that an action is proposed to me as good, bad, or indifferent."

Socrates' Divine Inner Voice—the Daemon

Socrates often mentions that he is guided by a daemon, a kind of divine spirit, oracle, or 'sign,' that takes the form of an 'inner voice' or non-vocal nudge. The guide never tells Socrates what to do; it only indicates when Socrates is not to do something. Socrates learned over time to listen to this inner divine voice. He acted in service to it. Nothing that he does in his life is untouched by this inner divine voice. He describes it in *The Apology of Socrates* as written by Plato:—

> "You have heard me speak at sundry times and in diverse places of an oracle or sign which comes to me and is the divinity which Meletus ridicules in the indictment. This sign, which is a kind of voice, first began to come to me when I was a child; it always forbids but never commands me to do anything which I am going to do. This is what deters me from being a politician."

We can define the Greek idea of the daemon in many ways derived from Greek religion, mythology, and philosophy: god, godlike, power, fate, lesser deity, or guiding spirit. Daemons were possibly seen as the souls of men of the Golden Age acting as tutelary deities, lesser divinities, or spirits, often personifications of abstract concepts or beings of the same nature as both mortals and deities, similar to ghosts, chthonic heroes, spirit guides, forces of nature, or the deities themselves, as found in Plato's *Symposium*:—

According to Hesiod's myth, "…great and powerful figures were to be honored after death as a daemon." In Hesiod's *Theogony*, Phaeton becomes an incorporeal daemon, or divine spirit and the people of the Golden Age were transformed into daemons by the will of Zeus to serve mortals benevolently as their guardian spirits; "…good beings who dispense riches, nevertheless, they remain invisible, known only by their acts." The daemons of venerated heroes were localized by the construction of shrines, so as not to wander restlessly, and were believed to confer protection and good fortune on those offering their respects.

Plato taught that a daemon existed within a person from their birth, and that each individual was obtained by a singular daemon prior to their birth by way of drawing a lot. In Plato's *Symposium*, the priestess Diotima teaches Socrates that love is not a deity; but rather a 'great daemon.' She goes on to explain that 'everything daemonic is between divine and mortal,' and she describes daemons as 'interpreting and transporting human things to the gods and divine things to men; entreaties and sacrifices from below, and ordinances and requitals from above.'

In Plato's *Apology of Socrates*, Socrates claimed to have a daemon (a 'divine being') that frequently warned him—in the form of a 'voice'—against mistakes but never told him what to do. By this he seems to indicate the true nature of the human soul, his newfound self-consciousness; somewhat of a kind of spiritual tact checking Socrates from any act opposed to his true moral and intellectual interests.

Regarding the charge brought against Socrates, Plato surmised:—

"Socrates does wrong because he does not believe in the gods in whom the city believes but introduces other daemonic beings."

This confusion concerning the budding consciousness of the human conscience shows the developmental nature of the evolution of conscience. The conscience is beginning to be acknowledged in Greek times as a part of the human soul. Or, as Heraclitus said: "…character is for man his daemon."

In the ancient Greek religion, daemon is a peculiar mode of activity: it is an occult power that drives humans forward or acts against them like the Furies chasing a guilty soul. Since the human daemon is the veiled countenance of divine activity, every deity can act through or as a daemon, much like the divine acting through the spiritual hierarchy.

For Plato, the daemon is a spiritual being who watches over each individual and is tantamount to a higher self, or an Angel. While Plato is called 'divine' by Neoplatonists, Aristotle is regarded as 'daemonios', meaning 'an intermediary to deities [daemons].'

For Proclus, daemons are the intermediary beings located between the celestial objects and the terrestrial inhabitants. Somewhat like a messenger, which is the original meaning for Angel.

The Greeks divided daemons into good and evil categories. They sometimes resemble the Arabic Genii in their humble efforts to help mediate the good and ill fortunes of human life. They also resemble the Christian Guardian Angels and the adversarial powers of evil, called Satan (Ahriman) and Lucifer. The comparable Roman concept is the 'genius' who accompanies and protects a person.

Xenocrates explicitly understood daemons as ranged along a scale from good to bad. Plutarch speaks of 'great and strong beings in the atmosphere, malevolent and morose, who rejoice in unlucky days, religious festivals involving violence against the self.' The Pythagoreans taught:—

> "The whole air is full of souls. We call them daemons and heroes, and it is they who send dreams, signs, and illnesses to men. It is towards these daemons that we direct purifications and holy rites, all kinds of divination, the art of reading chance utterances, and so on."

In the Greek 'ruler cult' that began with Alexander the Great, it was not the ruler but his guiding daemon that was venerated. In the Archaic or early Classical period, the daemon had been internalized for each person whom it served to guide, motivate, and inspire, as one possessed of such good spirits. Similarly, the first-century Roman imperial cult began by venerating the 'genius' or 'numen' of Caesars.

Daemons scarcely figure in Greek mythology or Greek art: they are felt, but their unseen presence can only be presumed by the individual inwardly.

In the *Old Testament*, evil spirits appear in the book of *Judges* and in *Kings*. The use of the idea of the daemon in the *New Testament's* original Koine Greek text caused the Greek word to be applied to the Judeo-Christian concept of an 'evil spirit' by the early second century A.D. Thus, the daemon faded into the Christian concepts of a conscience that is the 'Voice of God' in the heart of the human being, or an evil spirit tempting the soul.

Rudolf Steiner gives us many prose and poetic descriptions of conscience. He describes its origins, nature, and future development in relationship to human spiritual evolution in many of his lectures and books. We have extracted some of the most poignant remarks and present them in the selections below.

Rudolf Steiner's Indications Concerning Conscience

Once we have heard what great thinkers, theologians, poets, and philosophers have said about the nature of conscience in the human being, we can easily see that Cosmic Intelligence, has worked through the Spiritual Hierarchies in manifold ways. All the way from the ancient world when the Lord spoke to Elijah at Horeb (1 *Kings* 19:12) through the 'still small voice'; continuing up to the modern era as our personal experience of conscience. Moral Imagination, Moral Inspiration, and Moral Intuition can lead us to conscience but only the human ego can acknowledge or disregard what conscience whispers to the heart. The promptings of conscience are often drowned out by the temptations and cajoling of Lucifer and Ahriman. Nonetheless, it is ultimately through the moral 'ear' of the heart that we can listen for the voice of conscience.

Rudolf Steiner gives many indications about conscience and its place in human spiritual development. We have selected some indications that will define, describe, and place in time and space the significance of conscience as the voice of God on Earth.

Intuitive Thinking as a Spiritual Path: A Philosophy of Freedom, **Rudolf Steiner**, *The Idea of Freedom*, **subsection 24, pg. 148 (GA 4)**

"We described the stage of characterological disposition that works as pure thinking, or practical reason, as the highest. We have now described conceptual intuition as the highest motive. The expression of this voice is conscience."

Therapeutic Insights: Earthly and Cosmic Laws, **Rudolf Steiner, Lecture IV, July 2, 1921, GA 205**

"Something is reflected from the surface of the heart that is no longer merely a matter of habit or memory but is life that is already spiritualized when it reaches the outer surface of the heart. For what is thrown back from the heart are the pangs of conscience. This is to be considered, I would like to say, entirely from the physical aspect: the pangs of conscience that radiate into our consciousness are what is reflected by the heart from our experiences. Spiritual knowledge of the heart teaches us this."

An Occult Physiology, **Rudolf Steiner, *The Being of Man*, Prague March 20, 1911, GA 128**

"Although so close to man, because it concerns himself; the subject is a difficult one to approach. For if we turn our attention to the challenge 'Know thyself!' a challenge that has forced itself upon man through all the ages, as we may say, from mystic, occult heights, we see at once that a real, true self-knowledge is very hard of attainment. This applies not only to individual, personal self-knowledge, but above all to knowledge of the human being as such. Indeed it is precisely because man is so far from knowing his own being and has such a long way to go in order to know himself, that the subject we are about to discuss in the course of these few days will be in a certain respect something alien to us, something for which much preparation is necessary. Moreover, it is not without reason that I myself have only reached the point where I can at last speak upon this theme as the result of mature reflection covering a long period of time. For it is a theme which cannot be approached with any prospect of arriving at a true and honest observation unless a certain attitude, often left out of account in ordinary scientific observation, be adopted. This attitude is one of reverence in the presence of the essential nature and *Being of Man*. It is, then, of vital importance that we maintain this attitude as a fundamental condition underlying the following reflections.

"How can one truly maintain this reverence? In no other way, than by first disregarding what he appears to be in everyday life, whether it be oneself or another is of no consequence, and then by uplifting ourselves to the conception: Man, with all that he has evolved into, is not here for his own sake; he is here as revelation of the Divine Spirit, of the whole World. He is a revelation of the Godhead of the World! And, when a man speaks of aspiring after self-knowledge, of aspiring to become ever more and more perfect, in the spiritual-scientific sense which has just been indicated, this should not be due to the fact that he desires merely from curiosity, or from a mere craving or knowledge, to know what man is; but rather that he feels it to be his duty to fashion ever more and more perfectly this representation, this revelation, of the World Spirit through Man, so that he may find some meaning in the words, 'to remain unknowing is to sin against Divine destiny!' For the World Spirit has implanted in us the power to have knowledge; and, when we do not *will* to acquire knowledge, we refuse what we really ought

not to refuse, namely, to be a revelation of the World Spirit; and
we represent more and more, not a revelation of the World Spirit,
but a caricature, a distorted image of it. It is our duty to strive
to become ever increasingly an image of the World Spirit. Only
when we can give meaning to these words, 'to become an image
of the World Spirit'; only when it becomes significant for us in
this sense to say, 'We must learn to know, it is our duty to learn
to know,' only then can we sense aright that feeling of reverence
we have just demanded, in the presence of the Being of Man.
And for one who wishes to reflect, in the occult sense, upon
the life of man, upon the essential quality of man's being, this
reverence before the nature of man is an absolute necessity, for
the simple reason that it is the only thing capable of awakening
our spiritual sight, our entire spiritual faculty for seeing and
beholding the things of the spirit, of awakening those forces
which permit us to penetrate into the spiritual foundation of
man's nature. Anyone who, as seer and investigator of the Spirit,
is unable to have the very highest degree of reverence in the
presence of the nature of man, who cannot permeate himself to
the very fibers of his soul with the feeling of reverence before
man's nature, must remain with closed eyes (however open they
may be for this or that spiritual secret of the world) to all that
concerns what is really deepest in the Being of Man. There may
be many clairvoyants who can behold this or that in the spiritual
environment of our existence; yet, if this reverence is lacking,
they lack also the capacity to see into the depths of man's nature,
and they will not know how to say anything rightly with regard
to what constitutes the Being of Man."

Psychoanalysis in the Light of Anthroposophy, **Rudolf Steiner**, Lecture V, *Connections Between Organic Processes and the Mental Life of Man*, **Dornach, July 2, 1921, GA 205**

"If we study this thoroughly, we come at last to consider the human organism in its entirety. Take the lung organism, the liver organism, and so forth. Looking at them within, you reach a point when you survey, as it were, the surface of the several organs, naturally by means of spiritual sight. What exactly is this surface of the organs? It is nothing less than a reflecting apparatus for the soul life. Our perceptions, and also what we elaborate in thought are reflected upon the surface of all our inner organs; and this reflection makes known our recollections, our memory during life. Thus, after we have perceived and digested something in thought, it is mirrored upon the surface of our heart, liver, spleen, and so forth, and what is thus thrown back constitutes our memories. And with a not very extensive training you may notice how certain thoughts shine back in memory from the whole organism. Very different organs take part in this. If it is a question of remembering, let us say, very abstract conceptions, then the lung surface participates strongly. If it is a question of thoughts colored by feeling, of thoughts which have a nuance of feeling, then the surface of the liver is concerned. Thus, we can describe very well, and in detail, how the various organs take part in this reflection which makes its appearance as recollection, as the power of memory…

"In reality everything remembered with a strong ingredient of feeling or passion is also connected with what is reflected from the kidneys. If we consider lung or liver reflections we find them to be more often memory ideas, the memories proper. If we turn to the kidney system we see what sort of lasting habits we have in this incarnation; and within the kidney system are being prepared already the temperamental tendencies in the broadest sense which, by a detour through the head organization, are intended for our next incarnation.

"Let us study the heart with the same idea. For spiritual-scientific research, the heart is an extraordinarily interesting organ. You know that our trivial science is inclined to treat knowledge of the heart rather lightly. It looks upon the heart as a pump which pumps the blood through the body. Nothing more absurd can be believed, for the heart has nothing to do with pumping the blood. The blood is set in motion by the full agility of the astral body and ego, and the heart's movement is only the reflex of these activities. The movement of the blood is autonomous, and the heart only brings to expression the movement caused by these forces. The heart is in fact only the organ that manifests the movement of the blood, the heart itself having no activity in relation to this blood movement. The present natural scientists become very angry if you speak of this. Many years ago, I think in 1904 or 1905, on a journey to Stockholm I explained this to a scientist, a medical man, and he was furious about the idea that the heart should not be regarded as a pump, that the blood comes into movement through its own vitality, that the heart is simply inserted in the general blood movement, participates with its beat, and so on.

"Well, something is reflected from the surface of the heart which is not a matter of memory or of habit. The life processes become spiritualized when they reach the outer surface of the heart. For what is thrown back from the heart are the pangs of conscience. That is to be taken simply, entirely as the physical aspect. The pangs of conscience which radiate into our consciousness are that ingredient in our experiences which is reflected from the heart. Spiritual cognition of the heart teaches us this.

"But if we look into its interior, we see gathered there forces which again stem from the entire metabolic and limb organism, and because everything connected with the heart forces is spiritualized that is also spiritualized within it which has to do with our outer life and deeds. And however strange and paradoxical it may sound to anyone clever in the modern sense, the fact remains that what is thus prepared within the heart are the karmic propensities, the tendencies of our karma. It is revoltingly foolish to speak of the heart as a mere pumping mechanism, for the heart is the organ which, through mediation of the limb and metabolic system, carries what we understand as karma into the next incarnation."

The Waking of the Human Soul and the Forming of Destiny, Rudolf Steiner, Lecture I, Prague, April 28, 1923, GA 224

"Let us go back now to the first thing that the child learns: to walk, learning a balanced posture. There is more connected with this than is usually thought. Connected with it is the bringing about by the ego of a specific physical process which changes man from a creeping to a walking being. It is the ego that erects the human being; the astral body that is at work within the feeling for speech in the erect being; the etheric body that permeates all of this with the force of thinking. But all of these work into the physical body. When we consider the animal, which has its back parallel with the surface of the Earth, its action, its walking, its behavior—everything that proceeds out of the astral—is utterly unlike these things in man, who is a being with volition acting out of his upright, vertical nature. What comes about in man, taking place in the ego, astral body, etheric body—all of this is in the physical body a sort of combustion process. Here is a point where our physical science, if it was desirous of fulfilling itself, would be able to discover its union with Anthroposophy. It must be said that the combustion processes in man are altogether different from those in the animal. When the flame of the organic being works horizontally, it destroys what comes out of conscience; there cannot work into this what is derived from the moral out of conscience. The fact that, in the case of the human being, these processes are streamed through by the conscience is due to the fact that the flame of volition in man is perpendicular to the Earth. Within this striking in of the moral, of the nature of conscience, the child places himself just as into the external posture of balance. Together with the learning to walk, there darts into man the moral human nature—indeed, the religious permeation of the nature of man. These are truly lofty forces which are there at work when the child passes over from the creeping to the walking movement. These forces, if we follow them back through the darkness of the child's consciousness, lead us to a still loftier association of man with the Beings whom we call the Primal Forces, the Archai. Everything through which the human being has passed in the pre-earthly life is here reactivated. If to the prayer-like formula, for my thinking I thank the Angels, for language I thank the Archangels, we wish to attach a third unit, we must say: For my being placed within the earthly existence according to physical and moral forces, I thank the Archai—who have been endowed with this power by still loftier Beings.

"And now we can answer the question for ourselves:— *How is it that the human being, who possessed a brilliant consciousness before birth, brings with him here a dull consciousness?* Indeed, into this consciousness there dips down what we can combine under the concepts of walking capacity, speaking capacity, thinking capacity, which we have received into ourselves from the higher Hierarchies to be transformed by us. We see thus that what makes us human beings, that through which we are human beings among human beings, manifests our connection with the loftier divine-spiritual worlds. Into these divine-spiritual worlds we enter again and again in a certain way during our earthly existence. The truth is that we must say to ourselves: For the real nature of man, the state of sleep, out of which dreams come into play, is at least just as significant as the waking state. When man passes over from the waking state to the state of sleep, these three capacities that have been acquired in the manner described begin to grow silent: conceiving, speaking, action all grow silent. But we see then that, as thinking grows silent when we fall asleep, the human being, in the same degree in which thought disappears from his consciousness, comes near to the Angels, and, as his speaking capacity comes to an end, he approaches the Archangelic Beings. In the degree to which the human being has entered into complete stillness, he passes through the quieting of his activity into proximity with the Primal Beings, the Archai."

Wisdom of Man, of the Soul, and of the Spirit, **Rudolf Steiner, Part III,** *The Wisdom of Man,* **Lecture III,** *Imagination— "Imagination"; Inspiration—Self-fulfillment; Intuition— Conscience,* **Berlin, December 15, 1909, GA 115**

"When this has been intensified to the point of its full potentiality in life, this transition reveals what we can call the human *conscience.* All stirrings of conscience occur at the transition from emotions to intuition. If we seek the location of conscience, we find it at this transition. The soul is open laterally on the side of imagination and on that of intuition; but it is closed on the side where we encounter the impact, as it were, of outer corporeality through perception. It achieves a certain fulfillment in the realm of imagination, and another when it enters the realm of intuition—in the latter case through an event."

Spiritual Soul Instructions and Observation of the World, Rudolf Steiner, Lecture XV, What Does the Modern Human Being Find in Theosophy? Berlin, March 8, 1904, GA 52

"I want to mention another phenomenon, the conscience. This phenomenon is inexplicable at first. It becomes immediately clear to us if we look at its development. If we know that every soul shows a particular level of development, then we admit that the urge for figure [form] lives in the undeveloped soul. However, if the spirit has drawn the soul to itself, has united more and more with it, the spirit speaks at any moment of sympathy and antipathy. The human being *hears the spirit speaking from his soul*; he perceives this as the voice of conscience. This conscience can appear only on a particular level of human development. We never see the voice of conscience with primitive peoples. Later when the soul has gone through different personalities, the mind speaks to the soul."

The Education of the Child in the Light of Anthroposophy, Rudolf Steiner, GA 34

"What we call 'conscience' is nothing else than the outcome of the work of the Ego on the life-body through incarnation after incarnation. When man begins to perceive that he ought not to do this or that, and when this perception makes so strong an impression on him that the impression passes on into his etheric body, 'conscience' arises...

"With the change of teeth, when the etheric body lays aside its outer etheric envelope, there begins the time when the etheric body can be worked upon by education from without. We must be quite clear what it is that can work upon the etheric body from without. The formation and growth of the etheric body means the molding and developing of the inclinations and habits, of the conscience, the character, the memory, and temperament. The etheric body is worked upon through pictures and examples—i.e., by carefully guiding the imagination of the child. As before the age of seven we have to give the child the actual physical pattern for him to copy, so between the time of the change of teeth and puberty we must bring into his environment things with the right inner meaning and value. For it is from the inner meaning and value of things that the growing child will now take guidance. Whatever is fraught with a deep meaning that works through pictures and allegories, is the right thing for these years. The etheric body will unfold its forces if the well-ordered imagination is allowed to take guidance from the inner meaning it discovers for itself in pictures and allegories—whether seen in real life or communicated to the mind. It is not abstract conceptions that work in the right way on the growing etheric body, but rather what is seen and perceived—not indeed with the outward senses, but with the eye of the mind. This seeing and perceiving is the right means of education for these years.

"For this reason it matters above all that the boy and girl should have as their teachers persons who can awaken in them, as they see and watch them, the right intellectual and moral powers. As for the first years of childhood Imitation and Example were, so to say, the magic words for education, so for the years of this second period the magic words are Discipleship and Authority. What the child sees directly in his educators, with inner perception, must become for him authority—not an authority compelled by force; but one that he accepts naturally without question. By it he will build up his conscience, habits, and inclinations; by it he will bring his temperament into an ordered path. He will look out upon the things of the world as it were through its eyes. Those beautiful words of the poet, 'Every man must choose his hero, in whose footsteps he will tread as he carves out his path to the heights of Olympus,' have especial meaning for this time of life. Veneration and reverence are forces whereby the etheric body grows in the right way. If it was impossible during these years to look up to another person with unbounded reverence, one will have to suffer for the loss throughout the whole of one's later life. Where reverence is lacking, the living forces of the etheric body are stunted in their growth."

Health and Illness, **Volume II, Rudolf Steiner, Lecture I,** *Fever Versus Shock*, **Dornach, December 30, 1922, GA 348**

"It is indeed odd, you see, that something that people frequently call materialistic must be pointed out by spiritual science. But the reason for this is that when the human being is really observed, the spirit is revealed where others see only matter. Anthroposophy does not assume that the abdomen is only a chemical factory. I once told you that the liver is a wondrous organ, that the kidney with its functions is also a marvelous organ. Only by comprehending these organs will one find the spirit everywhere. If you stop finding the spirit in some area, if you think that digestion is a process that is too materialistic to be studied in a spiritual way, you then become a materialist. Indeed, materialism came into being through spiritual arrogance. I have told you this before, though it sounds remarkable: when the ancient Jews of the *Old Testament* had bad thoughts during the night, they did not blame the bad, unhealthy thoughts on their heads but on their kidneys. When they said, 'This night God has affected my kidneys,' they were more correct than today's medicine. The ancient Jews also said that God reveals Himself to man not through man's head but directly through the activity of his kidneys and generally through his abdominal activity.

"Considering this viewpoint, it is most interesting, though I don't know if you gentlemen have seen it, to watch an Orthodox Jew pray. When a devout Orthodox Jew prays, he does not take his phylactery out of a pocket that he wears over his heart or that hangs over his head. He wears his phylactery over his abdomen and prays with it in this position. People today naturally no longer know what the relationship is here, but those who long ago gave the ancient Jews their commandments were aware of the relationship. In western regions of Europe, people don't have much opportunity anymore to see this, but in eastern European regions it makes quite a special impression to observe how the old Jews pray. When they prepare for prayer, they take the phylactery out of the slit in their trousers; it then hangs around them and they pray.

"This knowledge that humanity once possessed by means of various dreamlike, ancient clairvoyant forces has been lost, and humanity today is not advanced enough to rediscover the spirit in all matter. You can comprehend nothing if you simply take your ordinary thoughts into a laboratory and mechanically execute experiments, and so on. You are not thinking at all while doing this. You must experiment in such a way that something of the spirit emerges everywhere; for that to happen, your experiments must be arranged accordingly. And so, one can say that it is funny that anthroposophy, the science of the spirit, has to point out how the human brain, the so-called noblest part, is connected with the lower abdomen, but it is simply so.

Only a true science leads to these facts. Similarly, any number of things can cause a disorder of the heart, for example. It can come through an internal irregularity; but in most cases an irregular activity of the heart can be traced to some disorder in the midbrain, where the feelings are particularly based (Diagram I). It is interesting to discover that just as the abdomen is related to the forebrain, so this forebrain is related, from the viewpoint of the soul, to the will, and the midbrain is related to feeling. Actually, only the back part of the brain is related to thinking. If we look into the brain, we see that the hindbrain is related to breathing and to thinking. Breathing has, in fact, a pronounced relationship to thinking."

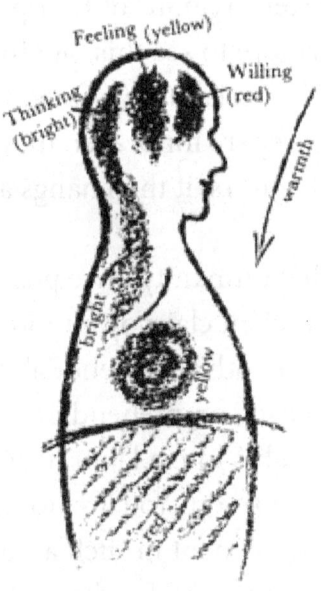

Diagram I

Health and Illness, **Volume II, Rudolf Steiner, Lecture V,**
*The Effect of Nicotine—Vegetarian and Meat Diets—On Taking
Absinthe—Twin Births,* **January 13, 1922, GA 348**

"The next consequence of a thickened heart is that the kidneys become ill, since it is due to the harmonious activities of heart and kidneys that the entire human bodily organization is kept functioning properly. The heart and kidneys must always work in harmony. Naturally, everything in the human being must harmonize, but the heart and kidneys are directly connected. It quickly becomes apparent that when something is amiss in the heart, the kidneys no longer function properly."

Conscience Arises from the Activity of the Cherubim in Our Blood

Lectures to the First Class, **Volume II, Rudolf Steiner, Lesson XIII, Dornach, May 17, 1924, GA 270**

"Now I must indicate something to you, my dear sisters and brothers, something you all know, for normal consciousness is already aware of it. It is what we call the voice of conscience in us. The voice of conscience! But the voice of conscience calls out in an indeterminate way to human consciousness. Usually, we do not rightly know what it is—in respect to our moral-psychological comportment—that comes from the mysterious depths of our souls and which we call the voice of conscience. With normal consciousness one does not penetrate so deeply into one's own being as to reach the voice of conscience. It ascends, but man does not reach it, so he does not look at it face to face.

"And when man penetrates meditatively to the distant world of the Cherubim [Spirits of Harmony], the wisdom filled beings who live and act throughout the Universe, he makes the great discovery that from the world of the Cherubim an impulse enters into him within which the voice of conscience lives. Oh, the voice of conscience is of high origin, high being. It actually lives in the world of the Cherubim. From that world of the Cherubim, it weaves itself into humanity and at first resounds from the depths of this humanity in an indeterminate way. But it is a great, mighty encounter when man, through intuition, can come into contact with the field of the Cherubim and encounter the world where his conscience lives and works. It is the greatest personal discovery anyone can make…

"…In truth it is the spirit from the field of the Cherubim that circulates in the blood that constitutes the voice of conscience. The blood is physical in all the parts of our bodies; but in that it is physical in all the parts of our bodies, it carries the voice of conscience, along with other things. And the waves of Cherubim life interweave in our blood."

The Origin of Conscience

At the Gates of Spiritual Science, **Rudolf Steiner, Lecture VIII,** *Good and Evil—Individual Karmic Questions,* **Stuttgart, August 29, 1906, GA 95**

"It is interesting to inquire whether in the historical evolution of mankind there has always been something comparable to what we call conscience. We find that in the earliest times, language had no word for it. In Greek literature it appears quite late, and in the language of the earlier Greeks no word for it exists. The same thing is true of the early periods of other civilizations. We may conclude, then, that the idea of conscience, in a more or less conscious form, came only gradually to be recognized. Conscience has developed fairly late in human evolution…

"Conscience is therefore the outcome of experiences spread over a number of incarnations. Fundamentally, all knowledge, from the highest to the lowest, is the outcome of what a man has experienced; it has come into being as a result of trial and error.

"An interesting fact is relevant here. Only since Aristotle has there been a science of logic, of logical thought. From this we must conclude that accurate thinking too, was born at a certain time. This is indeed so: thinking itself had first to evolve, and logical thinking arose in the course of time from fundamental observation of how thinking can go wrong. Knowledge is something mankind has acquired through many incarnations. Only after long trial and error could a store of knowledge be built up. All this illustrates the importance of the law of karma; here we have another example of something which has developed out of experience into a permanent habit and inclination. A motive such as conscience binds itself to the etheric body, becoming in time a permanent characteristic of it because the astral body has been so often convinced that this or that would not do."

The Riddle of Humanity, Rudolf Steiner, Lecture XII, August 27, 1916, GA 170

"But we must once more come into a relationship with the beings of the higher hierarchies, into a new relationship. During Old Moon and also during the first part of the Earth period, we were unconsciously, or subconsciously, dependent on them without being able to do anything about it. Spiritual beings of the higher hierarchies, and even some elemental beings directed their impulses into our consciousness. Now we are freeing ourselves from this. The period of imitation in early childhood remains as a kind of residue, a remnant.

"But we must again develop beyond a life of habit, both in the outer circumstances of our lives and in our moral behavior. I will simply refer you to the chapter in my *Philosophy of Spiritual Activity* which deals with moral tact. There you can read how our freedom is established on the basis of the habits we develop. We must be aware of what is really being developed in our life of habits! We still possess remnants of a connection with the spiritual beings of the higher hierarchies; but these are not fully apparent to our usual Earth consciousness. That world is unknown. We leave this unknown world behind when we pass through the gates of the senses into the world in which we live. But we originate in the world that is beyond the senses. Spiritual science enables us to lift the veil of the senses and rediscover it. And we do actually bear a remnant of this world within us. It is simply not apparent to our usual Earth consciousness. Up to the end of the Moon period, and on into Earth times, we still lived with the beings of the higher hierarchies in that spiritual world over yonder. In passing through the gates of the senses, we have left it behind. But not everything that our souls developed when we felt ourselves in the company of the beings of the higher hierarchies has been lost to us. We still carry an unconscious remnant with us. Among many other things, this unconscious remnant is also the basis of conscience. This is another way of viewing conscience. The whole of conscience is still inherited from the spiritual world. Only gradually, as we learn to understand the world once more and as we learn how to grasp it spiritually, will we discover a body of moral principles that will shed light on the more instinctive morality that is based on conscience. A morality that is increasingly filled with light will emerge—but, as goes without saying, only if humanity searches for it!"

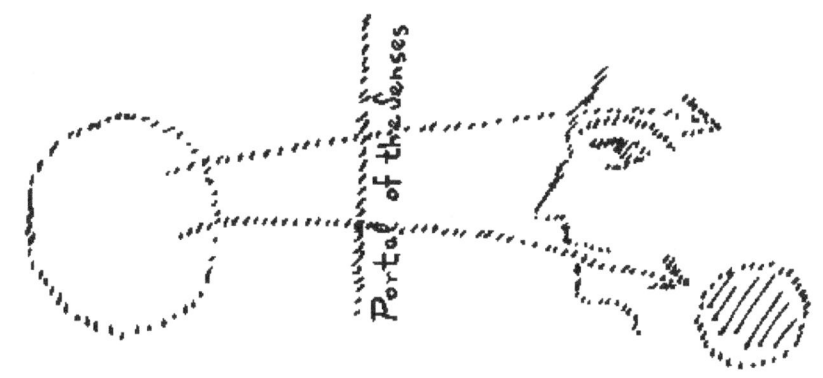

Macrocosm and Microcosm, **Rudolf Steiner, Lecture IX,**
Organs of Spiritual Perception—Contemplation of the Ego from
Twelve Vantage-points—The Thinking of the Heart, **Vienna**
March 29, 1910, GA 119

"An activity now begins of which it is important to take account
in connection with distinguishing between true and false pictures.
It can only be called *thinking of the heart*. This is something
that comes about in the course of the development of which
we spoke yesterday. In ordinary life we have the feeling that we
think with the head. That of course is a pictorial expression, for
we actually think with the spiritual organs underlying the brain;
but it is generally accepted that we think with the head. We
have a quite different feeling about the thinking that becomes
possible when we have made a little progress. The feeling then
is as if what had hitherto been localized in the head were now
localized in the heart. This does not mean the physical heart
but the spiritual organ that develops in the neighborhood of the
heart, the twelve-petalled lotus-flower. This organ becomes a
kind of organ of thinking in one who achieves inner development
and this thinking of the heart is very different from ordinary
thinking. In ordinary thinking everyone knows that reflection

is necessary in order to arrive at a particular truth. The mind moves from one concept to another and after logical deliberation and reflection reaches what is called 'knowledge.' It is different when we want to recognize the truth in connection with genuine symbols or emblems. They are before us like objects, but the thinking we apply to them cannot be confounded with ordinary brain-thinking. Whether they are true or false is directly evident without any reflection being necessary as in the case of ordinary thinking. What there is to say about the higher worlds is directly evident. As soon as the pictures are before us we know what we have to say about them to ourselves and to others. This is the characteristic of heart-thinking."

Wisdom of Man, of the Soul, and of the Spirit, Rudolf Steiner, Part III, *The Wisdom of Man,* Lecture III, *Imagination— "Imagination"; Inspiration—Self-fulfillment; Intuition— Conscience,* Berlin, December 15, 1909, GA 115

"Now, that is the process that takes place in the case of *intuition.* We can put it this way. When we can grasp with our own consciousness something that comes to full expression within this consciousness—not merely as knowledge but as an event, a world event—we are dealing with intuition, or more precisely, with intuition in the higher sense, such as is meant in my book, *Knowledge of the Higher Worlds and Its Attainment.* Within intuition, then, we are dealing with the governing will. While that shrewd psychologist, Brentano, finds only emotions within the soul, not will, because the will does not exist for ordinary consciousness, it remains for the consciousness that transcends ordinary consciousness to find something that is a higher event. It is the point at which the world enters and plays a part in consciousness. That is, intuition.

"Here again we have a sort of transition, only it is a little less readily noticeable than the one leading from imagination to 'imagination.' This transition sets in when we acquire such power of self-observation as to enable us not merely to will something and follow this by the deed, with thoughts and deeds standing dynamically side by side, so to speak, but to start expanding our emotions themselves over the quality of our deeds. In many cases this is even useful, yet it can happen in life that in performing an action we are gratified or disgusted by it. I don't believe an unprejudiced observer of life can deny the possibility of so expanding the emotions as to include likes and dislikes for one's own actions, but this co-experiencing of them in the emotions can be intensified.

"When this has been intensified to the point of its full potentiality in life, this transition reveals what we can call the human *conscience.* All stirrings of conscience occur at the transition from the emotions to intuition. If we seek the location of conscience, we find it at this transition. The soul is really open laterally on the side of imagination and on that of intuition, but it is closed on the side where we encounter the impact, as it were, of outer corporeality through perception. It achieves a certain fulfillment in the realm of imagination, and another when it enters the realm of intuition—in the latter case through an event."

Origin and Destination of Humanity, Rudolf Steiner, Lecture III, *Reincarnation and Karma,* Berlin, October 20, 1904, GA 53

"I would like to tell a phenomenon in addition, this is the phenomenon that we can exactly indicate the point in the European history of civilization where one speaks of conscience first. If you follow the whole ancient Greek world and trace the descriptions and accounts, you do not find a word, not even in the ancient Greek language, for conscience. One had no words for it. It may be especially remarkable to hear what Plato tells us about Socrates. In all Socratic dialogues the word is not yet included which appeared in Greece later only in the last century before Christ. Some think that the daimonion (daemon) is conscience.

"However, this can easily be disproved, and, hence, it cannot be considered seriously. We find conscience only in the Christian world. There is a drama trilogy, *Oresteia* by Aeschylus. If you pursue these this drama, you see that Orestes stands under the immediate impression of the matricide. He has murdered his mother because she killed his father. Now it is shown to us how Orestes is persecuted by the Furies, and it is shown how he turns to the court and the court acquits him. Nothing else appears than the concept of the gods taking revenge externally. There the process expresses itself in the fear of external powers. Nothing of that exists which the concept of conscience includes.

"Then Sophocles and then Euripides follow. With them Orestes faces us quite differently. Why he feels guilty this faces us here in another way. With these poets Orestes feels guilty because he now owns knowledge to have done something wrong. And from it the word conscience forms in Greek and also in Latin. Having a knowledge of one's own action, being able to observe oneself, being with one's own action this must have developed first. If now Paul Rée were right that conscience is a result of general human development that it develops out of that which the human being observes, because he is punished for that which harms to the fellow man, and, hence, harms to himself if he does anything that is not for the purposes of a reasonable world order. If this were the cause, this conscience would had undoubtedly to appear also in general. Because the external inducement takes place in the same sense, it would have to appear with bigger human masses; it would have to appear in a tribe at the same time, would develop as a general quality of the human species. Here one would have to study the Greek history as a soul history. At that time when in Greece with individual persons the concept developed which we do not yet find in older Greece, there was a period in which really the public unscrupulousness was the order of the day. Read the accounts of the time of the wars between Athens and Sparta! We cannot consider conscience as a general quality of the human species like the qualities of the animals."

The Christ Impulse and the Development of the Ego-Consciousness, Rudolf Steiner, Lecture I, *The Sphere of the Bodhisattvas,* Berlin, October 25, 1909, GA 116

"You will have heard the two Lectures just given by Dr. Unger, on the Ego in its relation to the Non-Ego in its comprehension of itself considered according to the *Theory of Knowledge.* Now do you suppose that what you then heard rendered by human lips and human thinking, could have been heard in this form 2,500 years ago? It would have been impossible in any part of the Earth to speak about the Ego in this form of pure thought. Suppose some individuality 2,500 years ago had desired to incarnate into our Earth-life, having made up their mind beforehand to speak of the Ego in that special way, well, it could not have done so! Anyone who supposes that anything of the kind could have been uttered by human lips, 2,500 years ago, entirely fails to recognize the actual progress and alteration in the development of civilization [and consciousness] since that time. For this to be possible it would not only be necessary for an individuality to resolve to incarnate in a human body, but it would also have been necessary that our Earth in her evolution should have produced a human body with a particular sort of brain, so that the truths, which in the higher worlds are quite of a different nature, could in that particular brain take the form which we call 'pure thought.' For the way in which Dr. Unger spoke of the Ego we call *the form of pure thought*. Around 2,500 years ago there would have been no human brain capable of being an instrument for translating these truths into such thoughts. The Beings who wish to descend to our Earth must make use of the bodies which this Earth-cycle itself produces. Our Earth, however, throughout the different periods of civilization has always brought forth bodies with ever different organizations; only in our Fifth Post-Atlantean Period of civilization, has it become possible to speak in the form of pure thought—the human race having produced the necessary bodies. Even in the Graeco-Latin Period it would not yet have been possible to speak like that along the lines of the theory of knowledge, for there would have been no instrument there to translate such thoughts into human language. That precisely is the task of our Fifth Post-Atlantean Period; it must gradually form the physical organization of man into an instrument through which those truths, which in other ages were grasped in quite other forms, can flow in ever purer and purer thought. We will take another example. When a man considers the question of good and evil at the present day, hesitating as to whether he should or should not do a certain thing, he says that a kind of inner voice speaks, telling him: 'You ought not to do this. You ought to do that!' and that this has nothing to do with any outer law. If we listen to this inner voice, we distinguish in it a certain impulse, an incitement to act in a certain way in a given case. We call this inner voice 'conscience.' If a man is of the opinion that the different periods of man's development were all exactly alike, he might easily believe that as long as man has inhabited the Earth, conscience has always existed. That would not be correct. We can, so to speak, prove historically that there was a beginning to the time when men began to speak of conscience. When this was, is clearly evident. It lay between the periods of two tragic poets: Aeschylus, who was born in the sixth century before our era, and Euripides, who was born in the fifth century. *You will find no mention of conscience previous to this.* Even in Aeschylus you will not as *yet* find what could be called the inner voice; what he writes of, still took the form of an astral, pictorial apparition; the Furies or Erinyes as vengeful beings, appeared to men. The time came, however, when the astral perception of the Furies was replaced by the inner-voice of conscience, Even in the Graeco-Latin period, in which a dim astral perception was still present, a man who had committed a wrong could perceive that every wrong act created astral forms in his environment, *whose presence filled him with anxiety and fear as to what he had done.* Those forms were man's educators at that time; they gave him his impulses. When he lost the last remains of his astral clairvoyance, this perception was replaced by the invisible voice of conscience; that means, that what was at first outside, then entered into the soul and became one of the forces now within it. The alteration that has taken place in mankind in the course of development comes from the fact that the external instrument of man, in which he seeks embodiment, has changed. Five thousand years ago, when a human soul did something wrong, the Furies were perceived; it could not then have heard the Voice of Conscience. In this way it learnt to establish an inner relation to good and evil. This same soul was born again and again, and at last it was born into a body possessing an organization in which the quality of conscience could approach it. In a future cycle of human development other forms and other capacities will be experienced in the soul."

Human History, **Rudolf Steiner, Lecture VII,** *Human History,*
Present, and Future in the Light of Spiritual Science, **Berlin,**
February 1, 1912, GA 61

"Then the Christian culture entered with necessity into that
age which has produced the ego-culture. It regards the Christ
Impulse as that by which the human ego receives the impulse to
manifest the spiritual in the future; just as the human being had
once descended from the spiritual. Someone who can realize
why Plato, Socrates and others were possible only in Greece, and
why at that time the ego-consciousness emerged at a specific
determining point, also understands why it was necessary for
the Mystery of Golgotha to take place during the Graeco-Roman
Period [747 B.C.–1414 A.D.] as the main focus of the entire
human development. Only someone who does not think about
these connections and does not know what human consciousness
means and how it changes can also not realize how the Christ
Impulse—characterized from another viewpoint in the previous
talk—positions itself in the course of human development from
the past through the present to the future. Just as in the ancient
Hebrew culture, the beginning appeared of that which appears
in the human ego. Now one can go into the details if one surveys
history that way. Philosophers often stated that the Greeks said,
any philosophy begins with marveling.

"Yes, it has to begin with the astonishment, as it appeared
in Greece. We can prove this if we look at history and at the
present in the right light. There something of the old clairvoyant
consciousness has remained that no longer works in the same
way as it once worked. *This is the dream.* The dream is the last,
decadent remnant of the old clairvoyance; because already the
conditions of the ego-consciousness work on it. What does the

dream lack? Observe the visions and how they surge up and down, you will realize that one thing is absent. We would never accept the way they come and go in the awakened consciousness. Why? Because the human being cannot be astonished in a dream; because within the culture of perception astonishment appears only with the ego-consciousness, and because something is contained in the dream *that comes from times without ego-consciousness.* The Greeks gave what appears as an ego-worldview with a miraculous characteristic saying, it begins with *marveling.* However, the dream still lacks another thing. While we are dreaming, we can do the most unbelievable things, *and conscience never torments us.* For conscience belongs to ego-consciousness; as it only appeared when the ego-consciousness had developed. One can prove this, while one compares, for example, the dramas of Aeschylus and Euripides. With Aeschylus there is never talk of conscience; but with Euripides the conscience already plays a role. *Conscience appears together with the ego-consciousness within human development, and the dream lacks conscience, it is only a remnant of the old clairvoyant consciousness.*

"We realize, while human history changed into the present, how from the old clairvoyant consciousness (from which language and myths have arisen) the intellectual consciousness gradually develops—*and which is now at a climax of its development.*"

Strengthening Conscience

The Original Impulse of Spiritual Science, **Rudolf Steiner, Lecture VII,** *Karma and Details of the Laws of Karma,* **Berlin, October 15, 1906, GA 96**

"A certain concept that can be explained in the light of karma, is particularly important here. It is the concept of conscience. What arises from a man's conscience is equally something that has been acquired. He has a conscience, an instinct for what is good, right, and true only because in his past lives, in his experiences during life, in his moral principles, he has molded this conscience. You can provide for the strengthening and enhancement of conscience if you undertake every day to deepen your moral conceptions. Moral conceptions become conscience in the next life and the one after that.

"So you see, that what the minute hand on the clock of life shows us becomes the hour hand in the next life. There must, however, be a certain strengthening of the moral principle and its realization in one life and then they are consolidated for the next. What is established in the etheric body of one life brings to maturity the attributes of the physical body of the next life. Good habits, good inclinations, good traits of character, prepare healthiness, physical proficiency, physical strength, therefore a healthy physical body, for the next life. A healthy physical body in one life indicates that the individual concerned prepared this physical body for himself in an earlier life through self-acquired habits and qualities of character. A particularly strong connection exists between a well-developed memory in one life and the physical body in the next life."

Conscience and Thinking

Preparing for a New Birth, **Rudolf Steiner, Stuttgart, June 21, 1923, GA 224**

"If we consider human existence on Earth, the most significant element in life must appear to be our capacity to think or make mental images—the capacity to think for ourselves about the world, our own actions and so forth. Any other view would be a self-deception. Certainly, there are temptations to consider other aspects of life as more valuable. We can feel, just below the threshold of consciousness, that our feelings about our own tasks, about our relationships and about the world, are more valuable than our thinking. And if we consider our moral existence, and the voice of conscience, we can tell ourselves that this conscience speaks to us from depths that thinking can never reach.

"We may feel all the more inclined to such a view when we see that even the most highly trained thinking, schooled in accordance with normal life, cannot arrive at the moral impulses of a simple, unschooled conscience. Still, we would be fooling ourselves if we imagined that thoughts are not the essence of human life on Earth.

"Certainly, the voice of conscience, the feeling of compassion, come from inexpressibly deeper sources than our thoughts. Yet these impulses that well up from the depths only find their right place in the human sphere when they are permeated by thought. The voice of conscience, too, only finds its true value by living within our thoughts, so that we clothe in thoughts what the voice of conscience says. Without overestimating thought, we still have to acknowledge, if we want to proceed in describing human consciousness without illusion, that it is thinking that makes us human. So Hegel is right, in a sense, when he says that thinking distinguishes man from beast."

Human Conscience Builds Christ's Physical Body

Ancient Wisdom and the Heralding of the Christ Impulse, **Rudolf Steiner, Lecture in Cologne, May 8, 1912, GA 143**

"These are questions which for the time being can only be hinted at. When the Christ Being descended to the Earth, He had to provide Himself with something similar to the sheaths of a human being: a physical body, an etheric body and an astral body. Gradually, in the course of the Epochs, something that corresponds to an astral, an etheric and a physical body formed around the originally purely spiritual Christ Impulse which descended at the Baptism by John. All these sheaths are formed from forces which have to be developed by humanity on Earth. What kind of forces are they?

"The forces of external science cannot produce a body for Christ because they are concerned only with things that will have disappeared in the future, *that will no longer exist*. But there is something that precedes knowledge and is infinitely more valuable for the soul than knowledge itself. It is what the Greek philosophers regarded as the beginning of all philosophy: *wonder or astonishment*. Once we have the knowledge, the experience which is of value to the soul has really already passed. People in whom the great revelations and truths of the spiritual world can evoke wonder, nourish this feeling of wonder, and in the course of time this creates a force which has a power of attraction for the Christ Impulse, which attracts the Christ Spirit: the Christ Impulse unites with the individual human soul when the soul can feel wonder for the mysteries of the world. Christ draws His astral body in earthly evolution from all those feelings which have lived in single human souls as wonder.

"The second quality that must be developed by human souls to attract the Christ Impulse is a power of *compassion*. Whenever the soul is moved to share in the suffering or joy of others, this is a force which attracts the Christ Impulse; Christ unites Himself with the human soul through compassion and love. Compassion and love are the forces from which Christ forms His etheric body until the end of earthly evolution. With regard to compassion and love one could, to put it crudely, speak of a program which Spiritual Science must carry out in the future. In this connection, materialism has evolved a pernicious science, such as has never previously existed on Earth. The very worst offence committed today is to correlate love and sexuality. This is the worst possible expression of materialism, the most devilish symptom of our time. Sexuality and love have nothing whatever to do with each other. Sexuality is something quite different from and has no connection at all with pure, original love. Science has brought things to a shameful point by means of an extensive literature devoted to connecting these two things which are simply not connected.

"A third force which flows into the human soul as if from a higher world to which man submits, to which he attributes a higher significance than that of his own individual moral instincts, is *conscience*.

"With man's conscience Christ is most intimately united. From the impulses which spring from the conscience of individual human souls Christ draws his physical body.

"The reality of an utterance in the *Bible* becomes very clear when we know that the etheric body of Christ is formed from men's feelings of compassion and love:—

'Inasmuch as ye have done it unto one of the least of these my brethren, ye have done it unto me.' (*Matthew* 25:40)

For to the end of the Earth's evolution Christ forms His etheric body out of men's compassion and love. As He forms His astral body out of wonder and astonishment, His physical body out of conscience, so does He form His etheric body out of men's feelings of compassion and love."

Faith—Love—Conscience

The Spiritual Foundation of Morality, **Rudolf Steiner, Lecture III, Norrköping, May 30, 1912, GA 155**

"We now see something appear which develops more and more, and which I have often spoken of in other connections, something which first appeared in the fourth Post-Atlantean Period [747 B.C.-1,414 A.D.], namely the Greek. It can be shown that in the old Greek dramas, for instance in Aeschylus, the Furies play a role which in Euripides is transformed into conscience. From this we see that in earlier times what we call conscience did not exist at all. Conscience is something that exists as a standard for our own actions when we go too far in our demands, when we seek our own advantage too much. It acts as a standard placed between our sympathies and antipathies.

"With this we attain to something which is more objective, which, compared with the virtues of truth, love and practical wisdom, acts in a much more objective, or outward manner. Love here stands in the middle, and acts as something which has to fill and regulate all life, also all social life. In the same way it acts as the regulator of all that man has developed as inner impulse. But that which he has developed as truth will manifest itself as the belief in super-sensible knowledge. Life-wisdom, that which originates in ourselves, we must feel as a divine spiritual regulator which, like conscience, leads securely along the true middle course…

"…Conscience is that which will enter as a regulator in the Consciousness- or Spiritual-Soul. Faith, love, conscience; these three forces will become the three stars of the moral forces which shall enter into human souls particularly through Anthroposophy. The moral perspective of the future can only be disclosed to those who think of these three virtues being ever more increased Anthroposophy will place moral life in the light of these virtues, and they will be the constructive forces of the future."

Conscience—The Voice of God

The Christ Impulse and the Development of the Ego-Consciousness, **Rudolf Steiner, Lecture VI,** *The Birth of Conscience*, **Berlin, May 2, 1910, GA 116**

"The question of the human conscience is one that must stir the very depths of our souls. For centuries philosophers and thinkers, the whole world over, have been more interested in this subject than in any other. With regard to the phenomenon of conscience one might easily succumb to the illusion of believing that everything to be found in the human soul today, was always to be found there. The human conscience too,—that precious possession of the human soul, which speaks like the voice of God in each individual man or woman, warning them of good or evil—even this precious gift was not always in man's inner being. Conscience, too, is something that has developed. And indeed, it is not so very long ago, comparatively speaking, that the human conscience announced its presence, since when it has developed more and more. Yet precious as this possession is to us, it is not intended that it should continue to live in the human soul in all the ages yet to come, just in its present form. It will develop further and take different forms; it will discover itself as something which man had to acquire, and which will bear fruit. And in later ages, when these fruits are his, it will be something upon which man can look back, saying: There once was a time when, in the course of my passage through the different incarnations, I was able to embody into my soul that which is now my conscience, and I am now enjoying the fruits of that! Just as we now look back at a time when our souls were in other incarnations and did not possess what we call conscience, so in later times our souls will look back at the present time and exclaim: Hail to that past! Thanks for the gifts which in the past became our human conscience! If we had not then been able to develop a human conscience in our souls, we should now lack what we need for our present life!

"From this we see that conscience forms part of the treasures of the soul at the present time, and if we understand something of the nature and being of the human conscience it gives us a sort of understanding of our age, and of its psychic life. Man's conscience came into being, that is a fact we have often referred to in various connections. If we go back a few centuries into ancient Greece, about five hundred years before the Christian era, we come to the great poet, Aeschylus. When we let the personages depicted by the mighty genius of the old Greek dramatist work upon us, we do not find what is today called conscience, or at any rate not designated by that name. Five hundred years before the Christian era the greatest dramatist then existing had no words to express what we now call the human conscience. If he wanted to express that process in the human soul which corresponds to what we now call conscience, he had to do so in this way:—

If a man committed the sin of murdering his mother, he was, through the might of the event made to see into the Spiritual worlds and there he perceived certain figures, which were known to the ancient Greek as the Erinyes and later to the Romans as the Furies.

Thus, according to Aeschylus, a man who had committed the evil deed of murdering his mother, did not, as he would today, hear the reproachful voice of conscience in his inner being; but something drove him to spiritual vision, and he saw around him figures, the avengers of his deed.

"This is one of the remarkable proofs to be found in the historical development of man, of what has just been asserted, that in olden times the capacities of the human soul were quite different. We have repeatedly emphasized that only gradually has the soul developed to its present power of perceiving the physical-sense world through the senses, and of using reason as it is used today. We stated that in olden times the soul possessed a certain clairvoyance as a normal capacity. At the time of Aeschylus this only appeared in special cases. For instance, it became clairvoyant when it was to see what it had brought about in the physical world by its wrongdoing. The soul of Orestes became clairvoyant after the murder of his mother. He then saw the spirits he had aroused in the spiritual world by his deed. They encompassed his soul on all sides. There was nothing of the nature of conscience in his soul; but a clairvoyant consciousness set in, enabling him to see the disorder brought about in the spiritual world by his wrongdoing. In olden times we find that when an evil deed was accomplished, no voice of conscience was heard, for in those days the soul was in a clairvoyant condition and could see what came about in the external world as a consequence of a wrong.

"What is it then that occurs when a wrong is done? Something is brought about by ourselves in the spiritual world. It is a purely materialistic belief that a wrong can take place without anything taking place in the spiritual world; it produces quite definite processes therein,—effects radiate from us which, though invisible to sense perception can be clearly seen by spiritual sight. These spiritual processes, radiating from one who has done wrong, provide nourishment for certain Spiritual Beings who are present in the spiritual world. Such Beings cannot approach man at all times; they can only do so when the radiations resulting from evil actions emanate from him. It is just the same as with a room—if it is quite clean no flies will enter it; there are no flies in a perfectly clean room; but if food is left about or dirt of any kind, the flies come immediately—so, the moment a man radiates certain spiritual emanations as a result of his evil action, he is surrounded by beings who feed on them. These are the beings whom Aeschylus, the great Greek dramatist, depicts around Orestes. What we today know as the inner-voice, Aeschylus represented in external forms because he was so conscious of it; for he knew that in special cases, a certain clairvoyant consciousness which was formerly the common possession of all men, could still be aroused...

"We need only trace Greek Art a little further, from Aeschylus to Euripides, who in his tragedies shows us that he already had the idea of conscience. In ancient Greece we can see how the idea of conscience gradually came into being during the last five hundred years before Christ. Look where you will in the *Old Testament* for a word corresponding to what we today call conscience: *you will not find one*. Conscience, as a quality, drew into the human soul; and if, instead of contemplating short spans-of-time we look at great periods, we see that conscience entered the human soul at about the same time as the Christ-impulse. We might say that conscience followed close on the Christ-impulse; it entered the historical development of the world almost like the shadow of that Impulse. In order to understand this, we must call to mind much that we have learned in the course of past years and make it fruitful for our understanding of what the human conscience really is…

"The Egyptian-Chaldean people waited for the spiritual or Consciousness Soul before they developed the ego; the Graeco-Latin peoples developed it in the Intellectual-Soul or soul of higher feeling; the culture of Northern Europe had prematurely developed the ego in the Sentient-Soul. That was in the human soul early in those countries; thus, the Sentient-soul and the ego-consciousness worked together there in a different way than anywhere else in the world. In Northern Europe they first made themselves felt in the development of mankind. What was the result of the Ego-consciousness being firmly established in the Sentient-Soul in the European peoples, before Christ had entered into the development of mankind, and before the latter had taken up what had been developed in Asia?

"Because of this a force had been developed in the soul of man, together with the Sentient Soul, which could only have been developed through the Sentient Soul being permeated with the ego-feeling while still quite virginal and uninfluenced by other civilizations. This permeation of the Sentient Soul with the sense of self (the ego-sense) has grown into man's conscience. This accounts for the wonderful innocence of conscience! How does it speak? It speaks in the same way in the simplest and most primitive of men, as it does in the most complex soul. It says quite simply: that is right, that is wrong, *without any theory or dogma*. When it says: that is right, or that is wrong, what it tells us works with the might of an instinct or an urge. You will only find it developed in this way in the West. Therefore, it throws its first rays like a rosy dawn, towards Greece and from thence towards Rome, where indeed we find it very strongly developed. We first meet with the word conscience,—*conscientia*—in the works of the Roman writers. Whereas among the Greeks we only find the first sporadic hints of it in Euripides, we find the Romans quite familiar with it, it had then become a word in general use. This is because of the influence of that strain of culture which came into being through the mutual inter-permeation of the Sentient Soul and ego-feeling; for the ego-feeling, which lifts men up from the lowest to the highest, already speaks in the Sentient Soul,—in which hitherto nothing spoke but instincts, desires, and passions,—and speaks there like a voice from God, urging man to do what is right that he may press up to the Higher Ego.

"In this way we can trace the first rise of conscience among the peoples of Europe. From thence it spreads its rays abroad to the other peoples of the Earth. Thus, through a wise world-guidance, humanity in one part of the world was so prepared that conscience could be added as a contribution to the whole collective development of humanity. We have now mentioned everything that can throw light upon conscience. We mentioned that indefinable attribute of conscience, its pressing forth from the depths of the soul. Conscience speaks like an urging impulse; but it is not an impulse. Those philosophers who so describe it, are far from hitting the mark. It speaks with the same power as does the Spiritual Soul itself when it appears—*but yet with elemental, original forces.*

"So, we see: Love appears on the Earth in the East; Conscience in the West. The two belong together; as Christ appears in the East, so Conscience awakens in the West, that through it Christ may be accepted. In the simultaneous occurrence of the fact of the Christ-event and the comprehension of it, and in the preparation for these two things in different parts of the Earth, we see the ruling of an infinite Wisdom guiding our development. We have thus indicated the past history of Conscience."

Conscience as a Teacher

Conscience and Astonishment as Indication of Spiritual Vision in Past and Future, **Rudolf Steiner, Breslau, February 3, 1912, GA 143**

"As a second fact from which we shall begin, we have the question of conscience. When a man does something, and with a sensitive nature even when he thinks, something stirs in him that we call conscience. This conscience is entirely independent of the external significance of events. We could for example have done something very advantageous to us, and yet this act might be condemned by our conscience. Everyone feels that when conscience goes into action something influences the judgment of an act that has nothing to do with its utility. It is like a voice that says within us: Truly, you should have done this, or you should not have done this—this is the fact of conscience, and we know how strong its warning power can be, and how it can pursue us through life. We know that the presence of conscience cannot be denied.

"Now we can consider again the life of dreams. Here we may do the strangest things which would cause us the most terrible pangs of conscience if we did them in waking life. Anyone can confirm this from his own experience, that he does things in dreams without his conscience stirring at all; while if he were to do them awake the voice of conscience would speak.

"Thus, these two facts, amazement and conscience, are excluded in a remarkable way from the life of dreams. Ordinarily man does not notice such things; nevertheless, they throw their light upon the depths of our existence...

"How is it with the conscience? Once more it is interesting, that the word 'conscience'—and therefore the concept too, for only when we have a conception of something does the word appear—is also only to be found in ancient Greece from a certain time onwards. It is impossible to find in earlier Greek literature, about up to the time of Aeschylus, a word that should be translated 'conscience.' But we find a word in the later Greek writers, for example Euripides. Thus, it can be pointed out precisely that conscience is something, just as is amazement about familiar things, known to man only from a certain period of ancient Greece onwards. What sprang up at this time as the activity of conscience was something quite different among the earlier Greeks. It did not then happen that the pangs of conscience appeared when a man had done something wrong. Men had then an original, elemental clairvoyance; going back only a short time before the Christian era we would find that all human beings still had this original clairvoyance. If a man then did something wrong, it was not followed by the stirring of conscience; but a demonic form appeared before the old clairvoyance, and a man was tormented by it. Such forms were called Erinys or Furies. Only when men had lost the capacity to see these demonic forms did they become able to feel, when they had done something wrong, the power of conscience as an inner experience...

"Astonishment, which did not exist in the ancient shadowy clairvoyance, cannot enter even today the consciousness of dreams. Astonishment and wonder cannot enter the life of dreams. We have them in the waking consciousness, which is directed to the external world. In his dreams, man is not in the external world; he is placed into the spiritual world and does not experience physical things. But it was in facing the physical world that man learned amazement. In dreams he accepts everything as it comes, as he did in the old clairvoyance. He could do this then because the spiritual powers came and showed him the good and evil that he had done; man did not then need wonder. Dreams thus show us by their own character that they are inherited from ancient times, when there was not yet any astonishment about everyday things, and not yet a conscience.

"Why was it necessary that man, having once been clairvoyant, could not remain so? Why has he descended? Did the gods perhaps drive him down unnecessarily? It is really so that man could never have acquired what lies in his capacity of wonder and what lies in his conscience, if he had not descended. Man descended in order to acquire knowledge and conscience; he could only do so through being separated for a time from these spiritual worlds. And he has achieved knowledge and conscience here, in order to ascend once more with them...

"...We really only feel something as a weight if it is outside us. So that if man feels his limbs beginning to become heavy as he falls asleep, this is a sign that man goes out of his body, out of his physical being.

"Much now depends upon a delicate observation, which can be made at the moment when the limbs grow heavy. A remarkable feeling appears. It tells us: 'You have done this—you have left this undone!' Like a living conscience the deeds of the previous day stand out. And if something is there that we cannot approve of we toss on our bed and cannot fall asleep. If we can be content with our action there comes a happy moment as we fall asleep, when a man says to himself: 'Could it always be so!' Then there comes a jolt—that is when man leaves his physical and ethereal body, and then a man is in the spiritual world.

"Let us observe the moment of this phenomenon, which is like a living conscience, more exactly. A man has not really any power to do something reasonable and tosses about on his bed. This is an unhealthy condition which prevents him from getting to sleep. It happens at the moment when we are about to leave the physical plane through falling asleep, in order to ascend into another world; but this is not willing to accept what we call our 'bad conscience.' A man cannot fall asleep because he is cast back by the world into which he should enter in sleep. Thus, if we say that we will listen to our conscience about some action, this means that we have a presentiment of what the human being will need to be in future in order to enter the spiritual world."

"Thus, we have in astonishment an expression of what we have seen at an earlier time, and conscience is an expression of a future vision in the spiritual world. Conscience reveals whether we shall be horrified or happy when we are able to behold our actions in the realm of spirit. Conscience is a presentiment that reveals prophetically how we shall experience our deeds after death.

"Astonishment and the impulse towards knowledge on the one hand, and the conscience on the other—these are living signs of the spiritual world. These phenomena cannot be explained without bringing in the spiritual worlds. A man will be more inclined to become an anthroposophist if he feels reverence and wonder before the facts of the world. The most developed souls are those which are able to feel wonder more and more. The less one can feel wonder, the less advanced is the soul…

"To be able to bring wonder everywhere—that is a memory of the vision before birth. To bring conscience everywhere into our deeds is to have a living presentiment that every deed which we fulfil will appear to us in the future in another form. Human beings who feel this are more predestined than others to find their way to Spiritual Science.

"This is still the case only with very few human beings; but certainly in the course of the twentieth century it will become widespread. It will take this form; let us assume that a man has done something and is troubled afterwards by a bad conscience. It is like this at the present time. But later, when the connection with the spiritual world has been restored, a man will feel impelled, after he has done this or that, to draw back from his action as if with blindfolded eyes. And then something like a dream picture, but one that is entirely living for him will arise; a future event, which will happen because of his deed. And men experiencing such a picture will say something like this to themselves: 'Yes, it is I who am experiencing this, but what I am seeing is no part of my past!'

"For all those who have heard nothing of spiritual science this will be a terrible thing. But those who have prepared for what all will experience will say to themselves: 'This is indeed no part of my past, but I will experience it in the future as the karmic result of what I have just done.'

"Today we are in the anteroom of that time, when the karmic compensation will appear to men in a prophetic dream-picture. And when you think of this experience in the course of time developing further and further, you can conceive the man of the future who will behold the karmic judgment upon his deeds.

"How does something like this happen—that human beings become capable of seeing this karmic compensation? This is connected with the fact that human beings once had no conscience but were tormented after evil deeds by the Furies.

This was an ancient clairvoyance which has passed away. Then came the middle period when they no longer saw the Furies, but what was brought about by the Furies previously now arose inwardly as conscience. A time is now gradually approaching in which we shall again see something—and this is the karmic compensation. That man has now developed conscience begins to enable him to behold the spiritual world consciously."

The Voice of Conscience After Death

Life Between Death and Rebirth, Rudolf Steiner, Lecture IX, *Life After Death*, Linz, January 26, 1913, GA 140

"In many people we find a propensity that in everyday life we denote as an immoral characteristic, and that is lack of conscience. In the voice of conscience, we have a wonderful regulator for the soul-life. A lack of conscience, the inability to listen to the warning voice of conscience, delivers us to yet other powers between the period of death and a new birth. The seer discovers souls who have become the servants of particularly evil spirit-beings after death."

Life Between Death and Rebirth, Rudolf Steiner, Lecture X, *Anthroposophy as the Quickener of Feeling and of Life*, Tübingen, February 16, 1913, GA 140

"If the seer looks back into the lives of such souls before death, he discovers why they are condemned to serve as servants to the spirits of death and disease. The cause lies in a lack of conscience in such souls during their earthly life. In accordance with the extent of their lack of conscience they condemn themselves to become servants of those evil beings. As truly as cause and effect obtain in the case of impinging billiard balls, so, too, must people who have no conscience become servants of these evil beings. That is indeed shattering!"

The Birth of Human Conscience

Metamorphosis of the Soul, Paths of Experience, **Volume II, Rudolf Steiner, Lecture VIII,** *Human Conscience*, **Berlin, May 5, 1910, GA 59**

"How often has the significance of conscience been brought out by the words, no matter whether they are taken literally or metaphorically: 'When conscience speaks in the human soul, it is the voice of God that speaks.' And one could scarcely find anyone, however unprepared to reflect on higher spiritual concerns, who has not formed some idea of what conscience is. Everyone feels vaguely that whatever conscience may be, it is experienced as a voice in the individual's breast which determines with irresistible power what is good and what is bad; what man must do in order to gain his own approval and what he must leave undone if he is not to despise himself. Hence, we can say: Conscience appears to every individual as something holy in the human breast, and that to form some kind of opinion about it is relatively easy...

"Now if light is thrown on those primordial times by means of clairvoyance in the way already described, what does the seer tell us concerning the human consciousness of those times when a man had, for example, committed an evil deed? His deed did not present itself to him as something he could inwardly assess. He beheld it, with all its harmfulness and shamefulness, as a ghostly vision confronting his soul. And when a feeling concerning his evil deed arose in his soul, the shamefulness of it came before him as a spiritual reality, so that he was as though surrounded by a vision of the evil he had wrought.

"Then, in the course of time, this dreamlike clairvoyance faded, and man's ego came increasingly to the fore. In so far as man found this central point of his being within himself, the old clairvoyance was extinguished, and self-consciousness established itself more and more clearly. The vision he had previously had of his bad and good deeds was transposed into his inner life, and deeds once clairvoyantly beheld were mirrored in his soul.

"Now what sort of forms were beheld in dreamy clairvoyance as the counterpart of man's evil deed? They were pictures whereby the spiritual powers around him showed how he had disturbed and disrupted the cosmic order, and they were intended to have a salutary effect. It was a counteraction by the Gods, who wished to raise him up and, by showing him the effect of his deed, to enable him to eliminate its harmful consequences. This was indeed a terrifying experience for him, but it was fundamentally beneficial, coming as it did from the cosmic background out of which man himself had emerged. When the time came for man to find in himself his ego-center, the external vision was transferred to his soul in the form of a reflected picture. When the ego first makes its appearance in the Sentient Soul, it is weak and frail, and man first has to work slowly upon himself in order that his ego may gradually advance towards perfection. Now what would have happened if, when the external clairvoyant vision of the effects of his misdeeds had disappeared, it had not been replaced by an inward counterpart of its beneficial influence? With his still frail ego, he would have been torn to and fro in his sentient soul by his passions, as though in a surging boundless sea. What, then, was it that was transferred at this historic moment from the external world to the inner life of the soul? If it was the great Cosmic Spirit that had brought the harmful effects of a man's deed before his clairvoyant consciousness as a healing influence, showing him what he had to make good, so that later on it was the same cosmic Spirit that powerfully revealed itself in his inner life at a time when his ego was still weak. Having previously spoken to man through a clairvoyant vision, the Cosmic Spirit withdrew into man's inner life and imparted to him what had to be said about correcting the distortion caused in the world-order. Man's ego is still weak, and the Cosmic Spirit keeps a perpetual, unsleeping watch over it and passes judgment where the ego could not yet judge. Behind the weak ego stands something like a reflection of the powerful Cosmic Spirit which had formerly shown to man through clairvoyant vision the consequences of his deeds. And this reflection is now experienced by him as conscience watching over him…

"But we may note that from about the first third of the Middle Ages and on through mediaeval philosophy, whenever conscience was spoken of, it was always said to be a power in the human soul which was capable of immediately declaring what a man should do and what he should leave undone. However, these mediaeval philosophers also say that underneath this power of the soul there is something else, something of finer quality than conscience itself. A personality often mentioned here, Meister Eckhart, tells of a tiny spark that underlies conscience; an eternal element in the soul which, if it is heeded, declares with unmistakable power the laws of good and evil.

"In modern times, we encounter once more the most varied accounts of conscience, including some which make a peculiar impression, for they clearly fail to recognize the serious nature of the divine inner voice that we call conscience. There are philosophers who say that conscience is something that a man acquires when, by extending continually his experience of life, he learns what is useful, harmful, satisfying and so on for himself. The sum of these experiences gives rise to a judgment which says: "Do this—don't do that.

"There are other philosophers who speak of conscience in terms of the highest praise. One of these is the great German philosopher, Johann Gottlieb Fichte, who pointed above all to the human ego not the transient personal ego but the eternal essence in man—as the fundamental principle of all human thought and being. At the same time, he held that the highest experience for the human ego was the experience of conscience, when a man hears the inward judgment: 'This you must do, for it would go against your conscience not to do it.' The majesty and nobility of this judgment, he believed, could not be surpassed. And if Fichte was the philosopher who laid the strongest emphasis on the power and significance of the human ego, it is characteristic of him that he ranked conscience as the ego's most significant impulse.

"The further we move on into modern times, and the more materialistic thinking becomes, the more do we find conscience deprived of its majesty—not in the human heart, but in the thinking of philosophers who are more or less imbued with materialism…

"A glance over the philosophers will show that in earlier times even the best of them thought of conscience differently from the way in which we are bound to think of it today. For when we say that conscience is a voice speaking out of a divine impulse in the breast of the simplest man, saying, 'This you must do—that you must leave undone' this is somewhat different from the teaching we find in Socrates and in his successor, Plato. They both insist that virtue can be learnt. Socrates, indeed, says that if a man forms clear ideas as to what he should and should not do, then gradually, through this knowledge of what virtue is, he can learn to act virtuously.

"Now one could easily object, from a modern standpoint, that things would go badly if we had to wait until we had learnt what is right and what is wrong before we could act virtuously. Conscience speaks with elemental power in the human soul and is heard by the individual as saying: 'This you must do, and that you must leave alone,' long before we learn to form ideas concerning good and evil and thus begin to formulate moral precepts. Moreover, conscience brings a certain tranquility to the soul on occasions when a man can say to himself: 'You have done something you can approve of.' It would be bad—many people might say—if we had to learn a lot about the nature and character of virtue in order to arrive at an agreed estimation of our behavior. Hence we can say that the philosopher to whom we look up as a martyr of philosophy, whose death crowned and ennobled his philosophical work—I mean Socrates—sets before us a concept of virtue which hardly tallies with our view of conscience today: and even with later Greek thinkers we always find the assertion that perfect virtue is something that can be learnt, a doctrine not in keeping with the primitive, elemental, power of conscience.

"How is it, then, that so pre-eminent and powerful a person as Socrates is not aware of the idea of conscience that we have today, although we feel whenever we approach him, as Plato describes him, that the purest morality and the highest degree of virtue speak through his words? The reason is, that the ideas, concepts, and inward experiences which feel today as though they were innate, were in fact acquired laboriously by the human soul in the course of time. When we trace the spiritual life of humanity back into the past, we find that our idea of conscience and our feeling for it were not present in the same way in ancient times, and therefore not among the Greeks. Conscience, in fact, was *born*...

"Now what sort of forms were beheld in dreamy clairvoyance as the counterpart of man's evil deed? They were pictures whereby the spiritual powers around him showed how he had disturbed and disrupted the cosmic order, and they were intended to have a salutary effect. It was a counteraction by the Gods, who wished to raise him up and, by showing him the effect of his deed, to enable him to eliminate its harmful consequences. This was indeed a terrifying experience for him, but it was fundamentally beneficial, coming as it did from the cosmic background out of which man himself had emerged. When the time came for man to find in himself his ego-center, the external vision was transferred to his soul in the form of a reflected picture. When the ego first makes its appearance in the sentient soul, it is weak and frail, and man first has to work slowly upon himself in order that his ego may gradually advance towards perfection. Now what would have happened if, when the external clairvoyant vision of the effects of his misdeeds had disappeared, it had not been replaced by an inward counterpart of its beneficial influence? With his still frail ego, he would have been torn to and fro in his sentient soul by his passions, as though in a surging boundless sea. What, then, was it that was transferred at this historic moment from the external world to the inner life of the soul? If it was the great cosmic Spirit that had brought the harmful effects of a man's deed before his clairvoyant consciousness as a healing influence, showing him what he had to make good, so, later on, it was the same cosmic Spirit that powerfully revealed itself in his inner life at a time when his ego was still weak. Having previously spoken to man through a clairvoyant vision, the cosmic Spirit withdrew into man's inner life and imparted to him what had to be said about correcting the distortion caused in the world-order. Man's ego is still weak, and the cosmic Spirit keeps a perpetual, unsleeping watch over it and passes judgment where the ego could not yet judge. Behind the weak ego stands something like a reflection of the powerful Cosmic Spirit which had formerly shown to man through clairvoyant vision the consequences of his deeds. And this reflection is now experienced by him as conscience watching over him.

"So, we see how true it is when conscience is naïvely described as the voice of God in man. At the same time, we see how Spiritual Science points to the moment when external vision became inward experience and conscience was born…

"It is not so very long since the time when the birth of conscience can be seen to occur. If we look back to the fifth and sixth centuries B.C., we encounter in ancient Greece the great dramatic poet Aeschylus; and in his work, we find a theme which is especially remarkable for the reason that the same subject was treated by a late Greek poet in a quite different way…

"Orestes sees before him, in dreamlike clairvoyance, the effect of his act of matricide in its external form. Apollo had approved the deed; but there is something higher. Aeschylus wished to indicate that a still higher cosmic ordinance obtains; and this he could do only by making Orestes become clairvoyant at that moment, for he had not yet gone far enough to dramatize what today we call an inner voice. If we study his work, we feel that he was at the stage when something like conscience ought to emerge from the whole content of the human soul, but he never quite reached that point. He confronts Orestes with dreamlike, clairvoyant pictures that have not yet been transformed into conscience. Yet we can see how he is on the verge of recognizing conscience. Every word that he gives to Klytemnestra, for example, makes one feel unmistakably that he ought to indicate the idea of conscience in its present-day sense; but he never quite gets that far. In that century, the great poet could only show how bad deeds rose up before the human soul in earlier times.

"Now we will pass over Sophocles and come to Euripides, who described the same situation only a generation later. Scholars have rightly pointed out—though Spiritual Science alone can show this in its true light—that in Euripides the dream-pictures experienced by Orestes are no more than shadowy images of the inward promptings of conscience—somewhat as in Shakespeare. Here we have palpable evidence of the stages whereby the idea of conscience was taken hold of by the art of poetry. We see how Aeschylus, great poet as he was, cannot yet speak of conscience itself, while his successor, Euripides, does speak of it. With this development in mind, we can see why human thinking in general could work its way only slowly towards a true conception of conscience. The force now active in conscience was active also in ancient times; the pictures showing the effects of a man's deeds rose before his clairvoyant sight. The only difference is that this force became internalized; but before it could be inwardly experienced, the whole process of human development, which led gradually to the concept of conscience, had to take its course."

"Thus, we see in conscience a faculty which comes to the fore by degrees and has to be acquired by man's own endeavors. Where, then, should we look for this most intense activity of conscience? At that point where the human ego was beginning to make itself known and was still weak, that is something which can be shown in human development. In ancient Greece it had already advanced to the stage of the Intellectual Soul. But if we look further back to Egypt and Chaldea outer history knows nothing of this, but Plato and Aristotle were clairvoyantly aware of it—we find that even the highest culture of those times was achieved without the presence of an inwardly independent ego. The difference between the knowledge that was nurtured and put to use by the sanctuaries of Egypt and Chaldea and our modern science is that our science is grasped by the Consciousness Soul, whereas in pre-Hellenic times it all depended on inspirations from the Sentient Soul. In ancient Greece the ego progressed from the Sentient Soul [2,907 B.C.-747 B.C.] into the Intellectual Soul [747 B.C.-1,414 A.D.]. Today we are living in the Consciousness Soul Period [1,414 A.D.-3,574 A.D.], which means that a real ego-consciousness arises for the first time. Anyone who studies the evolution of mankind, and in particular the transition from Eastern to Western culture, can see how human progress has been marked by ever-increasing feelings of freedom and independence. Whereas man had formerly felt himself entirely dependent on the Gods and the inspirations that came from them, in the West, culture first came to spring from the inner life."

"...The point is that in the West everything was designed to raise the ego from the Sentient Soul to the Consciousness Soul. In the East the ego was veiled in obscurity and had no freedom. In the West, by contrast, the ego works its way up into the Consciousness Soul. If the old dreamlike clairvoyance is extinguished, everything else tends to awaken the ego and to evoke conscience as guardian of the ego as a divine inner voice. Aeschylus was the cornerstone between the worlds of East and West...

"The elements necessary for understanding this were present in the stream of thought that came over from the East; they needed only to be raised to a higher level. It was in the West that souls were ripe to grasp and accept this impulse—the West, where experiences which had belonged to the outer world were transferred to the inner life most intensively, and in the form of conscience watched over a generally weak ego. In this way souls were strengthened and prepared to hear the voice of conscience now saying within them: The Divinity who appeared in the East to those able to look clairvoyantly into the world—this Divinity now lives in us!

"However, what was thus being prepared could not have become conscious experience if the inward Divinity had not spoken in advance in the dawning of conscience. So, we see that external understanding for the Divinity of Christ Jesus was born in the East, and the emergence of conscience came to meet it from the West. For example, we find that conscience is more and more often spoken of in the Roman world, at the beginning of the Christian era, and the further westward we go, the clearer is the evidence for the recognized existence of conscience or for its presence in embryonic form.

"Thus, East and West played into each other's hands. We see the Sun of the Christ-nature rising in the East, while in the West the development of conscience is preparing the way for understanding the Christ. Hence the victorious advance of Christianity is towards the West, not the East. In the East we see the spread of a religion which represents the final consequence—though on the highest level—of the Eastern outlook: Buddhism takes hold of the Eastern world. Christianity takes hold of the Western world because Christianity had first created the organ for receiving it. Here we see Christianity brought into relation with the deepened element in Western culture: the concept of conscience embodied in Christianity.

"...The highest spiritual consciousness says that when conscience speaks, it is truly the Cosmic Spirit speaking. And

Spiritual Science brings out the connection between conscience and the greatest event in the evolution of mankind, the Christ-event. Hence it is not surprising that conscience has thereby been ennobled and raised to a higher sphere. When we hear that something has been done for reasons of conscience, we feel that conscience is regarded as one of the most important possessions of mankind.

"Thus, we can see how natural and right it is for the human heart to speak of conscience as 'God in man.' And when Goethe says that the highest experience for man is when 'God-Nature reveals itself to him,' we must realize that God can reveal himself in the spirit to man only if Nature is seen in the light of its spiritual background. This has been provided for in human evolution, on the one hand by the light of Christ, shining from outside, and on the other by the divine light within us: the light of conscience. Hence a philosopher such as "Fichte, who studies human character, is justified in saying that conscience is the highest voice in our inward life. On this account, also, we are aware that our dignity as human beings is inseparable from conscience. We are human beings because we have an ego-consciousness; and the conscience we have at our side is also at the side of our ego. Thus, we look on conscience as a most sacred individual possession, inviolable by the external world, whose voice enables us to determine our direction and our goal. When conscience speaks, no other voice may intrude.

"So it is that on one side conscience ensures our connection with the primordial power of the world and on the other guarantees the fact that in our inmost self we have something like a drop flowing from the Godhead. And man can know: When conscience speaks in him, it is a God speaking."

The 'Consuming Fire of Shame'

Macrocosm and Microcosm, Rudolf Steiner, Lecture III,
*The Inner Path Followed by the Mystic—Experience the Cycle
of the Year*, March 23, 1910, Vienna, GA 119

"There is in man what is called the sense of Shame, the essence
of which is that in his soul he wants to divert the attention of
others from the thing or quality of which he is ashamed. This
sense of shame in connection with something he does not want
to be revealed is a faint indication of the feeling which would
be intensified to overpowering strength if he were to look
consciously into his own inner being. This feeling would take
possession of the soul with such power that it would seem to be
diffused over everything encountered in the external world; the
man would undergo an experience comparable with that of being
consumed by fire. Such would be the effect produced by this
feeling of shame…

"It is the comparison of the soul with what it would perceive if
it had sight of what spiritually underlies the physical and etheric
bodies that would evoke the intense feeling of shame; preparation
for this is made in advance through all the experiences undergone
by the mystic before he becomes capable of penetrating into
his inmost being. To realize for himself the imperfection of his
soul, to realize that his soul is weak, insignificant, and has still
an infinitely long path to travel, is bound to arouse a feeling
of humility and a yearning for perfection, and these qualities
prepare him to endure the comparison with the infinitely wise
structure into which he penetrates on waking. Otherwise, he
would be consumed by shame as if by fire.

"The mystic prepares himself by concentrating on the
following thoughts:—

'When I behold what I am and compare it with what the wise guidance of the Universe has made of me, the shame I feel is like a consuming fire.'

"This feeling gives rise outwardly to the flush of shame. This feeling would intensify to such an extent as to become a scorching fire in the soul if the mystic has not the strength to say to himself:—

'Yes, I feel utterly paltry in comparison with what I may become; but I shall try to develop the strength that will make me capable of understanding what the wisdom of the Universe has built into my bodily nature and to make myself spiritually worthy of it.'

"The mystic is made to realize by his spiritual teacher that he must have boundless humility. It may be said to him: Look at a plant. A plant is rooted in the soil. The soil makes available to the plant a kingdom lower than itself but without which it cannot exist. The plant can bow to the mineral kingdom, saying: I owe my existence to this lower kingdom out of which I have grown. The animal too owes its existence to the plant kingdom and if it were conscious of its place in the world would in humility acknowledge its indebtedness to the lower kingdom. And man, having reached a certain height, should say: I could not have attained this stage had not everything below me evolved correspondingly.

"When a man cultivates such feelings in his soul, the realization comes to him that he has a reason not only to look upwards—*but to look downwards with thankfulness to the*

kingdoms below him. The soul is then filled with this feeling of
humility and realizes how infinitely long is the path that leads
towards perfection. Such is the training for true humility.

"Then, secondly, the would-be mystic must develop another
feeling which makes him capable of enduring whatever obstacles
may lie in his path as he strives towards perfection. He must
develop a feeling of *resignation* in respect of whatever ordeals
he will have to endure in order to reach a certain stage of
development. For only by proving himself victorious over pain
and suffering for a long, long time can he develop the strong
powers needed by his soul to overcome the inevitable sense of
inferiority in face of what a wise World-Order has incorporated
in the etheric and physical bodies. The soul must say to itself over
and over again:—

'Whatever pain and suffering still await me, I will not waver;
for if I were willing to experience only what brings joy,
I should never develop the strength of which my soul is
actually capable.'

"Strength is developed only by overcoming obstacles, not by
simply submitting to conditions as they are. Forces of soul can be
steeled only when a man is ready to bear pain and suffering with
resignation. This strength must be developed in the soul of the
mystic if he is to become fit to descend into his inner being.

"Let nobody imagine that Spiritual Science demands that
a man living an ordinary, everyday life shall undergo such
exercises for they are beyond his power. What is being described
here is simply a narration of what those who voluntarily embark
upon such experiences can make of the soul, that is to say, they

can make the soul capable of penetrating into their own inmost being. In the course of normal life, however, the Sentient Body [Soul Body; Astral Body] intervenes between what it is possible for the mystic to experience inwardly and what is actually experienced in the external world. That is what protects a man from descending into his own inner self without preparation and being consumed by a feeling of shame. In the normal course of life a man cannot experience what is thus screened from him by the Sentient Body; for there he has already reached the frontier of the spiritual world. A spiritual investigator seeking to explore the inner nature of man must cross this frontier; he must cross the stream which diverts normal human consciousness from the inner to the outer world. This normal consciousness, while insufficiently mature, is protected from penetrating into man's inner self—*protected from being consumed in the fire of shame.* Man cannot see the Power which protects him from this experience every morning on waking. This Power is the first spiritual Being encountered by one who is about to pass into the spiritual world. He must pass this Being who protects him from being consumed by the inner sense of shame; he must pass this Being who deflects his inward-turned gaze to the external word, to the tapestry of sense-phenomena. Normal consciousness becomes aware of the effect of this Being; but man cannot see him. He is the first Being who must be passed by one who desires to penetrate into the spiritual world. This spiritual Being who every morning stands before man and protects him while he is still immature from the sight of his own inner self, is called in Spiritual Science, the Lesser Guardian of the Threshold. The path into the spiritual world leads past this Being."

The Effect of Occult Development Upon the Self and the Sheaths of Man, **Rudolf Steiner, Lecture V, The Hague, March 24, 1913, GA 145**

"In the case of a person who has undergone a theosophical development there comes a clear after-feeling regarding what he has said; he feels something like an inner shame when he has expressed what is not right in a moral or intellectual sense; and something like a sort of thankfulness—not satisfaction with himself—when he has been able to express something to which the wisdom he has attained can give assent. And if he feels—and for this, too, he acquires a delicate sensitiveness—that something like an inner self-satisfaction, a self-complaisance with himself arises when he has said something that is right, that is a sign that he still possesses too much vanity, which is no good in his development. He learns to distinguish between the feeling of satisfaction which follows when he has said something with which he can agree, and the self-complaisance which is worthless. He should try not to allow this latter feeling to arise; but only to develop the feeling of shame when he has said anything untrue or non-moral, and when he has succeeded in saying something suitable to the occasion, to develop a feeling of gratitude for the wisdom he now has part in, and to which he does not lay claim as his own, but receives as a gift from the Universe.

"Little by little the student feels in this way with respect to his own thinking. As has already been said, he must remain a man on the physical plane; and while not attaching too much value to the self-formed thoughts, he must still form them; but this self-thinking itself now alters, so much that he holds it under the self-control we have just described. Regarding a thought, of which he may say: 'I have thought that, and it is in keeping with the Wisdom'—regarding this thought he develops a feeling of gratitude towards the Wisdom. A thought which arises as a wrong, ugly, non-moral thought leads to a certain inner feeling of shame, and the student feels:—

'Can I really still be like this? Is it possible that I have still sufficient egotism to think this, in the face of the Wisdom that has entered into me?'

"It is extremely important for him to feel this kind of self-control in his inner being. The peculiarity of this self-control is that it never comes through the critical intellect—*but always appears in feeling, in perception.* Let us pay great attention to this, my dear friends: A man who is only clever, who only possesses the judgment of the outer life, who is critical, can never arrive at what we are now speaking of—*for this must appear as a feeling.* When he has acquired this feeling—when it arises as if from his own inner being—he identifies himself with this feeling either of shame or thankfulness, and feels that his own self is connected with this feeling. And if I were to make a diagram of what is thus experienced, it is as though one felt wisdom streaming in from above, coming towards one from above, streaming into one's head in front and then filling one from above downwards. On the other hand, a student feels that, as though coming from his own body, there streams towards that wisdom a feeling of shame, so that he identifies himself with this feeling, and addresses the wisdom as something given from outside; and feels within himself a region wherein this feeling, which is now the ego, meets the instreaming wisdom bestowed. (Diagram I)

"The pupil can inwardly experience the region where these two meet. To feel this meeting, proves a right inner experience of the etheric world; he experiences the thoughts pressing in from the external etheric world—for it is the wisdom streaming towards him from the external etheric world that presses in and is perceived by means of the two feelings—that is the rightly-perceived etheric world. And when he perceives it thus, he ascends to the higher Beings which only descend as far as to an etheric body and not to a physical human body. On the other hand, he may experience this etheric world wrongly, in a certain sense. Rightly, the etheric world is experienced between thinking and feeling, in the manner just described. The experience is purely an inner process in the soul. The elementary or etheric world may be experienced wrongly if it is experienced on the boundary between breathing and our own etheric body. If the student performs breathing exercises too soon, or in an incorrect way, he gradually becomes a witness of his own breathing-process. With the breathing process of which he is then aware (the act of breathing being usually unnoticed), he may acquire a breathing which perceives itself. And this feeling may be associated with a certain perception of the etheric world. By means of all kinds of breathing-exercises a person may gain the power of observing certain etheric processes which really are in the external world, but which belong to the lowest external psychic processes, and which, if experienced too soon, can never give the right idea of the true spiritual world.

"Of course, from a certain point in the esoteric practice a regulated breathing-process may also begin; *but this must be properly directed*. It then comes about that we perceive the etheric world, as has been described, on the border between thinking and feeling, and what we thus learn to recognize is only strengthened by our also coming to know the grosser etheric processes which take place on the border between the etheric world and our breathing-processes. For the matter is as follows: There is a world of genuine higher Spirituality, this we attain through the interaction which takes place—as we have described—between wisdom and feeling, there we come to the deeds accomplished in the etheric world by the beings belonging to the higher hierarchies. But there are a great number of all sorts of good and bad and hostile and horrible and dangerous elementary beings, which, if we become acquainted at the wrong time, obtrude themselves upon us as if they really were a valuable Spiritual World; while they are nothing more, in a certain sense, than the lowest dregs of the beings of the Spiritual World. He who wishes to penetrate into the Spiritual World must indeed become acquainted with these beings; but it is not well to become acquainted with them at the beginning. For the peculiarity is this: that if a person becomes acquainted with these beings at first, without traversing the difficult path of his own inner experience, he grows fond of them, has astonishing partiality for them; and it may then occur that a man who thus raises himself into the spiritual world in a wrong way, especially through such physical training as may be called a changing of the breathing-processes, will describe certain things pertaining to this spiritual world, as they appear to him. He describes them in such a way that many people may think them extremely beautiful, while to the occultist who perceives them in the inward experience, they may be horrible and loathsome. Such things are quite possible in the experience of the spiritual world."

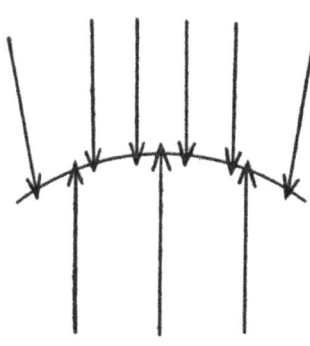

Diagram I

Divine Beings Speak Through Conscience

Anthroposophical Leading Thoughts, **Rudolf Steiner, XXVI,**
Memory and Conscience, **March, 1925 GA 26**

"In the present moment of cosmic evolution these Divine Spiritual Beings work in such a way as to impress the moral content of the Universe into the astral body and Ego of man during sleep. All the World-processes in sleeing man are really moral processes and cannot be spoken of as even remotely like the activities of Nature.

"In their after-effects, man carries these processes over from sleeping into waking. But the after-effects remain asleep. For man is awake in that part of his life only which inclines to the sphere of Thought. What actually takes place in his sphere of Will is wrapped in darkness even in the waking state, as the whole life of the soul is wrapped in darkness during sleep. But in this sleeping life of the Will, the Divine-Spiritual works on in the waking life of man. Morally, man is as good or as bad as he can be according to the nearness with which he approaches the Divine-Spiritual Beings when asleep. And he comes nearer to them, or remains farther away from them, according to the moral quality of his former lives on Earth.

"From the depths of the waking being of the soul's existence, that which was able to implant itself in the soul's existence, in community with the Divine-Spiritual world during sleep, sounds forth. *This is the voice of conscience.*

"We see how the very things which a materialistic view of the world is most inclined to explain merely from the natural side, are found to lie on the moral side of things when seen by spiritual knowledge.

"In Memory the Divine-Spiritual being works directly within the waking man. In Conscience the same Divine-Spiritual being works in the waking man indirectly—as an after-effect.

"The forming of memory takes place in the organization of nerves and senses. The forming of conscience takes place—albeit as a pure process of soul and spirit—in the metabolic and limb-system.

"Between the two there lies the rhythmic organization, whose activity is polarized in two directions. In the breathing rhythm it is in intimate relation to sense-perception and to thought. In the breathing of the lung the process is at its coarsest. Thence it grows finer and finer, till, as a highly refined breathing process, it becomes sense-perception and thought.

"Sense-perception is still very near to breathing; it is only a breathing through the sense-organs, not through the lungs. Thought, ideation, is farther removed from the lung-breathing, and is upheld by the thinking system of man. And that which reveals itself in the play of fancy is already very close to the rhythm of blood-circulation. It is a very inward breathing that comes into connection with the system of metabolism and the limbs. Psychologically, too, the activity of fancy reaches down into the sphere of Will, just as the circulatory system reaches down into the system of metabolism and the limbs.

"In the activity of fancy, the thinking system comes close up to the system of the Will. The human being dives down into that sphere of his waking life which is asleep—the Sphere of Will. Hence, in human beings who are especially developed in this direction, the contents of the soul appear like dreams in the waking state. Such a human organization was present in Goethe. Goethe once said that Schiller must interpret to him his own poetic dreams.

"In Schiller himself, a different human system was at work. He lived on the strength of what he brought with him from former lives on Earth. He had a strong life of the Will, and had to seek actively for the corresponding wealth of fancy.

"The Ahrimanic Power, in its world-intentions, counts upon those human beings who are especially developed in the sphere of fancy—whose perception of sense-reality quite naturally transforms into the pictures of fancy. With the help of such human beings, the Ahrimanic Power hopes to be able to cut off the evolution of mankind from the past and carry it on in the direction of its own, Ahrimanic intentions.

"The Luciferic Power reckons on those human beings who, while naturally more developed in the Sphere of Will, are inspired by an inner love for the ideal world-conception to transform their vision of sense-reality actively into pictures of creative fancy. Through such human beings the Luciferic Power would like to keep human evolution entirely within the impulses of the past. It would thus be able to preserve mankind from diving down into the sphere where the Ahrimanic Power must be overcome.

"In this our earthly existence, we stand between two opposite poles. Above us spread the stars. From thence there radiate the forces which are connected with all things calculable and regular in Earth-existence. The regular alternation of day and night, the seasons, the longer cosmic periods, are the earthly reflection of the real process in the stars.

"In this our earthly existence, we stand between two opposite poles. Above us spread the stars. From thence there radiate the forces which are connected with all things calculable and regular in Earth-existence. The regular alternation of day and night, the seasons, the longer cosmic periods, are the earthly reflection of the real process in the stars.

"The other pole radiates out from the interior of the Earth. Irregular activities are at work in it. Wind and weather, thunder and lightning, earthquakes and volcanic eruptions, are a reflection of this process of the Inner-Earth.

"Man himself is an image of this existence of the Stars and Earth. In his Thinking System lives the order of the Stars; in the Willing System of his limbs the chaos of the Earth. In the Rhythmic System he experiences in consciousness his own earthly being, in free balance and interplay between the two.

Further Leading Thoughts issued from the Goetheanum for the Anthroposophical Society (with regard to the foregoing study on Memory and Conscience)

"174. Man is organized in spirit and in body from two different sides. First, from the physical-etheric Cosmos. Whatever radiates from the Divine-Spiritual Being into this organization in man's nature, lives in it as the force of sense-perception, of the faculty of memory and of the play of fancy.

"175. Secondly, man is organized out of his own past lives on Earth. This organization is purely of the soul and spirit, and lives in him through the astral body and the Ego. Whatever enters of the life of Divine-Spiritual Beings into this human nature—its influence lights up in a man as the voice of conscience and all that is akin to this.

"176. In his rhythmic organization man has the constant union of the Divine-Spiritual impulses from the two sides. In life and experience of rhythm the force of memory is carried into the Willing-Life, and the might of conscience into the Life-in-Ideas."

Wonder, Compassion, and Conscience

Earthly and Cosmic Man, **Rudolf Steiner, Lecture VI,**
The Mission of the Earth. Wonder, Compassion and Conscience.
The Christ Impulse, **Berlin, May 14, 1912, GA 133**

"Conscience is a third power whereby the human being transcends what he is in the physical body. In ordinary life he will desire this or that; according to his impulses or needs he will pursue what is pleasing and thrust aside what is displeasing to him. But in many such actions he will be his own critic, in that his conscience, the voice of his conscience sounds a note of correction. Final satisfaction or dissatisfaction with what he has done also depends upon how the voice of conscience has spoken. This, in itself, is a proof that 'conscience' is a power whereby the human being is led out beyond the sphere of his impulses, his likes and dislikes.

"Wonder (amazement), Compassion (fellow-feeling), and Conscience are the three powers by means of which the human being, even while in the physical body, transcends his own limitations, for through these powers, influences which cannot find entrance into the human soul by way of the intellect and the senses, ray into physical life…

"…And Conscience could not be experienced as a spiritual force sending its voice into man's world of natural urges, passions, and desires, if the material body did not hanker after things against which warning must be given by another power. And so, the human being must be incarnated in a physical body in order that he may be able to experience wonder, compassion, and conscience…

"…The purpose of Earth-evolution is that there may be implanted into the evolutionary process, as a whole, powers which could otherwise never have come into existence: Wonder, Compassion and Conscience.

"I have told you how the birth of conscience can clearly be traced to a certain period of Greek culture. In the works of Aeschylus, what we call 'conscience' played no part; there were only remembrances of the avenging Furies, and not until we come to the works of Euripides is there any clear expression of 'conscience' as we know it now. The concept of conscience arose only very gradually during the Graeco-Latin Period [747 B.C.-1,414 A.D.]…

"…Man could not remain in those worlds because only by coming down into the physical world of Earth-evolution could he receive into himself the forces of wonder, love or compassion, and conscience or moral obligation…

"…*And if we lack this sharpness of conscience, if we do not feel, the most intense responsibility to the holiest truth, we shall make no progress on any other path…*

"We know that what we actually see in the kingdoms of Nature around us is not reality, but 'Maya,' the 'Great Illusion.' In the kingdom of the animals, we see the individual forms coming into being and passing away; the Group-Soul alone endures. In the plant kingdom, the individual plants appear and disappear, but behind them there is the Earth-Spirit which does not pass away. So it is, too, in the kingdom of the minerals. The Spiritual endures, but the Physical, whether in the animal, plant, or mineral kingdom, is transient, impermanent. Even the outer senses discern that the planet Earth is involved in a process of pulverization and will at some future time disintegrate into dust. We have spoken of how the Earth-body will be cast off by the Spirit of the Earth, as the human body is cast off by the individual human Spirit. What will remain as the highest substance of the Earth when its goal has been reached? The Christ Impulse was present on the Earth, so to say as 'spiritual Substance.' That Impulse endures and will be received into men during the course of Earth-evolution. But how does It live on? When the Christ Impulse was upon the Earth for three years, It had no physical body, no ether-body, no astral body of Its own, but was enveloped in the three sheaths of Jesus of Nazareth. When the goal has been reached, the Earth, like man, will be a fully developed being, a meet and fitting vehicle for the Christ Impulse. But from whence are the three sheaths of the Christ Impulse derived? From forces that can be unfolded only on the Earth. Beginning with the Mystery of Golgotha, whatever has unfolded on the Earth since the Fourth Post-Atlantean Period [747 B.C.-1,414 A.D.] as the power of wonder, whatever comes to life in us as wonder—passes, finally, to the Christ, weaving the Astral Body of the Christ Impulse. Love or Compassion in the souls of men weaves the Ether-Body of the Christ Impulse; and the power of conscience which from the time of the Mystery of Golgotha until the goal of the Earth is attained, lives in and inspires the souls of men, weaves the Physical Body—or what corresponds with the physical body—for the Christ Impulse. Love or Compassion in the souls of men weaves the etheric body of the Christ-impulse; and the power of Conscience which from the time of the Mystery of Golgotha until the goal of the Earth is attained, lives in and inspires the souls of men, weaves the physical body—or what corresponds with the physical body—for the Christ-impulse.

"The true meaning of words from the Gospel can only now be discerned:—

'Inasmuch as ye have done *it* unto one of the least of these My brethren, ye have done *it* unto Me.' (*Matthew* 25:40)

"The forces streaming from man to man are the units integrating the Ether-Body of Christ: love, or compassion, weaves the Ether-Body of Christ. Thus, when the goal of Earth-evolution is attained, He will be enveloped in the threefold vesture woven from the powers that have lived in men—and which, when the limitations of the 'I,' have been transcended, become the sheaths of Christ.

"And now think of how men live in communion with Christ. From the time of the Mystery of Golgotha to the attainment of the goal of Earth-evolution, man grows more perfect in that he develops to the stature that is within his reach as a being endowed with the power of the "I." But men are united with the Christ Who has come among them, in that they transcend their own "I"—and through wonder, build the Astral Body of Christ. Christ does not build His own astral body—but in the wonder that arises in their souls, men share in the forming of the astral body of Christ. His etheric body will be fashioned through the compassion and love flowing from man to man; and His physical body through the power of conscience unfolding in human beings. Whatever wrongs are committed in these three realms deprive the Christ of the possibility of full development on the Earth—that is to say, Earth-evolution is left imperfect. Those who go about the Earth with indifference and unconcern, who have no urge to understand what the Earth can reveal to them, deprive the astral body of Christ of the possibility of full development; those who live without unfolding compassion and love, hinder the etheric body of Christ from full development; and those who lack conscience hinder the development of what corresponds with the physical body of Christ ... *but this means that the Earth cannot reach the goal of its evolution.*

"The principle of Egotism has to be overcome in Earth-evolution. The Christ Impulse penetrates more and more deeply into the life and culture of humanity and the conviction that this Impulse has lived its way into mankind, free from every trace of denominationalism—as, for example, in the paintings of Raphael, this conviction will bear its fruit. How Christ may truly be portrayed is a problem still to be solved. Men on Earth will have to be greatly enriched in their life of feeling if, after the many attempts made through the centuries, another is to succeed to some slight extent in expressing what the Christ is as the super-sensible Impulse living on through Earth-evolution. The attempts made hitherto do not even suggest what form such a portrayal of Christ should take. For it would have to express how the enveloping sheaths woven of the forces of wonder, compassion and Conscience are gradually made manifest. The countenance of Christ must be so vital and living that it is an expression of the victory won over the sensory, desire-nature in men of Earth—victory achieved through the very forces which have spiritualized the countenance. There must be sublime power in this countenance. The painter or sculptor will have to express in the unusual form of the chin and mouth, the power of conscience unfolded to its highest degree. The mouth must convey the impression that it is not there for the purpose of taking food but to give utterance to whatever moral strength and power of conscience has been cultivated by men through the ages; the very structure of the bones around the teeth in the lower jaw will seem to form themselves into a mouth. All this will have to be expressed in the countenance. The form of the lower part of the face will have to express a power whose out-streaming rays seem to shatter the rest of the way that certain other forces are vanquished. With a mouth like this, it will be impossible to give the Christ Figure a bodily form similar to that possessed by the physical human being today. On the other hand, all the power of compassion will flow out of His eyes—the power that eyes alone can contain—not in order to receive impressions but to bear the very soul into the joys and sufferings of others. His brow will give no suggestion of thought based upon earthly sense-impressions. It will be a brow conspicuously prominent above the eyes, arching over that part of the brain; it will not be a 'thinker's' brow which merely works upon material already there. Wonder will be made manifest in this projecting brow which curves gently backwards over the head, expressing wonder and marvel at the mysteries of the world. It will be a head such as is nowhere to be found in physical humanity.

"Every true representation of the Christ must be a portrayal of the Ideal embodied in Him. When man reaches out towards this highest Ideal and strives through Spiritual Science to represent it in Art, this feeling will arise in greater and greater strength:—If you would portray the Christ, you must not look at what is actually there in the world, but you must let your whole being be quickened and pervaded by all that flows from contemplation of the spiritual evolution of the world, inspired by the three great impulses of Wonder, Compassion and Conscience."

Conscience and Spiritual Development

Spiritual Beings in the Heavenly Bodies and in the Kingdoms of Nature, **Rudolf Steiner, Lecture II, Helsinki, April 4, 1912, GA 136**

"We know that the ordinary unconscious condition, the ordinary sleep-condition of man, is caused by the fact that he leaves his physical and etheric bodies lying in the bed and draws out the astral body and the rest of what belongs to it; but the normal man is then unconscious. When, however, he devotes himself more and more to those exercises which consist of meditation, concentration, and so on, and further strengthens the slumbering hidden forces of his soul, then he can establish a conscious condition of sleep. Thus, when he has drawn his astral body out of his physical and etheric bodies, he is no longer unconscious, but has then around him—not the physical world, not even the world just described, the world of the nature-spirits—but another and still more spiritual world. When the time comes that a man, after he has freed himself from his physical and etheric bodies, feels his consciousness flash up, he then perceives quite a new order of spiritual beings. The next thing which strikes the occult vision thus far trained, is that the new spirits man now perceives have as it were command over the nature-spirits. Let us be quite clear as to how far this is the case. I have told you that those beings which we call the nature-spirits of the water, work especially in the budding and sprouting plant-world. Those which we may call the nature-spirits of the air, play their part in late summer and autumn, when the plants prepare to fade and die. Then these meteor-like air-spirits sink down over the plant-world and saturate themselves, as it were, with the plants, helping them to fade away in their spring and summer forms. The disposition that at one time the spirits of the water, and at another the spirits of the air should work in this or that region of the Earth, changes according to the different regions of the Earth—in the Northern part of the Earth it is naturally quite different from what it is in the South. The office of directing, as it were, the suitable nature-spirits to their activities at the right time, is carried out by those spiritual beings which we learn to know when the occult vision is so far trained that, when we have freed ourselves from our physical and etheric bodies, we can still be conscious of our environment. There are spiritual beings, for instance, working in connection with our Earth, with our Earth-planet, who allot the work of the nature-spirits to the seasons of the year, and thus bring about the alternations of the seasons for the different regions of the Earth, by distributing the work of the nature-spirits. These spiritual beings represent what we may call the astral body of the Earth, into which man plunges with his own astral body at night when he falls asleep. This astral body, consisting of higher spirits which hover round the Earth-planet and permeate it as a spiritual atmosphere, is united with the Earth; and into this spirit-atmosphere man's astral body plunges during the night-time.

"Now to occult observation there is a great difference of nature-spirits, the spirits of Earth, Water, [Air, Fire] etc., and those beings which on the other hand, direct these nature-spirits. The nature-spirits are occupied in causing the beings of nature to ripen and fade, in bringing life into the whole planetary Earth-sphere. It is different with those spiritual beings which in their totality can be called the astral body of the Earth.

"These beings are such that when man can become acquainted with them by means of his occult vision, he perceives them as beings connected with his own soul—with his own astral body. They exert such an influence upon the astral body of man—(as also upon the astral bodies of animals), that we cannot speak of a mere life-giving activity; their activity resembles the action of feeling and thought upon our own souls. The nature-spirits of water and air can be observed; we may say they are in the environment; but we cannot say of these spiritual beings of which we are now speaking, that they are in our environment; we are in fact always actually united with them, as if poured into them, when we perceive them. We are merged into them, and they speak to us in spirit. It is as though we perceived thoughts and feelings from the environment; impulses of will, sympathy and antipathy come to expression in what these beings cause to flow into us as thoughts, feelings, and impulses of will. Thus, in this category of spirits we see beings already resembling the human soul. If we turn back again to what has been stated, we may say that all sorts of regulations in time, of divisions in the relations of time and space, are also connected with these beings. An old expression has therefore been preserved in occultism for these beings, which in their totality we recognize as the astral body of the Earth, and this in English would be, 'Spirits of the Rotation of Time.' Thus, not only the seasons of the year, and the growing and the fading of the plants; but also the regular alternation which, in relation to the earth-planet, expresses itself in day and night, is brought about by these spirits, which are to be classed as belonging to the astral body of the Earth. In other words, everything connected with rhythmic return, with rhythmic alternation, with the repetitions of happenings in time, is organized by spiritual beings which collectively belong to the astral body of the Earth and to which the name 'Spirits of the Rotation of Time,' of our planet, is applicable. What the astronomer ascertains through calculation about the rotation of the Earth on its axis, is perceptible to occult vision, because the occultist knows that these spirits are distributed over the whole Earth, and are actually the bearers of the forces which rotate the Earth on its axis. It is extremely important that one should be aware that in the astral body of the Earth is to be found everything connected with the ordinary alternations between the blossoming and withering of plants and also all that is connected with the alternations between day and night,—between the various seasons of the year, and the various times of the day, etc. Everything that happens in this way calls up in the observer who has progressed so far that he can, with his astral body, go out of his physical and etheric bodies and still remain conscious—an impression of the spiritual beings belonging to the Spirits of the Rotation of Time.

"We have now, as it were drawn aside the second veil, the veil woven of the nature-spirits. We might say that when we draw aside the first veil, woven of material physical impressions, we come to the etheric body of the Earth, to the nature-spirits, and we can then draw aside a second veil and come to the Spirits of the Rotation of Time, who regulate everything subject to rhythmic rotation. Now we know that in our own astral body is embedded what may be called the higher principles of man's nature, which at first we understand as the ego embedded in our astral body. We have already said that our astral body is plunged into the region of the Spirits of the Rotation of Time; that it is immersed in the surging sea, as it were, of these spirits; but as regards the normal consciousness our ego is still more asleep than the astral body. A man who is developing occultly and progressing esoterically becomes aware of this, because in the spiritual world into which he plunges and which consists of the Spirits of the Rotation of Time, he first learns to penetrate into the perceptions of the astral body. In a certain respect this perception is really a dangerous reef in esoteric development, for the astral body of man is, in itself, unity; but everything in the realm of the Spirits of the Rotation of Time is, fundamentally, multiplicity, plurality. And since, in the way described, man is united with and immersed in this plurality, if he is still asleep in his ego and awake in his astral body, he feels as if he were dismembered in the world of the Spirits of the Rotation of Time. That must be avoided in a properly ordered esoteric development. Hence those who are able to give instruction for such development, see that the necessary precautions are taken that the man should not if possible allow his ego to sleep when his astral body is already awake; for he would then lose inner cohesion and would, like Dionysos, be split up into the whole astral world of the Earth, consisting of the Spirits of the Rotation of Time. In a regular esoteric development precautions are taken that this should not occur. These consist in care being taken that the student, who through meditation, concentration, or other esoteric exercises is to be stimulated to clairvoyance, should retain two things in the whole sphere of clairvoyant, occult observation. In every esoteric development it is especially important that everything should be so adjusted that two things that man has in ordinary life should not be lost— which he might however very easily lose in esoteric development if not rightly guided. If rightly guided he will not lose them. First, he should not lose the recollection of any of the events of his present incarnation, as ordinarily retained in his memory. *The connection with memory must not be destroyed.* This connection with memory means very much more in the sphere of occultism than it does in the sphere of ordinary life. In ordinary life we only understand by memory, the power of looking back and not losing consciousness of the important events of one's life. In occultism a right memory means that a man only values with his perceptions and feelings what he has already accomplished in the past, so that he applies no other value to himself or to his deeds than the past deeds themselves entitle. Let us understand this quite correctly, *for this is extremely important.* If a man in the course of his occult development were suddenly driven to say to himself 'I am the reincarnation of this or the other spirit,'—without there being any justification for it through any action of his—then his memory in an occult sense would be interrupted. An important principle in occult development is that of attributing no other merit to oneself, than what comes from one's actions in the physical world in the present incarnation. That is extremely important. Any other merit must only come on the basis of a higher development, which can only be attained if one first of all stands firmly on the ground that one esteems oneself for nothing but what one has accomplished in this incarnation. This is quite natural if we look at the matter objectively; for what we have accomplished in the present incarnation is also the result of earlier incarnations; it is that which Karma has, so far, made out of us. What Karma is still making of us we must first bring about; we must not add that to our value. In short, if we would set a right value on ourselves, we can only do so, at the beginning of esoteric development, if we ascribe merit only to what is inscribed in our memory as our past. That is the one element which we must preserve, if our ego is not to sleep while our astral body is awake.

"The second thing which we as men of the present day must not lose is the degree of conscience we possess in the external world. Here again is something which it is extremely important to observe. You must have often experienced that someone you know has gone through an occult development, and if it is not guided and conducted in the right way, you find that, in relation to conscience, your friend takes things much more lightly than he did before his occult training. His education, his social connection guided him before, so that he did this thing or that, or dared not do it. After beginning an occult development, many people begin to tell lies who never did so before, and as regards questions of conscience, they take things more lightly. We ought not to lose an iota of the conscience we possess. As regards memory, we must only value ourselves according to what we have already become; not according to any reliance on the future, or

on what we are still going to do. As regards conscience, we must
retain the same degree as we acquired in the ordinary physical
world. If we retain these two elements in our consciousness:
a healthy memory which does not deceive us into believing
ourselves to be other than our actions prove us to be, and a
conscience which does not allow us morally to take things more
lightly than before,—indeed if possible we should take them more
seriously—if we retain these two qualities, our ego will never be
asleep when our astral body is awake.

"We shall carry the connection with our ego into the world
in which we awaken with our astral body, if we can, as it were,
remain awake in our sleep, preserve our consciousness and carry
it with us into the condition in which with our astral body we
are freed from the physical and etheric bodies. Then, if we awake
with our ego, not only do we feel our astral body to be connected
with all the spiritual beings we have today described as the Spirits
of the Rotation of Time belonging to our planet; but we feel in
a quite peculiar way, that we actually no longer have a direct
relation to the individual who is the bearer of the physical body
and etheric body in which we usually live. We feel, so to speak, as
if all the qualities of our physical and etheric bodies were taken
from us. Then too we feel everything taken from us which can
only live externally in any one country of our planet. For that
which lives on a particular territory of our planet is connected
with the Spirits of the Rotation of Time. Now, however, when we
waken with our ego, we feel ourselves not only poured out into
the whole world of the Spirits of the Rotation of Time—*but we
feel ourselves one with the whole undivided spirit of the planet itself;
we awaken in the undivided spirit of the planet itself.* It is extremely
important that we should feel ourselves as belonging to the whole
of our planet. For example, when our occult vision is sufficiently

awakened, and we are so far advanced that we can awaken our ego and astral body simultaneously, then our common life with the planet so expresses itself that, just as during the waking hours in the sense-world, we can follow the Sun as it passes over the heavens from morning till night, so it no longer now disappears when we fall asleep. When we sleep the Sun remains connected with us; it does not cease to shine but takes on a special character, so that whilst we are actually asleep during the night, we can still follow the Sun. Man is of such a nature that he is connected with the changing conditions of the planet only insofar as he lives in his astral body. When however, he becomes conscious of his ego, he has nothing to do with them. He then becomes conscious of all the conditions which his planet can go through. He then pours himself into the whole substance of the planetary spirit. When I say that a man becomes one with the planetary spirit, that he lives in union with this planetary spirit, you must not suppose that this implies an advanced degree of clairvoyance—*this is but a beginning.* For when a man awakens in the manner described, he really only experiences the planetary spirit as a whole; whereas it consists of many, many differentiations—of wonderful, separate, spiritual beings—as we shall hear in the following lectures. The different parts of the planetary spirit, the special multiplicities of this spirit, of these he is not yet aware. What he realizes first of all, is the knowledge:—

"I live in the planetary spirit as though in a sea, which spiritually laves the whole Earth planet and itself is the spirit of the whole Earth."

"One may go through immensely long development in order further and further to experience this unification with the planetary spirit; but to begin with, the experience is as has been described. Just as we say with regard to man: 'behind his astral body is his ego'—so do we say that behind all that we call the totality of the Spirits of the Rotation of Time is hidden the Spirit of the Planet itself, the Planetary Spirit. Whereas the Spirits of the Rotation of Time guide the nature-spirits of the elements in order to call forth the rhythmic change and repetitions in time—the alterations in space of the Earth-planet—the Spirit of the Earth has a different task. It has the task of bringing the Earth itself into mutual relation with the other heavenly bodies in the environment, to direct it and guide it, so that in the course of time it may come into the right relations to the other heavenly bodies. The Spirit of the Earth is, as it were, the great sense-apparatus of the Earth, through which the Earth-planet enters into the right relationship with the Cosmos. If I were to sum up the succession of those spiritual beings with whom we on our Earth are first of all concerned, and to whom we can find the way through a gradual occult development, I must say:—

'As the first external veil we have the sense-world, with all its multiplicity, with all we see spread out before our senses and which we can understand with our human mind. Then, behind this sense-world, we have the world of nature-spirits. Behind this world of nature-spirits we have the Spirits of the Rotation of Time, and behind these the Planetary Spirit.'

"If you wish to compare what is known to the normal consciousness concerning the structure of the Cosmos, with the structure of the Cosmos itself, you may make that clear in the following way. We will take it that the most external veil is this world of the senses, behind that is the world of the nature-spirits, and behind that the Spirits of the Rotation of Time and behind that the Planetary Spirit. Now we must say that the Planetary Spirit in its activity, in a certain respect penetrates through to the sense-world; so that in a certain way we can perceive its image in the sense-world; this also applies to the Spirits of the Rotation of Time, as well as to the nature-spirits. So that if we observe the sense-world itself with normal consciousness, we can see in the background as it were, the impression, the traces, of those worlds which lie behind; as if we drew aside the sense-world as the outermost skin, and behind this we had different degrees of active spiritual beings. The normal consciousness realizes the sense-world by means of its perceptions; the world of nature-spirits expresses itself from behind these perceptions as what we call the Forces of Nature. When science speaks of the forces of nature, we have there nothing actually real; to the occultist the forces of nature are not realities but *Maya* [Illusion], they are the imprints of the nature-spirits working behind the world of sense.

"Again the imprint of the Spirits of the Rotation of Time is what is usually known to ordinary consciousness as the *Laws of Nature*. Fundamentally all the laws of nature are in existence because the Spirits of the Rotation of Time work as the directing powers. To the occultist the laws of nature are not realities. When the ordinary natural scientist speaks of the 'laws of nature' and combines them externally, the occultist knows that these laws are revealed in their reality when, in his awakened astral body, he listens to what the Spirits of the Rotation of Time say, and hears how they order and direct the nature-spirits. That is expressed in Maya, in external semblance, as the laws of nature, and the normal consciousness, as a rule, does not go beyond this. It does not usually reach the imprint of the Planetary Spirit in the external world. The normal consciousness of present-day humanity speaks of the external world of perception, of the facts that can be perceived; speaks of the forces of nature, light, warmth, magnetism, electricity, and so on; of the forces of attraction and repulsion, of gravity, etc. *These are the beings of Maya, behind which, in reality, lies the world of the nature-spirits—the etheric body of the Earth.* External science also speaks of the Laws of Nature; that again is a Maya. Underlying these laws is what we have today described as the world of the Spirits of the Rotation of Time. Only when we penetrate still further do we come to the stamp or imprint of the Planetary Spirit itself in the external sense-world. Science today does not do this. Those who still do so are no longer quite believed. The poets, the artists do; they seek for a meaning behind things. Why does the plant-world blossom? Why do the different species of animals arise and disappear? Why does man inhabit the Earth? If we thus inquire into the phenomena of nature, and wish to analyze the meaning, and to combine the external facts as even a deeper philosophy still sometimes tries to do, we then approach the imprint of the Planetary Spirit itself in the external world. Today, however, nobody really believes any longer in this seeking after the meaning of existence. Through feeling, one still believes a little, but science no longer wishes to know of what could be discovered about the laws of nature by studying the passage of the phenomena.

"If we still seek a meaning as to the laws of nature in the things of the world perceptible to our senses, we should be able to interpret this meaning as the imprint of the Planetary Spirit in the sense-world. That would be the external Maya. In the first place the sense-world itself is an external Maya; for it is what the etheric body the Earth, the substance of the nature-spirits, drives out of itself. A second Maya is what appears to man of the nature-spirits in the forces of nature. A third Maya is that which appears as the laws of nature, coming from the Spirits of the Rotation of Time. A fourth Maya is something which, in spite of its Maya-nature, speaks to the soul of man because, in the perception of the purpose of nature, man at any rate feels himself united with the Spirit of the whole planet, with the Spirit which leads the planet through cosmic space, and gives meaning in fact to the whole planet. In this Maya lies the direct imprint of the Planetary Spirit itself.

"Thus we may say that we have today ascended to the undivided Spirit of the Planet. If again we wish to compare what we have now discovered for the planet, with man, we may say:—

'The sense-world corresponds to the physical body of man; the world of nature-spirits to the etheric body, the world of the Spirits of the Rotation of Time to the astral body, and the Planetary Spirit to the ego of man.'

"Just as the ego of man perceives the physical environment of Earth, so does the Planetary Spirit perceive everything in the periphery, and in cosmic space as a whole outside the planet; it adjusts the acts of the planet and also the feelings of the planet, of which we shall speak tomorrow, according to these perceptions of cosmic space. For what a planet does outside in space when it passes on its way in cosmic distances, and what it effects its own body, in the elements of which it consists, that again is the result of the observations of the Planetary with regard to the external world. Just as the individual human soul lives in the world of the Earth side-by-side with other men, and adjusts himself to them, so does the Planetary Spirit live in its planetary body, which is the ground on which we stand; but this Planetary Spirit lives in fellowship with other planetary Spirits, other Spirits of the heavenly bodies."

Conscience and Supersensible Knowledge

Supersensible Knowledge, **Rudolf Steiner, Lecture II,** *Anthroposophy and the Ethical-Religious Conduct of Life,* **Vienna, September 29, 1923, GA 84**

"At the moment when we ascend to a direct experience of the health-giving or the disease-bringing spiritual life, we come into contact with the very roots of the moral life of man, the roots of the whole moral existence. We come into contact with these roots of the moral existence only when we have reached the perception that the physical life of the senses and that which flows out of the human being is really, from the point-of-view of a higher life, a kind of dream, related to this higher life as the dream is related to the ordinary life. And that which we sense out of the indefinite depths of our human nature as *conscience,* which enables us to conduct our ordinary life, which determines whether we are helpful or harmful for our fellow men, that which shines upward from the very bottom of our human nature, stimulating us morally or immorally, becomes luminous; it is linked up in a reality just as the dream is linked up in a reality when we wake. We learn to recognize the conscience as something existing in man as a dimly mirrored gleam of the sense and significance of the spiritual world—of that super-sensible world to which we human beings belong, after all, in the depths of our nature. We now understand why it is necessary to take what the knowledge of the sense world can offer us as a point of departure and to proceed from this to a super-sensible knowledge, when we are considering the moral order of the world and desire to arrive at the reality of this moral world order…

"…When we learn to see now through super-sensible knowledge that what is rooted in us as our conscience is, in its essence, the mirroring within our inner-being of the real spiritual world which weaves and breathes throughout the world of the senses, we then learn to recognize the moral nature of man as that which forever unites us without our knowing this, even when we sense it only as a 'still small voice' within us, with that spiritual world which can be laid open to us through super-sensible knowledge. Especially will one who sees that the ancient spiritual traditions, super-sensible knowledge handed down from primeval times and continuing until now, have faded away and continue their existence today as pale religious creeds, will be able to see that man stands in need of a new stimulus in this very sphere."

Occultism and Initiation, **Rudolf Steiner, Helsinki, April 12, 1912, GA 136**

"Here I am confronted by a deep mystery of life. It is all the deeper because, if our feelings are of a moral nature, our consciousness does not vanish and we are not dazed when passing over into the consciousness of another soul. Indeed, how far I am able to maintain my own consciousness to a full extent, when experiencing the sorrows and joys of another soul, and not my own, is a standard of measure for my morality. It is even a moral defect for my consciousness to be dazed by the joys and sorrows of another soul; for then we have a situation similar to that of facing one's own creative activity taking place during sleep. Consciousness falls asleep, as it were, in the face of another person's sorrows and joys.

"The second experience which pertains to the moral sphere and leads us out of our ordinary consciousness, is *conscience*. If we observe conscience in an unprejudiced way, we can say the following: In life we may love or hate, do or leave certain things undone, under the influence of our instincts and passions, or of sympathy and antipathy, or perhaps we may follow the dictates of education or of social relations—these appear to us from outside. But there is something which never speaks to us from outside, and this we call conscience.

"Conscience comes to us from a world—we can feel and experience this—that speaks to us inwardly and can be heard by us inwardly. Conscience influences our ordinary perceptible world; for everything which we can perceive is open to correction when the super-sensible demands of conscience impel us to action. Conscience bears witness to the fact that, in the moral sphere, our soul can be told something which transcends our consciousness. And, again, we find that it is a moral defect if our soul falls into a kind of sleep when conscience begins to speak and does not listen to its voice but only listens to what speaks from the physical environment through sympathy or antipathy, so that these promptings govern the soul's impulses to action. If we can thus transcend our ordinary consciousness without feeling dazed, conscience is a phenomenon that speaks to the human soul in such a way that it need not take its impulses from any influence coming from the external world.

"In regard to beings outside our own self, in regard to experiences transcending our knowledge and our consciousness, we have in the moral sphere the possibility to penetrate into them through compassion and love. Through conscience we listen, as it were, to truths which do not come from the world of the senses.

"If it is possible in this way to penetrate into beings outside our own and to take into our soul's truths of the kind uttered by conscience, then there is a prospect of penetrating into a world which is not the one given to us during our waking consciousness from the moment of waking-up to the moment of falling asleep. It is possible, and this prospect opens out to us through methods we call the methods of initiation. In regard to thinking, feeling, and willing, these methods of initiation consist in other forms of soul-activity than those to which we are accustomed in our ordinary life for the acquisition of an external knowledge concerning the world…

"This is, however, connected with something else, though I can only give a brief description of these stages of initiation. Little by little, the whole process forces us to renounce something the ordinary clairvoyant does not like to renounce. The ordinary clairvoyant is so glad to live in this world of visions, he or she takes such indulgent pleasure in these experiences of a higher world, and they are so suggestive that he or she easily takes them for reality. This can lead to a nervous breakdown. But if through, the above effort of will we remain fully conscious that 'all this is produced by our own self,' if our consciousness never falls asleep, something arises that is a source of regret to many—namely, the power lying at the foundation of that effort of our will falls destructively upon this whole imaginative world, disposes of it and many things which the ordinary clairvoyant holds very precious are thus blotted out. In other words, the following happens. Although in *Imaginative Consciousness* we have an element really setting forth the forces constituting a creative process (for we do not let it go beyond the limit where the destructive process would set in)—and we really transcend our ordinary consciousness, as we normally do when we feel compassion or love—the decision, or the effort of will by which we bring destruction (but also structure and order) into our visionary world leads to the development of an activity that does not exist anywhere in the external physical world, and that very soon reveals itself as the creative activity within our own being, lying beyond the reach of our ordinary consciousness. It is the activity which may be seen in our soul-spiritual being when it works upon our organism by drawing regenerating forces out of its spiritual environment; it is the soul-spiritual core which lives in the Spiritual Cosmos.

"In the next stage, which is technically designated as *Inspiration*, we learn to recognize the soul-spiritual core of our being, and how it lives within the creative forces of the Cosmos. Whereas *Imagination*, the first stage of initiation, only led us into our inner being by conjuring up a merely visionary world, the process of *Inspiration* leads us to a higher stage. A flash of light breaks in upon our whole visionary world, something that really seems to come out of the spiritual Cosmos, as does conscience, and we observe that it speaks to us in the same way in which conscience speaks to us in our ordinary consciousness. Conscience may be compared to the way in which Inspiration speaks to the imaginative consciousness; but then Imagination passes over to the stage of Inspiration, and we enter a real, super-sensible world...

"The methods gained through initiation, whose prototypes were compassion and conscience, i.e., experiences of our ordinary consciousness, thus give us an immediate knowledge of processes of the super-sensible world connected with the human being. Initiation therefore becomes the path leading us up into the super-sensible worlds."

Rudolf Steiner makes it very clear that conscience is the bridge between the physical and spiritual worlds through human willpower which is the most mysterious part of the threefold soul capacities of thinking, feeling, and willing. Conscience descended from the Cherubim, like bolts of lightning in the night sky, into the dreamless sleep of human willpower to awaken it to the spiritual dialogue between the Cherubim and human beings. Steiner refers to the Cherubim as 'The Divine Spiritual' again and again. Of course, we know that the Archai, in particular, also work in the hidden realms of human willpower. But to add to the efforts of the Archai, the efforts of the Cherubim speaking with the 'Voice of God,' makes *conscience* a tremendously elevated spiritual activity, as if a god had come down to speak to a human.

One might wonder if there will be further developments of conscience in the future that go beyond a 'one way conversation,' wherein conscience tells the ego what is wrong. Perhaps the Divine Spiritual 'Voice of God' will evolve into a continuous dialogue with spiritual beings about the forewarnings of karmic consequences from actions about to be taken; and also, the karmic outcomes of those actions.

Dr. Steiner tells us that Sophia and Christ will someday walk next to us and engage in moral conversations about spiritual matters that are personal to the individual. In the 6th Post-Atlantean Period, Sophia will be a personal friend who is concerned with every step taken on the path of spiritual development. She will continue to be the spiritual midwife of the soul. In the 7th Post-Atlantean Period, Christ will walk beside the human being helping, guiding, and revealing the karmic outcomes of human deeds before they are even taken. Christ will broaden His duties as the Lord of Karma and the Guardian of the Threshold and become the spiritual companion, along with Sophia, who helps tame the astral body and purify the ego.

It is incumbent upon each human soul to incline their ear and their heart towards the 'still, small voice of god' that speaks to them like a

Cherubim with flaming words. Ignorance cannot stand in the presence of the fiery Cherubim, the Spirits of Harmony. Their duty is to bring balance into the Cosmos, and this includes the karma of humanity. The promptings of the Cherubim, through Christ, balance the temptations of Lucifer, Ahriman, and the Asuras and point toward the proper 'way' in each ethical situation that the human being is faced with. Christ Jesus said, *"I am the way and the truth and the life. No one comes to the Father except through me."*; which is exactly what is needed in every action a human being takes. Christ shows the 'Way' through example; but in the future, He will show the Christian 'Way' to go in every situation. Sophia brings the Wisdom (Sophia) of Christ as the 'Truth' of the Cosmic Christ's deeds for the spiritual evolution of humanity. If we listen to Sophia and Christ now, we can hear the voice of conscience. In the future, we will walk and talk with them as loving counselors who guide us towards the Spiritual Divine.

From Cosmic Intelligence to Spiritual Hierarchies to the 'voice of god' in conscience, humans continue to grow towards their 'Celestial Parents' in heaven. Moral Imagination, Moral Inspiration, Moral Intuition, tempered with Wonder, Compassion, and Conscience help us ascend the ranks of Spiritual Hierarchies. *It is a long and painful road of experience that ultimately leads to Wisdom.* Gathering that Wisdom, through Freedom and Love will accelerate human Ascension and bring us back to our original home in heaven. The greatest comfort on that path is that the Holy Trinity, the Nine Spiritual Hierarchies, and the entire ascended realm of humans are always ready and able to guide us with a helping hand to ascend Jacob's Ladder to the spiritual world. Our job is simple, and yet most difficult; to quit selfishness and empty oneself to the 'selfless Cosmic Ego' inside of us; and then, surrender to the outpouring of the spirit.

What is the price of Experience? Do men buy it for a song?

Or wisdom for a dance in the street? No, it is bought with the price

Of all that a man hath, his house, his wife, his children

Wisdom is sold in the desolate market where none come to buy

And in the wither'd field where the farmer ploughs for bread in vain…

William Blake, *The Four Zoas*

The Soul's Probation, Scene 10, by Rudolf Steiner

A Voice (representing Spirit-Conscience):

Feel now what thou hast seen,

Live o'er what thou hast done

Refreshed from Being's source;

Thine own life hast thou dreamed.

Work out this deed in thee

With noble spirit-light

Regard thy daily task

With force of spirit-sight.

BIBLIOGRAPHY

- Andreæ, Johann Valentin. *Reipublicæ Christianopolitanæ descriptio.* Argentorati: Sumptibus hæredum Lazari Zetzneri, Strasbourg, 1619.

- Andreæ, Johann Valentin. *Johann Valentin Andreae's Christianopolis; an ideal state of the seventeenth century.* translated from the Latin of Johann Valentin Andreae with an historical introduction. by Felix Emil Held. The Graduate School of the University of Illinois, Urbana- Champaign, 1916.

- Arnold, Edwin Sir. *The Light of Asia, or The Great Renunciation (Mahâbhinishkramana): Being the Life and Teaching Gautama, Prince of India and Founder of Buddhism (As Told in Verse by an Indian Buddhist).* Kegan Paul, Trench, Trübner & Co., London, 1879.

- Avari, Burjor. *India: The Ancient Past: A History of the Indian Sub-Continent.* Routledge, New Edition, 2007.

- Barnwell, John. *The Arcana of the Grail Angel: The Spiritual Science of the Holy Blood and of the Holy Grail.* Verticordia Press, Bloomfield Hills, 1999.

- Barnwell, John. *The Arcana of Light on the Path: The Star Wisdom of the Tarot and Light on the Path.* Verticordia Press, Bloomfield Hills, 1999.

- Blavatsky, H. P. (Helena Petrovna). *Isis Unveiled: A Master-Key to the Mysteries of Ancient and Modern Science and Theology.* J. W. Bouton. New York, 1878.

- Blavatsky, H. P. (Helena Petrovna). *The Key to Theosophy: Being a Clear Exposition, in the Form of Question and Answer, of the Ethics, Science and Philosophy for the Study of Which the Theosophical Society Has Been Founded.* The Theosophical Publishing Company, Ltd. London, 1889.

- Blavatsky, H. P. (Helena Petrovna). *The Secret Doctrine: The Synthesis of Science, Religion and Philosophy.* The Theosophical Publishing Company, Ltd. London, 1888.

- Blavatsky, H. P. (Helena Petrovna). *The Voice of Silence: Being Extracts from the Book of the Golden Precepts.* Theosophical University Press, 1992.

- Bockemuhl, Jochen. *Toward a Phenomenology of the Etheric World: Investigations into the Life of Nature and Man.* Anthroposophic Press, Spring Valley, N. Y., 1977.

- Campanella, Tommaso. *The City of the Sun.* The ProjectGutenberg Ebook, David Widger, 2013.

- Colum, Padriac. *Orpheus: Myths of the World.* Floris Books. Colum, Padriac. *The Children's Homer.* MacMillan Co., 1946.

- Colum, Padriac. *The Tales of Ancient Egypt.* Henry Walck Incorporated, New York,1968.

- Crawford, John Martin. *The Kalevala: The Epic Poem of Finland.* John B. Alden, New York, 1888.

- Gabriel, Douglas. *The Eternal Curriculum for Wisdom Children: Intuitive Learning and the Etheric Body.* Our Spirit, Northville, 2017.

- Gabriel, Tyla. *The Gospel of Sophia: The Biographies of the Divine Feminine Trinity,* Volume, Our Spirit, Northville, 2014.

- Gabriel, Tyla. *The Gospel of Sophia: A Modern Path of Initiation,* Volume 2. Our Spirit, Northville, 2015.

- Gabriel, Tyla and Douglas. *The Gospel of Sophia: Sophia Christos Initiation,* Volume 3. Our Spirit, Northville, 2016.

- Gabriel, Douglas. *The Spirit of Childhood.* Trinosophia Press, Berkley, 1993.

- Gabriel, Douglas. *The Eternal Ethers: A Theory of Everything.* Our Spirit, Northville, 2018.

- Gabriel, Douglas. *Goddess Meditations.* Trinosophia Press, Berkley, 1994.

- Gebser, Jean. *The Ever Present Origin.* Ohio University Press, 1991.

- Green, Roger Lancelyn & Heather Copley. *Tales of Ancient Egypt.* Puffin Books, New York, 1980.

- Harrison, C. G. *The Transcendental Universe; Six Lectures on Occult Science, Theosophy, and the Catholic Faith.* George Redway, London 1893.

- Harrison, C. G. *The Transcendental Universe; Six Lectures on Occult Science, Theosophy, and the Catholic Faith.* Delivered Before the Berean Society, edited with an introduction by Christopher Bamford. Lindesfarne Press, Hudson, 1993.

- Hamilton, Edith. *Mythology.* Little Brown And Co., Boston, 1942.

- Harrer, Dorothy. *Chapters from Ancient History.* Waldorf Publications, Chatham, 2016.

- Hazeltine, Alice Isabel. *Hero Tales from Many Lands.* Abingdon Press, New York, 1961.

- Heidel, Alexander. *The Babylonian Genesis: The Story of Creation.* University of Chicago Press, Chicago, 1942.

- Hiebel, Frederick. *The Gospel of Hellas.* Anthroposophic Press, New York, 1949.

- Jocelyn, Beredene. *Citizens of the Cosmos: Life's Unfolding from Conception through Death to Rebirth.* Continuum, New York, 1981.

- König, Karl. *Earth and Man.* Bio-Dynamic Literature, Wyoming, Rhode Island, 1982.

- Kovacs, Charles. *Ancient Mythologies and History.* Resource Books, Scotland, 1991.

- Kovacs, Charles. *Greek Mythology and History.* Resource Books, Scotland, 1991.

- Landscheidt, Theodor. *Sun-Earth-Man a Mesh of Cosmic Oscillations: How Planets Regulate Solar Eruptions, Geomagnetic Storms, Conditions of Life, and Economic Cycles.* Urania Trust, London, 1989.

- Laszlo, Ervin and Kingsley, Dennis L. *Dawn of the Akashic Age: New Consciousness, Quantum Resonance, and the Future of the World.* Inner Traditions, Rochester Vermont, 2013

- Plato. *The Republic.* Dover Thrift Editions, 2000.

- Sister Nivedita (Margaret E. Noble) & Coomaraswamy, Ananda K.. *Myths of the Hindus and Buddhists.* Henry Holt, New York 1914.

- Steiner, Rudolf. *Ancient Myths: Their Meaning and Connection with Evolution.* Steiner Book Center, 1971.

- Steiner, Rudolf. *Christ and the Spiritual World: The Search for the Holy Grail.* Rudolf Steiner Press, London, 1963.

- Steiner, Rudolf. *Foundations of Esotericism*. Rudolf Steiner Press, London, 1983.

- Steiner, Rudolf. *Isis Mary Sophia: Her Mission and Ours*. Steiner Books, 2003.

- Steiner, Rudolf. *Man as a Being of Sense and Perception*. Steiner Book Center, Vancouver, 1981.

- Steiner, Rudolf. *Man as Symphony of the Creative Word*. Rudolf Steiner Publishing, London, 1978.

- Steiner, Rudolf. *Occult Science*. Anthroposophic Press, NY, 1972.

- Steiner, Rudolf. *Rosicrucian Esotericism*. Anthroposophic Press, NY, 1978.

- Steiner, Rudolf. *Rosicrucian Wisdom: An Introduction*. Rudolf Steiner Press, London, 2000. GA 425

- Steiner, Rudolf. *The Bridge between Universal Spirituality and the Physical Constitution of Man*. Anthroposophic Press, NY, 1958.

- Steiner, Rudolf. *The Evolution of Consciousness*. Rudolf Steiner Press, London, 1926.

- Steiner, Rudolf. *The Goddess from Natura to the Divine Sophia*. Sophia Books, 2001.

- Steiner, Rudolf. *The Holy Grail: from the Works of Rudolf Steiner*. Compiled by Steven Roboz. Steiner Book Center, North Vancouver, 1984.

- Steiner, Rudolf. *The Influence of Spiritual Beings Upon Man*. Anthroposophic Press, NY, 1971.

- Steiner, Rudolf. *The Reappearance of Christ in the Etheric*. Anthroposophic Press, NY, 1983.

- Steiner, Rudolf. *The Risen Christ and the Etheric Christ*. Rudolf Steiner Press, London, 1969.

- Steiner, Rudolf. *The Search for the New Isis the Divine Sophia*. Mercury Press, N.Y., 1983.

- Steiner, Rudolf. *The Spiritual Hierarchies and the Physical World*. Anthroposophic Press, N.Y., 1996.

- Steiner, Rudolf. *The Tree of Life and the Tree of Knowledge*. Mercury Press, NY, 2006.

- Steiner, Rudolf. *The True Nature of the Second Coming*. Rudolf Steiner Press, London, 1971.

- Steiner, Rudolf. *Theosophy*. Anthroposophic Press. New York, 1986.

- Steiner, Rudolf. *Wonders of the World, Ordeals of the Soul, Revelations of the Spirit*. Rudolf Steiner Press, London, 1963.

- Steiner, Rudolf. *World History in Light of Anthroposophy*. Rudolf Steiner Press, London, 1977.

- Tappan, Eva March. *The Story of the Greek People*. Houghton Mifflin Co., Boston 1908.

- van Bemmelen, D. J. *Zarathustra: The First Prophet of Christ*, 2 Vols. Uitgeverij Vrij Geestesleven, The Netherlands, 1968.

- Watson, Jane Werner (Vālmīki). *Rama of the Golden Age: An Epic of India*. Garrard Pub., Champaign.

APPENDIX

Diagram 1

Elohim †
Incarnations of the Earth

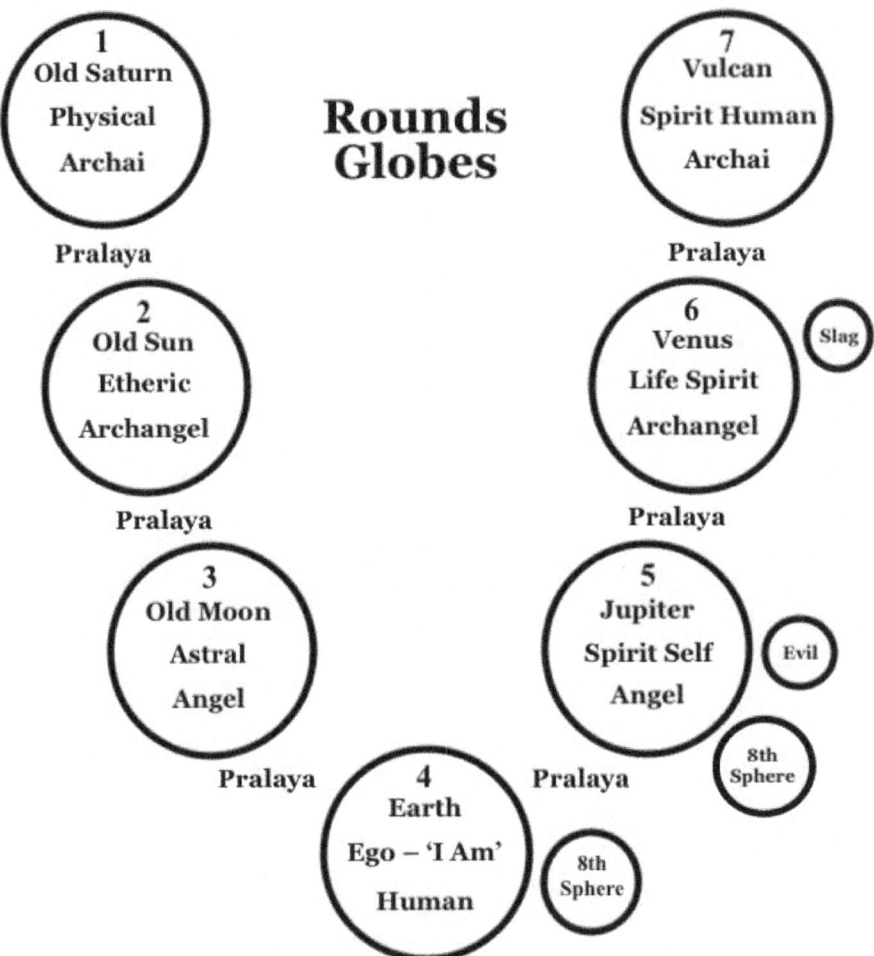

1
Old Saturn
Physical
Archai

**Rounds
Globes**

7
Vulcan
Spirit Human
Archai

Pralaya

Pralaya

2
Old Sun
Etheric
Archangel

6
Venus
Life Spirit
Archangel

Slag

Pralaya

Pralaya

3
Old Moon
Astral
Angel

5
Jupiter
Spirit Self
Angel

Evil

8th
Sphere

Pralaya

4
Earth
Ego – 'I Am'
Human

Pralaya

8th
Sphere

† Spirits of Form, Greek: Exousíai, ἐξουσίαι; Latin: Potestates; English:
Powers, Authorities; Hebrew: ʾĔlōhīm, אֱלֹהִים - plural of אֱלוֹהַּ, ʾĔlōah.
"God(s), Heavenly Power(s)."

Diagram 2

7 Conditions of Consciousness

"Neither can they die any more: for they are equal unto the angels;
and are the children of God, being the children of the resurrection." Luke (20:36)

Old Saturn
Deep Trance
Consciousness
Upper
Devachan

Old Sun
Dreamless Sleep
Consciousness
Lower
Devachan

Old Moon
Dream
Consciousness
Astral World

"Each condition of consciousness
can only run its course in seven
conditions of life; each condition
of life in seven conditions of
form. That is 7 x 7 x 7 conditions.
In fact, an entire evolution such
as that of the Earth passes
through 7 x 7 x 7 conditions of
form. Our Earth was once
Saturn; this went through seven
conditions of life and each
condition of life through seven
conditions of form, Therefore
you have forty-nine conditions of
form upon Saturn, forty-nine
upon the Sun, forty-nine upon
the Moon, etc.; 7 x 49 = 343
conditions of form. Man passes
through 343 conditions of form
in the course of his evolution." †

"Jesus answered them,
Is it not written
in your law, I said,
Ye are gods?"
John (10:34)

Atman
Vulcan
Moral
Intuition
Universal
Consciousness

Budhi
Venus
Moral
Inspiration
Hearing
Music of the
Spheres

Manas
Jupiter
Moral
Imagination
Psychic or Soul
Consciousness

Earth
Waking
Consciousness

† Rudolf Steiner,
The Apocalypse of St. John,
Lecture X June 28th, 1908 (CW 104)

Diagram 3

7 Main Epochs of Earth Evolution

Polarian Epoch
Hyperborean Epoch
Lemurian Epoch
Atlantean Epoch
5th Post-Atlantean Epoch ←
6th Post-Atlantean Epoch
7th Post-Atlantean Epoch

7 Post-Atlantean Periods

1st Post-Atlantean Period
Old Indian Period
2nd Post-Atlantean Period
Old Persian Period
3rd Post-Atlantean Period
Egypto-Chaldean Period
4th Post-Atlantean Period
Greco-Roman Period
5th Post-Atlantean Period
Anglo-Germanic Period
6th Post-Atlantean Period
Russian Period
7th Post-Atlantean Period
American Period

The 5th Post-Atlantean Epoch is divided into
7 Post-Atlantean Periods of 2,160 years

Diagram 4

7 Atlantean Periods (Sub-Races)

1st Rmoahals
2nd Tlavtlis
3rd Toltecs
4th Original Turanians
5th Ur Semites
6th Akkadians
7th Mongolians

7 Post-Atlantean Periods

1st Old Indian Period
1st Old Persian Period
3rd Egypto-Chaldean-Babylonian-Hebrew Period
4th Greco-Roman Period
5th Anglo-Germanic Period
6th Russian Period
7th American Period

"Today the idea of civilization has already superseded the idea of race"
Rudolf Steiner, Munich, May 8th, 1907

"To this [Atlantean] Root-Race belong the following Sub-Races:
Firstly the Rmoahals, secondly the Tlavtlis, thirdly the Toltecs,
fourthly the original Turanians, fifthly the original Semites,
sixthly the Akkadians, seventhly the Mongols. Still further back
we come to the continent of Lemuria, between Africa, Asia and
Australia." Rudolf Steiner, *The Foundations of Esotericism*
Lecture XXIV – Berlin, October 26th, 1905 (CW 93a)

Diagram 5

7 Post-Atlantean Periods

The Age of Cancer
Old Indian Period ♋ **The Etheric Body**
7,227 B.C.-5,067 B.C.

The Age of Gemini
Old Persian Period ♊ **The Astral Body**
5,067 B.C.-2,907 B.C.

The Age of Taurus
Egypto-Chaldean Period ♉ Sentient-Soul
2,907 B.C.-747 B.C.

The Age of Aries
Greco-Roman Period ♈ **Intellectual-Soul**
747 B.C.-1,414 A.D.

The Age of Pisces
Anglo-Germanic Period ♓ **Consciousness-Soul**
1,414 A.D.-3,574 A.D.

The Age of Aquarius
E. European Period ♒ **Spirit-Self**
3,574 A.D.-5,734 A.D.

The Age of Capricorn
American Period ♑ **Life-Spirit**
5,734 A.D.-7,894 A.D.

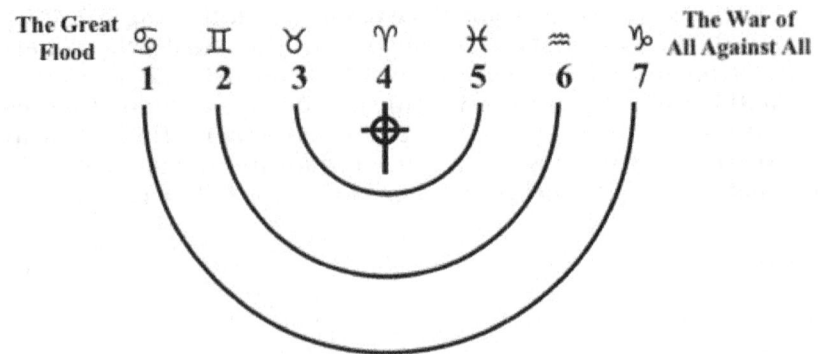

Diagram 6

The Cosmic Year – Post-Atlantean Epochs

5th Post Atlantean Period   7,227 B.C.-7,894 A.D.

1. ♋ 2. ♊ 3. ♉ 4. ♈ 5. ♓ 6. ♒ 7. ♑

6th Post Atlantean Period   7,894 A.D.-23,014 A.D.

1. ♐ 2. ♏ 3. ♎ 4. ♍ 5. ♌ 6. ♋ 7. ♊

7th Post Atlantean Period   23,014 A.D.-38,134 A.D.

1. ♉ 2. ♈ 3. ♓ 4. ♒ 5. ♑ 6. ♐ 7. ♏

"What is important for us is the fact that the position of the Sun at the spring equinox moves backward, passing through the whole Zodiac little by little. It traverses the whole Zodiac until it finally returns to the original position, taking approximately 25,920 years. These 25,920 years are termed the Platonic Year, the Cosmic Year. The exact figure varies according to the various methods of calculation. However, we are not concerned with exact figures but with the rhythm this precession entails. You can imagine that a cosmic rhythm must lie in this movement which repeats itself every 25,920 years. We can say that these 25,920 years are very important for the life of the Sun, for during this time the life of the Sun passes through one unit, a proper unit. The next 25,920 years are then a repetition. We have a rhythm in which one unit measures 25,920 years....

"On average, a human being takes eighteen breaths a minute. Not all breaths are equal, for those in youth differ from those in old age, but the average is eighteen breaths a minute. Eighteen times a minute we rhythmically renew our life. Multiply this by 60 and you have 1,080 times an hour. Now multiply by 24, and the number of breaths in twenty-four hours comes to 25,920!"

"A year has 365¼ days and if we divide 25,920 by 365.25 the answer is: nearly 71. Let us say 71 years, which is the average life-span of the human being. The human being is free, however, and often lives much longer; but you know that the patriarchal life-span is given as 70 years. The span of a human life is 25,920 days, 25,920 great breaths, and so we have another cycle wonderfully depicting the macrocosm in the microcosm. We could say that by living for one day, taking 25,920 breaths, we depict the Platonic Cosmic Year, and by living for 71 years, waking up and going to sleep 25,920 times — a breathing on a larger scale — we once again depict the Platonic Year." Rudolf Steiner, Dornach 28th, January 1916

Diagram 7

Nine-Fold Constitution of the Human Being

1. *Old Saturn*
Thrones – Warmth Ether
Spirits of Will
Primal Physical Body as Warmth

Sphere of Planet Saturn
Mineral Kingdom
4th Stage of the Archai

2. *Old Sun*
Kyriotetes – Light Ether
Spirits of Wisdom
Primal Etheric Body as Light

Sphere of Planet Jupiter
Plant Kingdom
4th Stage of the Archangels

3. *Old Moon*
Dynamis – Sound Ether
Spirits of Motion
Primal Astral Body as Movement

Sphere of Planet Mars
Animal Kingdom
4th Stage of the Angels

4. *Earth*
Exusiai – Life Ether
Donate "I Am" – Ego

Human – Earth & Moon
Sentient-Soul
Intellectual-Soul
Consciousness-Soul

5. *Future Jupiter*
Heavenly Sound Ether
Angel Stage

Jupiter + Two Moons
Holy Spirit – Wisdom
Spirit-Self (Manas)

6. *Future Venus*
Heavenly Light Ether
Archangel Stage

Venus + One Moon
Son – Love
Life-Spirit (Budhi)

7. *Future Vulcan*
Heavenly Warmth Ether
Archai Stage

Vulcan – No Moon
Father – Will
Spirit-Human (Atman)

ABOUT
DR. RUDOLF STEINER

Rudolf Steiner was born on the 27th of February 1861 in Kraljevec in the former Kingdom of Hungary and now Croatia. He studied at the College of Technology in Vienna and obtained his doctorate at the University of Rostock with a dissertation on Theory of Knowledge which concluded with the sentence: "The most important problem of human thinking is this: to understand the human being as a free personality, whose very foundation is himself." He exchanged views widely with the personalities involved in cultural life and arts of his time. However, unlike them, he experienced the spiritual realm as the other side of reality. He gained access through exploration of consciousness using the same method as the natural scientist uses for the visible world in his external research. This widened perspective enabled him to give significant impulses in many areas such as art, pedagogy, curative education, medicine, agriculture, architecture, economics, and social sciences, aiming towards the spiritual renewal of civilization.

He gave his movement the name of "Anthroposophy" (the wisdom of humanity) after separating from the German section of the Theosophical Society, where he had acted as a general secretary. He then founded the Anthroposophical Society in 1913 which formed its center with the construction of the First Goetheanum in Dornach, Switzerland. Rudolf Steiner died on 30th March 1925 in Dornach. His literary work is made up of numerous books, transcripts and approximately 6000 lectures which have for the most part been edited and published in the Complete Works Edition.

Steiner's basic books, which were previously a prerequisite to gaining access to his lectures, are: *Theosophy, The Philosophy of Freedom, How to Know Higher Worlds, Christianity as a Mystical Fact,* and *Occult Science.*

ABOUT THE AUTHOR, DR. DOUGLAS GABRIEL

Dr. Gabriel is a retired superintendent of schools and professor of education who has worked with schools and organizations throughout the world. He has authored many books ranging from teacher training manuals to philosophical/spiritual works on the nature of the divine feminine.

He was a Waldorf class teacher and administrator at the Detroit Waldorf School and taught courses at Mercy College, the University of Detroit, and Wayne State University for decades.

He then became the Headmaster of a Waldorf School in Hawaii and taught at the University of Hawaii, Hilo. He was a leader in the development of charter schools in Michigan and helped found the first Waldorf School in the Detroit Public School system and the first charter Waldorf School in Michigan.

Gabriel received his first degree in religious formation at the same time as an associate degree in computer science in 1972. This odd mixture of technology and religion continued throughout his life. He was drafted into and served in the Army Security Agency (NSA) where he was a cryptologist and systems analyst in signal intelligence, earning him a degree in signal broadcasting. After military service, he entered the Catholic Church again as a Trappist monk and later as a Jesuit priest where he earned PhD's in philosophy and comparative religion, and a Doctor of Divinity. He came to Detroit and earned a BA in anthroposophical studies and history and a MA in school administration. Gabriel left the priesthood and became a Waldorf class teacher and administrator in Detroit and later in Hilo, Hawaii.

Douglas has been a sought-after lecturer and consultant to schools and businesses throughout the world and in 1982 he founded the Waldorf Educational Foundation that provides funding for the publication of educational books. He has raised a great deal of money for Waldorf schools and institutions that continue to develop the teachings of Dr. Rudolf Steiner. Douglas is now retired but continues to write a variety of books including a novel and a science fiction thriller. He has four children, who keep him busy and active and a wife who is always striving towards the spirit through creating an "art of life." She is the author of the Gospel of Sophia trilogy.

The Gabriels' articles, blogs, and videos can currently be found at:

OurSpirit.com
Neoanthroposphy.com
GospelofSophia.com
EternalCurriculum.com

TRANSLATOR'S NOTE

The Rudolf Steiner quotes in this book can be found, in most cases, in their full-length and in context, through the Rudolf Steiner Archives by an Internet search of the references provided. We present the quoted selections of Steiner from a free rendered translation of the original while utilizing comparisons of numerous German to English translations that are available from a variety of publishers and other sources. In some cases, the quoted selections may be condensed and partially summarized using the same, or similar in meaning, words found in the original. Brackets are used to insert [from the author] clarifying details or anthroposophical nomenclature and spiritual scientific terms.

We chose to use GA (Gesamtausgabe — collected edition) numbers to reference Steiner's works instead of CW (Collected Works), which is often used in English editions. Some books in the series, *From the Works of Rudolf Steiner*, have consciously chosen to use a predominance of Steiner quotes to drive the presentation of the themes rather than personal remarks and commentary.

We feel that Steiner's descriptions should not be truncated but need to be translated into an easily read format for the English-speaking reader, especially for those new to Anthroposophy. We recommend that serious aspirants read the entire lecture, or chapter, from which the Steiner quotation was taken, because nothing can replace Steiner's original words or the mood in which they were delivered. The style of speaking and writing has changed dramatically over the last century and needs updating in style and presentation to translate into a useful tool for spiritual study in modern times. The series, *From the Works of Rudolf Steiner* intends to present numerous "study guides" for the beginning aspirant, and the initiate, in a format that helps support the spiritual scientific research of the reader.

Made in the USA
Las Vegas, NV
22 March 2025

19949031R00184

NUTRITION AND RECOVERY GUIDE FOR CROSSFIT

Charles de Blatz

Table of Contents

Intro to CrossFit Nutrition

CrossFit is a unique fitness regimen that combines various elements of strength training, cardiovascular conditioning, and gymnastics, all with the goal of increasing general physical preparedness (GPP). To meet the demands of CrossFit, athletes must not only train hard but also fuel their bodies in the right way. Nutrition is arguably one of the most important factors in determining an athlete's performance and recovery. Without proper fuel, even the most dedicated training efforts can fall short.

CrossFit involves high-intensity, full-body workouts that require endurance, strength, and power. From Olympic lifts like the clean and jerk to bodyweight exercises such as pull-ups and burpees, these diverse movements push your body in all directions and demand maximum exertion. It is this intensity that makes CrossFit so effective in building functional fitness, but it also places significant stress on the body. To perform well and recover properly, athletes need a nutrition plan that complements this intensity, provides energy for the workouts, and supports muscle recovery afterward.

Nutrition is not just about eating enough food to fuel the body, it's about eating the right foods in the right amounts, at the right times, to maximize performance and recovery. This is where CrossFit nutrition comes into play. It is the science and art of fueling your body for optimal performance while also allowing it to recover efficiently between workouts. Understanding the fundamentals of nutrition, and how to adjust them to meet the specific needs of CrossFit, is key to achieving the best results.

- **The Role of Nutrition in CrossFit**

CrossFit's intensity demands a significant amount of energy. During a typical CrossFit workout, athletes burn calories at a high rate, and without adequate nutrition, the body will run low on energy. In addition to fueling intense workouts, proper nutrition also supports recovery, reduces fatigue, builds muscle, and helps prevent injuries. Nutrition is the foundation of performance because it directly influences an athlete's strength, endurance, mental clarity, and overall recovery.

CrossFit also requires a diverse set of physical capabilities—strength, power, speed, agility, endurance, and coordination. Each of these traits is impacted by your diet. For example:

- **Strength** is supported by protein to repair and build muscle tissue after heavy lifting.

- **Endurance** relies on carbohydrates, which provide the body with fast-acting fuel during long workouts or cardio-intensive training sessions.
- **Speed and power** require proper fueling with a combination of fast-digesting carbohydrates and lean protein.
- **Recovery** is dependent on getting the right nutrients to repair muscles, replenish glycogen stores, and reduce inflammation after a workout.

Given the varied demands of CrossFit, athletes need a well-rounded nutrition strategy that includes all three macronutrients: carbohydrates, proteins, and fats, in the right proportions. Each macronutrient plays a unique role, and understanding how to balance them is essential.

- **Macronutrients and Their Role in CrossFit**
- **Carbohydrates: The Primary Fuel Source**

Carbohydrates are the body's primary energy source, especially during high-intensity activities like CrossFit. When you perform explosive movements, like sprinting, jumping, or lifting heavy weights, your body taps into glycogen—stored glucose in muscles and the liver—as its immediate fuel. Without enough glycogen, performance drops, and fatigue sets in quickly.

Carbs are crucial for CrossFit athletes because they provide:

- **Energy for anaerobic activities**: Many CrossFit exercises are done at maximal intensity for short periods (such as 30 seconds to a minute), relying on anaerobic energy systems. Glycogen stored in the muscles fuels these short bursts of activity.
- **Glycogen replenishment**: After a workout, replenishing glycogen stores is essential for recovery, especially if you plan to train again soon. Consuming carbs post-workout helps your muscles recover and maintain performance for the next session.

The amount of carbohydrates you need depends on the volume and intensity of your training. For moderate-intensity CrossFit, aim to consume between 3 to 6 grams of carbs per kilogram of body weight per day, with higher carb intake on heavy training days.

Sources of carbohydrates include:

- Whole grains (brown rice, oats, quinoa)
- Fruits (bananas, apples, berries)
- Vegetables (sweet potatoes, leafy greens)
- Legumes (lentils, chickpeas)
- Dairy (yogurt, milk)
- **Proteins: Muscle Repair and Growth**

Proteins are essential for the repair and growth of muscle tissue, making them a critical part of any CrossFit nutrition plan. Every time you lift weights, perform high-intensity interval training (HIIT), or do bodyweight exercises, you cause small tears in muscle fibers. Your body needs protein to rebuild these fibers, making them stronger and more resilient.

Protein helps with:

- **Muscle recovery**: After CrossFit workouts, your muscles undergo a repair process, which is where protein comes in. Consuming sufficient protein post-workout helps stimulate muscle protein synthesis (MPS), which leads to muscle growth and recovery.
- **Preventing muscle breakdown**: In CrossFit, your muscles are under constant stress. Eating enough protein ensures that your body has the tools to repair and maintain muscle mass, reducing the risk of muscle loss or injury.

To maximize muscle recovery, it's recommended to consume about 1.2 to 2 grams of protein per kilogram of body weight per day. High-quality protein sources include:

- Lean meats (chicken, turkey, lean beef)
- Fish and seafood (salmon, tuna, shrimp)
- Eggs and egg whites
- Dairy products (cottage cheese, Greek yogurt, milk)
- Plant-based proteins (lentils, beans, quinoa, tofu)
- **Fats: Supporting Long-Term Energy and Hormonal Health**

Fats are often misunderstood but play an essential role in CrossFit nutrition. While they are not the body's primary source of energy during intense workouts, they serve important functions like:

- **Providing sustained energy**: Fats are a slower-burning energy source than carbohydrates and provide long-lasting fuel for moderate and low-intensity activity. While CrossFit workouts are typically high-intensity, incorporating healthy fats into your diet helps to ensure that energy levels remain stable throughout the day.
- **Supporting recovery and immune function**: Healthy fats help reduce inflammation after intense training sessions and support overall recovery. They also play a critical role in maintaining hormonal balance, which is key for muscle growth, fat loss, and overall health.

Fats should make up about 20-30% of your total daily caloric intake. Focus on consuming healthy fats from sources such as:

- Avocados
- Nuts and seeds (almonds, walnuts, chia seeds)
- Olive oil, coconut oil, and nut butters
- Fatty fish (salmon, mackerel, sardines)

- **Nutrition Timing for CrossFit Athletes**

When it comes to CrossFit nutrition, it's not just about what you eat, but when you eat it. Properly timing your meals and snacks is critical for fueling performance, optimizing recovery, and reducing fatigue.

- **Pre-Workout Nutrition**

Before you hit the gym, your body needs fuel to perform at its best. A balanced pre-workout meal should include a combination of carbohydrates, protein, and a small amount of healthy fats. Carbs will give you quick energy, while protein will help with muscle preservation. Fats should be kept minimal as they digest more slowly, which can cause discomfort during intense workouts.

A good pre-workout meal should be consumed about 60 to 90 minutes before your workout. For example, a banana with a scoop of whey protein or a small bowl of oatmeal with nuts would be excellent choices.

- **Post-Workout Nutrition**

Post-workout nutrition is where the magic happens. After an intense CrossFit session, your muscles are primed to absorb nutrients that will help them recover and grow. Aim to consume a meal that is rich in protein to promote muscle repair and carbohydrates to replenish glycogen stores.

It's best to consume your post-workout meal within 30 minutes to two hours after exercise, as this is when your body is most responsive to nutrient intake (the "anabolic window"). A protein shake with a piece of fruit or a chicken and rice meal are great post-workout options.

- **Conclusion: The Foundation of CrossFit Success**

CrossFit nutrition is an essential component of your overall fitness strategy. With the right balance of carbohydrates, protein, and fats, you can fuel your body to perform at its best during workouts and ensure optimal recovery afterward. Nutrition is the foundation upon which your CrossFit success will be built. By fueling your body with the right nutrients at the right times, you will improve performance, increase strength, prevent injury, and ensure you're ready for whatever challenge CrossFit throws your way.

Understanding the relationship between nutrition and CrossFit will enable you to tailor your diet to meet your unique training needs, optimize your results, and support your long-term fitness goals. In the next chapters, we will dive deeper into how to adjust your nutrition for different training frequencies, competition prep, and recovery—helping you reach your full CrossFit potential.

Basics of Nutrition for CrossFit

Understanding the fundamentals of CrossFit nutrition is essential for achieving optimal performance, ensuring proper recovery, and supporting long-term health. Nutrition isn't just about what you eat—it's about how your body uses the nutrients you provide to fuel intense workouts, repair muscles, and keep you healthy and energized. CrossFit is a highly demanding sport that requires you to perform at your peak every day, and the fuel you give your body will directly impact your performance.

To unlock your full potential as a CrossFit athlete, it's essential to understand the three primary macronutrients—carbohydrates, proteins, and fats—and how to balance them effectively for training, recovery, and performance. Each of these macronutrients plays a specific role in how your body functions, and knowing how much of each you need, and when to consume them, will make a big difference in the results you achieve.

In this chapter, we will break down the basics of CrossFit nutrition, including macronutrients, calorie requirements, the role of micronutrients, hydration, and how to structure your diet to support the varied demands of CrossFit training.

- **The Role of Macronutrients in CrossFit Nutrition**
- **Carbohydrates: The Primary Fuel for CrossFit**

Carbohydrates are the most immediate and preferred source of energy for CrossFit athletes. When you push your body to its limits during intense workouts, your muscles rely on stored carbohydrates (glycogen) for fuel. The body breaks down carbohydrates into glucose, which is used to generate energy, particularly during high-intensity, short-duration activities like CrossFit training.

CrossFit involves a mix of strength training, aerobic conditioning, and anaerobic exercise, all of which demand a significant amount of glycogen. Without an adequate supply of glycogen, performance will suffer, and fatigue will set in much quicker. This is why carbohydrates are considered the backbone of CrossFit nutrition.

Key Benefits of Carbohydrates for CrossFit:

- **Energy for High-Intensity Workouts**: CrossFit involves multiple high-intensity movements (sprints, jumps, heavy lifts), all of which require glucose for quick energy.
- **Glycogen Replenishment**: After a workout, your glycogen stores are depleted. Consuming carbohydrates post-workout helps replenish those stores and aids in recovery.
- **Endurance**: For longer training sessions or Metabolic Conditioning (MetCon) workouts, carbs help sustain energy and delay the onset of fatigue.

How to Incorporate Carbs:

- Carbohydrates should make up approximately 40-60% of your daily caloric intake, depending on your activity level.
- For athletes training once a day, you may need around 3-5 grams of carbs per kilogram of body weight.
- For athletes training multiple times a day, you may require 6-10 grams of carbs per kilogram of body weight.

Ideal Carb Sources for CrossFit:

- Whole grains like oats, quinoa, and brown rice.
- Root vegetables such as sweet potatoes, yams, and carrots.
- Fruits like bananas, berries, apples, and oranges.
- Vegetables like leafy greens, broccoli, and spinach.

- **Protein: Building and Repairing Muscle**

Protein is crucial for muscle repair and growth, especially after the intense strain placed on muscles during CrossFit workouts. Every time you lift weights, do bodyweight exercises, or perform high-intensity intervals, you create microtears in your muscles. Protein provides the building blocks (amino acids) needed to repair those tears and promote muscle growth.

CrossFit athletes need protein to help with:

- **Muscle Recovery**: The body uses protein to repair muscle fibers damaged during exercise, facilitating muscle growth and recovery.
- **Preventing Muscle Breakdown**: During periods of intense exercise, muscle breakdown can occur if protein intake is inadequate. Protein helps protect muscle mass from catabolism (breakdown).
- **Supporting Immune Function**: Intense training can stress the immune system. Adequate protein intake ensures that your body's immune system functions properly.

The amount of protein you need depends on your training intensity, muscle mass, and goals. Generally, CrossFit athletes should aim for around 1.2 to 2.0 grams of protein per kilogram of body weight per day, with higher amounts needed during periods of intense training or muscle-building.

Ideal Protein Sources:

- Lean meats like chicken, turkey, and beef.
- Fatty fish like salmon and tuna.
- Eggs, especially egg whites.
- Plant-based sources like lentils, chickpeas, and tofu.
- Dairy products such as Greek yogurt and cottage cheese.
- Protein powders (whey, casein, or plant-based protein) for convenience.

- **Fats: Long-Term Energy and Hormonal Health**

While carbohydrates provide quick energy during CrossFit, fats serve as a slower, more sustained source of energy. Fats are important for overall health and play a critical role in supporting various bodily functions, including hormone production, cell structure, and inflammation management. They are especially important for CrossFit athletes who train at higher volumes or for long durations, as they provide energy for low- to moderate-intensity activity and endurance.

Fats are also crucial for:

- **Hormonal Health**: Fats are needed to produce hormones like testosterone and cortisol, which are essential for muscle recovery, strength, and overall performance.
- **Reducing Inflammation**: Healthy fats, particularly omega-3 fatty acids, can help reduce the inflammation caused by intense CrossFit training.
- **Sustained Energy**: During longer training sessions or MetCon workouts, your body can tap into fat stores for slow-burning energy.

Fats should make up about 20-30% of your total daily calories, depending on your energy needs. Focus on consuming healthy fats from whole food sources rather than processed foods.

Ideal Sources of Healthy Fats:

- Avocados.
- Nuts and seeds like almonds, walnuts, chia seeds, and flaxseeds.
- Olive oil, coconut oil, and avocado oil.
- Fatty fish like salmon, mackerel, and sardines.
- Nut butters (peanut, almond, cashew).

- **Caloric Needs for CrossFit Athletes**

Understanding how many calories your body needs is the first step in optimizing your nutrition for CrossFit. The intensity and frequency of your workouts play a major role in determining how many calories you should consume.

To calculate your caloric needs, you need to factor in your Basal Metabolic Rate (BMR) and the calories you burn during exercise.

1. **Calculate Your BMR**: This is the number of calories your body needs to maintain basic functions at rest. It can be estimated using various formulas like the Harris-Benedict Equation.

2. **Estimate Your Total Daily Energy Expenditure (TDEE)**: Once you have your BMR, multiply it by an activity factor (based on how active you are). For CrossFit athletes, this factor can range from 1.5 (for moderate activity) to 2.5 (for very high activity, such as multiple daily training sessions).

For example:

- A moderately active CrossFit athlete with a BMR of 1,800 calories and a moderate activity factor of 1.8 would need around 3,240 calories per day.

- **Micronutrients: Vitamins and Minerals**

Micronutrients, including vitamins and minerals, are essential for overall health, performance, and recovery. While they are required in smaller amounts than macronutrients, they are crucial for maintaining metabolic functions, immune health, and muscle repair.

For CrossFit athletes, certain vitamins and minerals play an especially important role:

- **Vitamin D**: Crucial for bone health and immune function. CrossFit athletes often require higher levels of vitamin D due to the intensity of their training.
- **Magnesium**: Supports muscle function, reduces cramps, and helps with recovery.
- **Calcium**: Important for bone health, especially given the weight-bearing nature of CrossFit.
- **Electrolytes (Sodium, Potassium, Calcium, Magnesium)**: Help maintain fluid balance, nerve function, and muscle contraction during high-intensity workouts.

A well-rounded diet with plenty of fruits, vegetables, lean proteins, and whole grains will typically provide all the vitamins and minerals you need. However, supplementation may be necessary in certain cases (e.g., vitamin D during winter months or magnesium for athletes prone to cramps).

- **Hydration: The Key to Performance**

Proper hydration is often overlooked, but it is one of the most important aspects of CrossFit nutrition. Dehydration can lead to fatigue, muscle cramps, impaired performance, and even heat exhaustion during intense training sessions.

CrossFit athletes should drink water regularly throughout the day, aiming for about 3-4 liters of water daily, depending on body size, workout intensity, and environmental conditions. Additionally, during prolonged workouts or in hot conditions, replenishing electrolytes lost through sweat with an electrolyte drink or a supplement may be beneficial.

- **Conclusion**

Understanding the basics of CrossFit nutrition is key to maximizing performance, enhancing recovery, and achieving long-term success in the sport. By focusing on the right balance of macronutrients—carbohydrates for energy, protein for muscle repair, and fats for sustained fuel—you'll ensure your body is properly fueled for the high-intensity demands of CrossFit.

Additionally, ensuring proper hydration, getting the necessary vitamins and minerals, and understanding your caloric needs will further support your goals as a CrossFit athlete. In the next chapters, we'll delve deeper into how to tailor your diet to specific training phases, such as training for competition, the off-season, and recovery. Proper nutrition is not just about looking good—it's about performing at your peak, recovering quickly, and staying healthy for the long haul.

Nutrition for One Workout a Day (OWOD)

For many CrossFit athletes, the standard training routine involves one intense workout per day, often referred to as "One Workout a Day" (OWOD). Whether you're a seasoned athlete or someone just starting out, understanding how to fuel your body for maximum performance during a single training session is essential for success. CrossFit is demanding, and the intensity of the workouts can lead to significant physical stress, so nutrition becomes an important part of the equation for sustaining energy levels, improving performance, and optimizing recovery.

In this chapter, we will explore the nutritional strategies for OWOD athletes, including how to balance macronutrients, when to eat, hydration needs, and meal timing. We'll also provide practical tips on how to structure your diet for the best results, taking into account the energy demands of CrossFit training.

- **Understanding the Energy Demands of CrossFit Workouts**

CrossFit is a high-intensity fitness regimen designed to increase general physical preparedness (GPP) through a combination of strength training, endurance, flexibility, and gymnastics. A typical CrossFit workout might include a combination of Olympic lifting, bodyweight exercises, and cardiovascular conditioning—all within a 20-45-minute window. The workouts may vary in duration and intensity, but regardless of the specific WOD (Workout of the Day), the energy demands are substantial.

- **Anaerobic Energy**: CrossFit includes exercises that challenge your anaerobic energy system (short bursts of high-intensity work) like lifting heavy weights or doing sprints. These activities primarily rely on glycogen (carbohydrates) stored in the muscles.

- **Aerobic Energy**: CrossFit also includes endurance-focused exercises that challenge your aerobic system, such as rowing, running, or jump rope. These activities rely on a combination of glycogen and fat for energy.

For OWOD athletes, the key to fueling these workouts lies in balancing macronutrients—carbs, protein, and fats—in a way that maximizes energy and performance.

- **Macronutrient Breakdown for One Workout a Day (OWOD)**
- **Carbohydrates: Fueling Energy for Performance**

Carbohydrates are the body's primary source of energy during high-intensity activities like CrossFit. When you perform explosive movements such as sprints, heavy lifts, or box jumps, your body taps into its glycogen reserves. Glycogen is stored glucose that is stored in muscles and the liver, and it's crucial for fueling CrossFit workouts. Without enough glycogen, you'll experience early fatigue, reduced performance, and prolonged recovery times.

Carbohydrates are especially important for OWOD athletes because:

- **Immediate Energy**: CrossFit workouts typically involve quick bursts of power, strength, and speed, all of which are fueled by glycogen. Carbohydrates provide fast, readily available energy to meet the demands of these workouts.
- **Glycogen Replenishment**: After a workout, glycogen stores are depleted, and replenishing them is vital to ensuring that you're ready for your next training session.

For OWOD athletes, it's recommended to consume a moderate amount of carbohydrates in your pre-workout meal to ensure your body is adequately fueled. Post-workout, consuming carbs helps to restore glycogen levels and speed up recovery.

Ideal Carb Intake for OWOD:

- Aim for 3-5 grams of carbohydrates per kilogram of body weight.
- A typical meal or snack before your workout should contain 30-60 grams of carbs, depending on your body size and workout intensity.
- Post-workout meals should prioritize carbs in the range of 40-70 grams, depending on your workout and calorie needs.

Sources of Carbohydrates for CrossFit:

- **Whole Grains**: Oats, quinoa, brown rice, and whole wheat bread are excellent sources of slow-digesting carbs, providing sustained energy.
- **Fruits**: Bananas, apples, berries, and oranges are rich in quick-digesting sugars that provide fast energy and essential vitamins and minerals.
- **Root Vegetables**: Sweet potatoes, yams, and beets are nutrient-dense carb sources that provide long-lasting energy.
- **Legumes**: Beans, lentils, and chickpeas offer both carbs and protein, which help with recovery after a workout.

- **Protein: Repairing and Building Muscle**

Protein plays a crucial role in muscle recovery and growth. During CrossFit workouts, your muscles experience microtears, and protein helps to repair these fibers, making them stronger and more resilient. Adequate protein intake is essential for ensuring that your body has the building blocks (amino acids) it needs to recover properly after a workout.

For OWOD athletes, the goal is not only to optimize recovery but also to preserve lean muscle mass while continuing to build strength and endurance. CrossFit is known for its full-body workouts, and maintaining a high protein intake will help you meet these demands.

Protein recommendations for OWOD athletes:

- **Daily Protein Intake**: Aim for 1.2 to 2.0 grams of protein per kilogram of body weight each day. Higher protein intake can be beneficial during periods of intense training, muscle building, or fat loss.
- **Pre-Workout Protein**: Consuming protein before a workout, such as a small serving of lean chicken or Greek yogurt, can help prepare your muscles for the work ahead and reduce muscle breakdown.
- **Post-Workout Protein**: A post-workout meal or shake with 20-30 grams of protein is ideal for muscle repair and recovery. Consuming protein within 30-60 minutes after exercise is particularly effective in boosting muscle protein synthesis.

Sources of Protein:

- **Lean Meats**: Chicken breast, turkey, and lean cuts of beef and pork.
- **Fish and Seafood**: Salmon, tuna, shrimp, and white fish are excellent sources of high-quality protein.
- **Eggs**: A complete protein that contains all nine essential amino acids. Whole eggs are particularly rich in nutrients.
- **Dairy**: Greek yogurt, cottage cheese, and milk provide both protein and beneficial fats.
- **Plant-Based Proteins**: Tofu, tempeh, legumes (lentils, beans), and quinoa are excellent plant-based sources of protein.
- **Fats: Essential for Recovery and Hormonal Health**

While fats aren't as immediately used for energy during CrossFit workouts, they are still essential for overall health and performance. Healthy fats support long-term energy and help the body recover more effectively from intense exercise. Fats also support hormone production, including hormones like testosterone, which play a key role in muscle growth and fat loss.

For OWOD athletes, fats are particularly beneficial because they provide sustained energy throughout the day and help reduce inflammation post-workout.

Recommended Fat Intake for OWOD:

- Aim for 20-30% of your total daily calories to come from healthy fats.
- Avoid excessive consumption of trans fats and highly processed oils, as these can promote inflammation and hinder recovery.

Sources of Healthy Fats:

- **Avocados**: Packed with monounsaturated fats, avocados are great for promoting heart health and reducing inflammation.

- **Nuts and Seeds**: Almonds, walnuts, chia seeds, and flaxseeds are great sources of healthy fats and also provide fiber and protein.
- **Olive Oil and Coconut Oil**: Both oils are rich in monounsaturated and medium-chain triglycerides (MCTs), which are great for overall health.
- **Fatty Fish**: Salmon, mackerel, sardines, and trout are rich in omega-3 fatty acids, which help reduce inflammation and improve recovery.

- **Pre-Workout Nutrition: Fueling Your Body for Peak Performance**

Before any CrossFit workout, you want to ensure that your body is properly fueled to perform at its best. Pre-workout nutrition is key to maximizing your energy and reducing fatigue during the workout. The goal is to provide a combination of easily digestible carbohydrates and moderate protein to fuel your muscles and provide a steady energy source.

When to Eat:
- Ideally, you want to eat a pre-workout meal 60-90 minutes before your training session. This allows time for digestion and ensures that your body has the fuel it needs.

Pre-Workout Meal Composition:
- **Carbohydrates**: 30-60 grams of carbs will provide your muscles with immediate energy.
- **Protein**: 15-20 grams of protein to support muscle repair and growth.
- **Minimal Fat**: Keep fats low in the pre-workout meal, as they can slow digestion and cause discomfort during high-intensity training.

Examples of Pre-Workout Meals:
- Oatmeal with a scoop of protein powder, chia seeds, and berries.
- A banana with a scoop of peanut butter and a serving of whey protein.
- A smoothie made with Greek yogurt, spinach, a banana, and some almond butter.

- **Post-Workout Nutrition: Rebuilding and Recovery**

After CrossFit workouts, your muscles are primed to absorb nutrients that will promote muscle repair, replenish glycogen stores, and help with recovery. Post-workout nutrition is essential for reducing soreness, preventing muscle breakdown, and preparing your body for the next workout.

When to Eat:
- Aim to eat within 30-60 minutes after your workout. This is when your body is most receptive to nutrients and when your muscle protein synthesis is heightened.

Post-Workout Meal Composition:
- **Carbohydrates**: 40-70 grams to replenish glycogen stores and restore energy levels.
- **Protein**: 20-30 grams to stimulate muscle repair and growth.

- **Hydration**: Rehydrate with water or an electrolyte drink to replace fluids and minerals lost during exercise.

Examples of Post-Workout Meals:

- A protein shake with banana and almond milk.
- Grilled chicken with sweet potatoes and leafy greens.
- Quinoa with black beans, avocado, and salsa.

- **Hydration: The Key to Performance and Recovery**

Hydration is crucial for optimal performance and recovery. Dehydration can lead to fatigue, cramping, and impaired muscle function. During high-intensity CrossFit workouts, you lose fluids and electrolytes through sweat, which need to be replaced to maintain performance.

Hydration Tips:

- **Before Your Workout**: Drink water throughout the day to stay hydrated, aiming for 3-4 liters of water.
- **During Your Workout**: Sip water during your session to maintain hydration levels.
- **After Your Workout**: Rehydrate with water and consider adding an electrolyte drink if you've had a particularly sweaty session.

- **Conclusion**

Nutrition for OWOD athletes is about fueling your body for peak performance, ensuring efficient recovery, and supporting overall health. By balancing your macronutrients—carbohydrates, protein, and fats—you will optimize energy levels during your CrossFit workouts and promote muscle growth and repair afterward. Proper timing of pre- and post-workout meals is essential for maximizing results, and staying hydrated will ensure that your body performs at its best.

In the next chapters, we will delve into how nutrition strategies differ when training multiple times a day, preparing for competition, and managing your off-season. By understanding the nuances of nutrition for each phase of your training, you can ensure that you're always working toward your goals, whether that's improving your strength, endurance, or overall CrossFit performance.

Nutrition for Multiple Workouts a Day (MWOD)

For many advanced CrossFit athletes, the training load increases, often involving multiple workouts per day (MWOD). This type of training regimen can be extremely taxing on the body and requires a strategic approach to nutrition in order to ensure maximum performance during each session, adequate recovery between sessions, and optimal long-term health. Training multiple times a day is often employed by competitive athletes or those aiming to push their limits and achieve rapid improvements in strength, conditioning, and skill.

In this chapter, we will explore the nutrition requirements and strategies for athletes who perform multiple CrossFit workouts a day. We will cover the critical role of macronutrients, meal timing, hydration, and recovery strategies to ensure you are able to recover between workouts, fuel each session, and stay healthy throughout this intense training cycle.

- **Understanding the Demands of Multiple Workouts a Day**

Multiple workouts a day are often used by athletes who have specific training goals, such as increasing performance in certain aspects of CrossFit (strength, endurance, power, or skill) or preparing for a competition. This level of training can put a lot of stress on the body, and without proper nutrition, athletes risk overtraining, burnout, and injury.

- **Energy Demands**: Each workout taxes the body's glycogen stores and puts significant stress on the muscular and cardiovascular systems. With multiple workouts, glycogen depletion happens faster, and muscle recovery becomes even more critical.

- **Recovery Time**: The recovery between workouts is limited, which means the window for rehydrating, replenishing glycogen, and rebuilding muscle tissue is shorter. Nutrition becomes key to maximizing recovery in between sessions and ensuring you can maintain performance.

- **Physical Stress**: The stress of multiple workouts increases your need for calories, macronutrients, and micronutrients to support the body's recovery processes. Over time, training multiple times a day can elevate inflammation and stress hormone levels, which is why optimal nutrition is important to prevent this from affecting performance or health.

For athletes who train multiple times a day, the goal is not only to fuel each workout properly but also to recover and prepare for the next session while maintaining overall health and performance.

- **Macronutrient Breakdown for Multiple Workouts a Day (MWOD)**

The same macronutrients—carbohydrates, protein, and fats—are critical when training multiple times a day, but their importance and timing vary slightly in this scenario. Athletes who train multiple times a day typically need more energy from carbohydrates to fuel intense workouts and support rapid recovery, as well as protein to repair muscles and optimize recovery between sessions.

- **Carbohydrates: Primary Fuel Source for Multiple Workouts**

Carbohydrates remain the most important macronutrient for athletes doing multiple workouts a day. CrossFit involves both high-intensity anaerobic work and aerobic endurance, both of which rely heavily on glycogen as the primary source of energy. When glycogen stores are depleted, athletes experience fatigue, reduced performance, and slower recovery. For MWOD athletes, having enough carbs in the system at all times is crucial for sustaining performance across multiple training sessions.

- **Carb Loading Between Workouts**: For MWOD athletes, you need to consume carbohydrates throughout the day to ensure glycogen stores are replenished between workouts. If you're doing two or three workouts in a day, you'll likely need to consume carbohydrates after each session to restore glycogen levels.
- **Energy for High-Intensity Efforts**: The body's demand for glycogen increases with the intensity of the workout, so the more demanding the WOD (especially those that include Olympic lifts, gymnastics movements, or sprints), the more carbs you'll need. Without sufficient carbs, your performance will suffer, and recovery time will increase.

Ideal Carb Intake for MWOD:
- Aim for 5-7 grams of carbohydrates per kilogram of body weight per day, or even higher depending on the intensity of your training.
- After each workout, aim to consume 40-70 grams of carbohydrates to quickly restore glycogen levels.

Carbohydrate Sources:
- **Whole Grains**: Oats, quinoa, brown rice, and whole wheat pasta.
- **Fruits and Vegetables**: Bananas, berries, apples, and leafy greens provide both quick-digesting and slow-digesting carbohydrates.
- **Starchy Vegetables**: Sweet potatoes, squash, and beets offer a nutrient-dense carb option for sustained energy.

- **Legumes**: Beans, lentils, and chickpeas provide fiber along with carbs for energy.
- **Protein: Ensuring Muscle Repair and Growth**

Protein is essential for repairing the muscle breakdown that occurs during intense CrossFit workouts. For MWOD athletes, protein consumption becomes even more crucial, as multiple workouts mean more microtrauma to the muscles that must be repaired in a short period of time. The body needs ample protein to rebuild the muscle fibers and stimulate muscle growth, especially in the hours following intense training.

Protein Recommendations for MWOD:

- **Daily Protein Intake**: For MWOD athletes, the ideal protein intake ranges from 1.4 to 2.0 grams per kilogram of body weight per day, depending on the volume and intensity of training.
- **Protein Timing**: Aim to consume protein with each meal to support muscle repair and recovery. After each workout, prioritize a protein-rich meal or shake with around 20-30 grams of protein to maximize recovery and prevent muscle breakdown.

Protein Sources for CrossFit:

- **Lean Meats**: Chicken, turkey, lean beef, and pork provide high-quality protein.
- **Fish and Seafood**: Salmon, tuna, shrimp, and cod offer protein along with healthy omega-3 fatty acids.
- **Eggs**: Whole eggs or egg whites are an excellent source of high-quality protein.
- **Dairy**: Greek yogurt, cottage cheese, and milk provide slow-digesting protein for sustained muscle repair.
- **Plant-Based Protein**: Tofu, tempeh, legumes, quinoa, and edamame offer non-animal sources of protein.
- **Fats: Supporting Hormonal Health and Sustained Energy**

Fats are essential for the body's overall health, particularly for the production of hormones like testosterone and estrogen, which are critical for muscle growth and repair. While fats are not the body's primary fuel source during high-intensity efforts, they are still important for maintaining sustained energy, supporting recovery, and improving overall health.

For MWOD athletes, fats should be consumed primarily for recovery, inflammation management, and overall well-being. Too much fat right before a workout can slow digestion and cause discomfort, so it's best to consume fats in meals spaced away from training sessions.

Ideal Fat Intake for MWOD:

- Fat intake should constitute about 20-30% of total daily calories.
- Focus on healthy fats, as they can help manage inflammation and promote recovery between sessions.

Sources of Healthy Fats:

- **Avocados**: Packed with monounsaturated fats, they support heart health and reduce inflammation.
- **Nuts and Seeds**: Almonds, walnuts, chia seeds, and flaxseeds are great sources of healthy fats and fiber.
- **Olive Oil**: Rich in monounsaturated fats, it can be used in cooking or as a dressing.
- **Fatty Fish**: Salmon, mackerel, and sardines provide omega-3 fatty acids, which have anti-inflammatory properties.

- **Meal Timing and Structuring for Multiple Workouts**

When you train multiple times a day, meal timing and frequency become crucial. With limited recovery time between sessions, strategically timing your meals and snacks can optimize performance and recovery.

- **Pre-Workout Nutrition: Preparing for Success**

Pre-workout meals for MWOD athletes should focus on providing quick, digestible carbohydrates for energy and moderate protein for muscle preservation. The meal should be consumed 60-90 minutes before the workout to allow for digestion and to ensure a steady supply of energy during the training session.

Key Elements:
- **Carbohydrates**: Aim for 30-60 grams of carbs to fuel high-intensity effort.
- **Protein**: Aim for 10-20 grams of protein to support muscle function and prevent catabolism.
- **Low Fat**: Keep fats to a minimum to avoid slowing digestion.

Pre-Workout Meal Examples:
- A smoothie with banana, protein powder, and almond milk.
- Oatmeal with whey protein and blueberries.
- A rice cake with peanut butter and a banana.

- **Post-Workout Nutrition: Accelerating Recovery Between Sessions**

After each workout, prioritize replenishing glycogen stores and repairing muscle tissue. The post-workout window (the 30-60 minutes following exercise) is when the body is most primed to absorb nutrients. For MWOD athletes, consuming the right foods at the right times can dramatically improve recovery and ensure that you are able to perform at your best in your next training session.

Key Elements:
- **Carbohydrates**: 40-70 grams of fast-digesting carbohydrates to replenish glycogen.
- **Protein**: 20-30 grams of protein to facilitate muscle repair.
- **Hydration**: Replenish lost fluids and electrolytes.

Post-Workout Meal Examples:
- A protein shake with fruit and a scoop of carbohydrate powder (like dextrose or maltodextrin).
- Grilled chicken with quinoa and sweet potatoes.

- Greek yogurt with honey and granola.
- **Recovery Nutrition Between Workouts**

If you have a short recovery window between workouts (such as 4-6 hours), it's essential to refuel with balanced meals that combine carbohydrates, protein, and fats. This will ensure that you're ready for the next training session without compromising recovery.

Key Elements:

- **Carbohydrates**: For glycogen replenishment.
- **Protein**: For muscle repair and recovery.
- **Fats**: For sustained energy and reducing inflammation.

Meal Examples:

- Turkey and avocado sandwich on whole-grain bread.
- A quinoa and chickpea salad with olive oil and mixed greens.
- A rice and chicken stir-fry with vegetables and olive oil.

- **Hydration: Staying Hydrated Between Workouts**

With multiple workouts a day, hydration becomes even more important. Proper hydration helps maintain performance, reduce fatigue, prevent muscle cramps, and support recovery. Dehydration can significantly impair both strength and endurance, and it can lead to decreased motivation, cognitive impairment, and an increased risk of injury.

- **Hydration Guidelines:**
- **Before Exercise**: Drink 500-600 ml of water 2-3 hours before a workout.
- **During Exercise**: Aim to drink 150-250 ml of water every 15-20 minutes during your workout.
- **After Exercise**: Rehydrate with water or an electrolyte drink immediately after exercise to replace fluids lost during training.

Electrolyte drinks containing sodium, potassium, and magnesium can help replace lost minerals and support muscle function, especially after intense, sweat-inducing workouts.

- **Conclusion**

Nutrition for athletes who engage in multiple workouts per day (MWOD) requires a careful balance of macronutrients, meal timing, hydration, and recovery strategies. By prioritizing carbohydrates for fueling workouts, protein for muscle repair, and healthy fats for sustained energy, MWOD athletes can optimize their training and recovery. Proper nutrition throughout the day, with strategically timed meals and snacks, will ensure that the body remains fueled and ready to tackle each training session.

In the next chapters, we will explore nutrition for athletes during the off-season, during competition preparation, and other important aspects of fueling performance. By understanding the specific needs of each phase of your training, you can continue to progress and maximize your CrossFit potential.

Nutrition for the Off-Season

The off-season in CrossFit is often viewed as a time for athletes to rest, recover, and recharge after a competition season or intense training cycle. It's also an opportunity to rebuild strength, work on weak areas, and focus on addressing injuries or mobility issues. Nutrition during the off-season plays a vital role in helping the athlete restock energy stores, repair muscle tissue, and set the stage for a successful upcoming season. During this phase, the nutritional approach differs from peak competition prep or during periods of intense training, as the focus shifts from peak performance to building a solid foundation for the next training cycle.

This chapter delves into the specific nutritional strategies you can use to make the most out of your off-season and build a well-rounded, sustainable approach to nutrition for recovery, muscle growth, and general well-being.

1. The Purpose of the Off-Season

The off-season is the period of time between competition seasons or high-intensity training blocks. It is typically a lower-intensity phase where athletes can afford to focus more on maintenance, recovery, and addressing individual weaknesses. While many athletes may find it tempting to continue pushing their training to peak levels, the off-season provides an opportunity to step back and focus on longer-term goals rather than short-term performance.

The primary objectives of the off-season are to:

2. **Recover and Rest**: Your body needs time to recover from the cumulative effects of previous training and competition. This period allows the central nervous system, muscles, and joints time to rest and repair.

3. **Strengthen Weak Points**: Whether it's a specific movement, mobility issue, or addressing injuries, the off-season allows for targeted improvement in these areas.

4. **Maintain General Fitness**: While intense WODs may decrease, maintaining a reasonable level of fitness and strength will keep your body from detraining significantly.

5. **Build a Foundation for the Upcoming Season**: Nutrition plays a significant role in setting the stage for the next training phase by restoring muscle mass, improving hormonal balance, and preparing the body to tackle more intense training.

By adjusting your nutrition during this phase, you can optimize recovery, build muscle mass, and ensure you're in the best shape possible when the competition season or next training block begins.

6. **Macronutrient Strategy During the Off-Season**

While the off-season is generally a lower-intensity phase, your body still requires an appropriate balance of macronutrients to rebuild, maintain muscle mass, and ensure overall health. Since you will likely be training at a lower intensity or frequency compared to the competition season, your calorie needs will be reduced, but the quality of your food and nutrient timing are just as crucial for long-term progress.

7. **Carbohydrates: Balancing Energy Needs**

In the off-season, carbohydrates are still important, but they should be adjusted according to your activity level. With fewer high-intensity workouts, your body's immediate need for glycogen will be lower, but you still need enough carbs to fuel moderate-intensity sessions, daily movement, and recovery.

Carb Recommendations:

- **Moderate Carb Intake**: Since training volume tends to be lower in the off-season, aim for 3-5 grams of carbohydrates per kilogram of body weight, depending on how active you are during this period.
- **Carbohydrate Timing**: Even during the off-season, try to consume carbs around your workouts, as they remain an essential fuel source for muscle recovery. After training, carbs help replenish glycogen stores and reduce muscle protein breakdown.
- **Focus on Low Glycemic Index Carbs**: Since you're not engaging in intense workouts, your focus should be on whole grains, vegetables, fruits, and legumes that provide sustained energy over the course of the day.

Carb Sources:

- **Whole Grains**: Brown rice, quinoa, oats, barley, whole wheat pasta, and buckwheat.
- **Starchy Vegetables**: Sweet potatoes, potatoes, butternut squash, and other root vegetables.
- **Legumes**: Lentils, chickpeas, black beans, and peas are excellent plant-based carb sources.

8. **Protein: Recovery and Muscle Maintenance**

Protein remains crucial in the off-season to rebuild muscle, address any muscle imbalances, and maintain strength while lowering training volume. Though your body may not be subjected to the same intense demands as during the competition season, you still need protein to maintain lean muscle mass and prevent muscle loss.

Protein Recommendations:

- **Moderate Protein Intake**: Aim for 1.4-1.8 grams of protein per kilogram of body weight per day. You may not need as much protein as during periods of intense competition preparation or high-volume training, but it remains necessary to maintain muscle and facilitate repair during the off-season.
- **Protein Timing**: Distribute protein intake throughout the day to support continuous muscle repair. Aim for 20-30 grams of high-quality protein per meal, and ensure post-workout protein intake for optimal recovery.

Protein Sources:
- **Animal-Based**: Chicken breast, lean beef, turkey, eggs, fish, and dairy (Greek yogurt, cottage cheese).
- **Plant-Based**: Tofu, tempeh, edamame, lentils, quinoa, chickpeas, and plant-based protein powders.

9. **Fats: Hormonal Health and Sustained Energy**

Fats become even more important in the off-season, as they support hormonal health, cognitive function, and energy levels. Maintaining healthy levels of fat will also allow for better recovery and reduced inflammation, which is particularly important if you've had any lingering injuries from the competitive season.

Fat Recommendations:
- **Healthy Fat Intake**: Fat should still make up about 25-30% of your total daily caloric intake during the off-season, focusing on unsaturated fats and omega-3 fatty acids.
- **Fat Sources**: The focus should be on whole, nutrient-dense fat sources, including avocado, nuts, seeds, and fatty fish, which help maintain stable hormone levels and contribute to reduced inflammation.

Fat Sources:
- **Healthy Oils**: Olive oil, coconut oil, and avocado oil are good choices for cooking or dressing meals.
- **Fatty Fish**: Salmon, mackerel, sardines, and other oily fish are rich in omega-3s, which help manage inflammation and support brain health.
- **Nuts and Seeds**: Almonds, walnuts, chia seeds, flaxseeds, and hemp seeds are excellent sources of healthy fats and provide important minerals like magnesium and zinc.
- **Avocados**: A great source of monounsaturated fats, which help to reduce inflammation and provide long-lasting energy.

---

10. **Hydration: Restoring Fluids Without Overtraining**

Even in the off-season, hydration is important for recovery, digestion, and supporting overall health. Training, even at lower intensities, still leads to fluid loss. Dehydration can affect energy levels, mood, and muscle function, which can negatively impact recovery and performance.

11. **Hydration Recommendations:**
- **Water**: Aim to drink at least 2.5 to 3 liters of water per day. If you are engaging in moderate-intensity activity, you may need more to replace the fluid lost through sweat.
- **Electrolytes**: In the off-season, if your training is less intense, you may not need as many electrolytes as during peak training seasons, but it's still important to replenish sodium, potassium, and magnesium. Consider adding an electrolyte drink to your post-workout meal if you've done intense training.

Hydration Tips:

- Drink water regularly throughout the day, not just around your workouts.
- If you are training at lower intensities but still working hard, aim to drink water with a pinch of salt or an electrolyte drink to help maintain fluid balance.

---

12. Meal Timing and Frequency in the Off-Season

While training intensity and volume might be lower, you still need to be mindful of your meal timing and frequency. In the off-season, the goal is to maintain a steady supply of nutrients to support muscle maintenance, recovery, and general health.

13. Meal Timing:

- **Pre-Workout Meal**: Eat a light meal or snack 60-90 minutes before training that includes a moderate amount of carbohydrates and protein. This meal should be easy to digest and provide sustained energy.
- **Post-Workout Meal**: Your post-workout meal is important for muscle recovery and replenishing glycogen. Aim to eat a balanced meal with carbohydrates and protein within 30-60 minutes after training.
- **Frequent Meals**: In the off-season, you may not need to eat as often as during intense competition prep. However, aim for 3-4 balanced meals a day with snacks if necessary to keep your energy levels steady.

---

14. Supplements During the Off-Season

While supplements should never replace whole foods, they can be useful in addressing specific nutritional needs during the off-season. In this phase, supplementation can focus on muscle repair, inflammation management, and joint health.

15. Key Supplements to Consider:

- **Whey Protein**: A convenient and fast-digesting protein source for muscle repair, particularly useful in the post-workout period.
- **Creatine**: Beneficial for building strength and muscle mass, creatine can still be used in the off-season to support muscle maintenance.
- **Omega-3 Fatty Acids**: Found in fish oil, omega-3s help reduce inflammation, improve cardiovascular health, and support overall recovery.
- **Vitamin D**: Many athletes are deficient in Vitamin D, especially during the winter months. A vitamin D supplement can help support immune function, bone health, and hormone production.
- **Collagen**: A great supplement for supporting joint health, especially if you've experienced any injuries during the competitive season.

---

16. Conclusion

The off-season in CrossFit is an essential time for recovery, rebuilding, and preparing for the next cycle of competition or intense training. Nutrition during this phase is vital to ensure you maintain muscle mass, restore energy levels, and set the stage for future performance. By adjusting your carbohydrate, protein, and fat intake, staying hydrated, and timing meals strategically, you can maximize your recovery, address weaknesses, and return to the competitive season stronger, healthier, and more prepared.

In the next chapters, we'll explore nutrition for competition preparation and how to fuel your body for maximum performance when training intensity increases again.

Nutrition for Competition

Competition season is the time when all of your hard work in the gym, at the table, and during recovery comes to a head. CrossFit athletes are often pushing their limits, testing strength, endurance, mental toughness, and agility in a single event or across several days of competition. The demands on the body during this time are high, and your nutritional approach plays a significant role in maximizing performance, maintaining energy levels, and ensuring you recover quickly between events.

This chapter will dive deep into how to fuel for competition day(s), optimize recovery, and tweak your daily nutrition to keep your energy, strength, and stamina high during the competitive grind. Whether you're preparing for a local throwdown, regionals, or the CrossFit Games, the principles covered here will help you approach your nutrition with a strategy that enhances your performance rather than leaves you scrambling for energy or dealing with digestive discomfort.

1. The Importance of Nutrition During Competition

In CrossFit competitions, where athletes are required to perform a variety of physical tasks that test different domains of fitness (strength, stamina, gymnastics, endurance, etc.), optimal nutrition is non-negotiable. Poor fueling or recovery strategies can leave you depleted during a workout, hinder your ability to perform at your best, and delay recovery, which can affect subsequent events or performances.

In competition, nutrition is needed for two primary purposes:

2. **Energy to Perform**: You need to have enough energy stored in your muscles and liver to power through the physical demands of each event.
3. **Recovery Between Events**: CrossFit competitions often consist of multiple events over several hours or days. Quick recovery becomes crucial so you can show up ready for the next challenge.

Getting nutrition right during this time can be the difference between a podium finish and crashing out early.

4. Carbohydrates: Your Fuel for Performance

Carbohydrates are the primary fuel source for high-intensity exercise like CrossFit. Glycogen, the stored form of carbohydrates in your muscles and liver, provides quick and easily accessible energy for explosive movements and endurance efforts. During competition, it's essential to ensure that glycogen stores are topped up before, during, and after each event.

5. Carb Loading for the Competition

If your competition spans multiple days or involves intense multiple events in a day, carbohydrate loading is a strategy that can help you increase your glycogen stores leading into the competition. Carbohydrate loading involves gradually increasing your carb intake in the days leading up to the competition and tapering off training to allow your muscles to store more glycogen than usual.

Carbohydrate Loading Strategy:

- **3-4 Days Before the Competition**: Increase your daily carbohydrate intake to 6-10 grams per kilogram of body weight. Focus on complex carbohydrates like whole grains, sweet potatoes, legumes, and fruits to gradually boost glycogen levels.

- **Day Before the Competition**: Maintain a high-carb diet with moderate protein intake (around 1.2-1.5 grams per kilogram of body weight). Avoid heavy, fatty foods, as they may slow digestion and lead to discomfort during the competition.

6. Carbs During Competition

Once competition starts, you'll need to keep your glycogen levels high to maintain performance. Eating carbohydrates during the event can prevent energy crashes and keep you going strong through long days or intense back-to-back workouts.

Intra-Workout Carbs:

- **Quick-Digesting Carbs**: For events that involve longer periods of exertion, include fast-digesting carbohydrate sources like sports drinks, gels, fruit, or energy bars. These can be easily consumed between events or during short rest periods to replenish glycogen quickly.

- **Amount**: Aim for about 30-60 grams of carbs per hour during intense efforts lasting longer than 60 minutes.

Carb Sources:

- Bananas, apples, oranges, and grapes.
- Sports drinks with a high carbohydrate content (e.g., Gatorade or Skratch Labs).
- Energy gels or chews.
- Simple homemade snacks like rice cakes, honey sandwiches, or oat bars.

7. Protein: Preserving Muscle Mass and Promoting Recovery

While carbohydrates are the go-to energy source during a competition, protein remains critical for muscle repair, preservation, and overall recovery. Competition days are often physically demanding, and the muscles go through a lot of wear and tear, so having sufficient protein available to aid in muscle repair is essential.

8. Pre-Competition Protein

You don't need to overthink protein intake the night before a competition. Aim for a balanced meal with moderate protein intake, ensuring your body has enough amino acids in circulation to support muscle repair throughout the event.

Pre-Event Meal:

- **Protein**: 20-30 grams of high-quality protein, such as chicken, turkey, eggs, or a whey protein shake.
- **Carbs**: Pair protein with easily digestible carbohydrates for a good balance of fuel and recovery (e.g., brown rice with chicken or a smoothie with fruit and protein powder).

9. Post-Competition Protein

Post-event recovery is just as important as fueling during the competition. Within 30-60 minutes after each event, you should aim to consume a meal or shake containing a high-quality protein source to initiate muscle recovery.

Post-Event Meal:

- **Protein**: 20-30 grams of fast-digesting protein (e.g., whey protein or a lean protein source like chicken or fish).
- **Carbs**: Combine protein with carbohydrates to replenish glycogen stores (e.g., a protein shake with fruit, or rice and lean protein).
- **Amount**: Aim for 1.2-1.5 grams of protein per kilogram of body weight each day during competition for muscle maintenance and repair.

Protein Sources:

- Whey protein shakes (fast-digesting).
- Chicken breast, fish, turkey, lean beef.
- Tofu, tempeh, or plant-based protein sources for vegan athletes.

---

10. Fats: Maintaining Long-Term Energy and Hormonal Balance

Fats, while not the primary fuel source for CrossFit competitions, still play an essential role in maintaining energy levels, supporting cognitive function, and ensuring hormonal balance. Healthy fats also support anti-inflammatory responses and can aid recovery during rest periods.

11. Fat Intake Before and During Competition

During competition days, fat intake should be moderate but not excessive, as fats take longer to digest and can leave you feeling sluggish or bloated. Keep fat consumption to lower levels before events and focus on carbs and protein.

Before the Competition:

- A small amount of fats can be beneficial in providing sustained energy, but don't overdo it. Examples of healthy fats to include are avocado, nuts, and olive oil. Aim for 10-15 grams of fat with your pre-event meal.

During the Competition:

- Keep fat intake minimal during the competition to avoid sluggishness. Focus primarily on carbs and proteins for fast energy and recovery.

Fat Sources:
- Avocados, olive oil, and coconut oil.
- Nuts and seeds.
- Fatty fish (like salmon or mackerel) in meals around rest periods.

---

12. Hydration: Staying Optimally Hydrated for Peak Performance

Hydration is crucial for every aspect of CrossFit, but it becomes even more important during competition, especially when multiple events are stacked back-to-back. Dehydration can severely impair physical performance, mental clarity, and recovery between events. Ensuring you're hydrated before, during, and after each competition will help you maintain your strength, focus, and stamina throughout the day.

13. Pre-Competition Hydration

Begin hydrating well before the competition starts. Aim to drink at least 500 milliliters of water 1-2 hours before your first event to ensure you're properly hydrated. In the days leading up to the competition, aim to drink a minimum of 3 liters of water daily to ensure hydration stores are full.

14. Hydration During Competition

During events, especially if there's a break between workouts, you'll need to drink water consistently to prevent dehydration. If you're competing outdoors in hot conditions or sweating heavily, you may need to supplement water with an electrolyte solution to maintain your sodium, potassium, and magnesium balance.

Electrolyte Recommendations:
- **Intra-Workout**: Consume an electrolyte drink (e.g., Nuun, Skratch Labs, or coconut water) to help maintain hydration during the events.
- **Post-Workout**: Continue to hydrate with water or an electrolyte-rich drink to speed recovery and avoid cramping.

---

15. Supplements: Enhancing Performance During Competition

Supplements can help fill nutritional gaps, enhance performance, and support recovery during competition. While whole foods should be your primary source of nutrition, certain supplements can give you an edge when used correctly.

16. Key Supplements to Consider for Competition:
- **Pre-Workout**: A pre-workout supplement with caffeine, beta-alanine, and creatine can help increase energy, endurance, and mental focus during events.
- **Creatine**: Although it's not typically considered an "immediate" performance booster, creatine supplementation can support power production, particularly in strength-focused events.
- **Branched-Chain Amino Acids (BCAAs)**: Consuming BCAAs during the event can help reduce muscle fatigue and damage.

- **Electrolytes**: Electrolyte tablets or drinks can help replace the salts lost through sweat and prevent dehydration, cramping, and muscle fatigue.

17. Conclusion

Competition nutrition is about ensuring that you have the right fuel in place to sustain peak performance, minimize fatigue, and recover quickly between events. By emphasizing the right balance of carbohydrates, protein, fats, hydration, and supplements, you can optimize your energy stores and muscle repair, giving you the edge when the intensity ramps up.

Competition nutrition isn't just about eating the right foods, but also about timing, hydration, and recovery strategies that will help you stay on top of your game throughout the entire competition. In the next chapters, we'll discuss strategies for recovery after the competition ends and how to return to your training cycles with a solid nutritional foundation.

Sleep and Recovery

Sleep and recovery are often the unsung heroes of any athlete's journey, but they are crucial in ensuring sustained performance, longevity in training, and resilience during competition. While rigorous training and disciplined nutrition are essential components of achieving your CrossFit goals, without adequate recovery, both physical and mental, you'll eventually hit a plateau, and performance may start to decline. This chapter will dive into the importance of sleep, recovery strategies, and how you can optimize both for maximal performance.

1. **The Role of Sleep in Performance**

Sleep is when the body repairs itself, replenishes glycogen stores, strengthens muscle tissue, and regulates hormones involved in muscle growth, fat loss, and overall recovery. During deep sleep, the body produces growth hormone, which is responsible for tissue growth and repair—vital after intense CrossFit training. Furthermore, sleep is integral to cognitive function, reaction time, and decision-making ability, which are all critical in competitive settings.

2. **How Sleep Affects Athletic Performance**

Adequate sleep is the foundation upon which all training and nutrition strategies are built. The effects of poor sleep extend far beyond just feeling tired. Research shows that sleep deprivation leads to:

3. **Decreased Strength and Endurance**: A lack of sleep impairs muscle recovery, reduces strength output, and affects your aerobic capacity. This could result in lower performance during WODs or competition events.

4. **Impaired Recovery**: Sleep allows the body to repair muscle fibers damaged during training, synthesize proteins to grow stronger muscle tissue, and reduce inflammation. Without proper sleep, muscle recovery is incomplete, leaving you vulnerable to overtraining and injury.

5. **Cognitive Impairment**: Sleep plays a crucial role in mental clarity, focus, and mood regulation. In CrossFit, where decision-making speed, mental resilience, and tactical thinking are needed, sleep deprivation can impair these skills, potentially undermining your performance.

6. **Hormonal Imbalance**: Chronic sleep deprivation disrupts the balance of hormones like cortisol (the stress hormone) and growth hormone. Elevated cortisol levels over extended periods can lead to muscle breakdown and fat storage, while reduced growth hormone secretion inhibits muscle repair and growth.

7. **Immune System Function**: Sleep is vital for maintaining a strong immune system. If you're not getting enough sleep, your immune function is

compromised, leaving you at higher risk of illness, injury, and delayed recovery.

8. How Much Sleep Do CrossFit Athletes Need?

The ideal amount of sleep varies for each individual, but most athletes benefit from **7-9 hours of sleep per night**. Some highly trained athletes may require up to 10 hours of sleep to feel fully rested and recover from intense training or competition. During heavy training periods or following intense competitions, your body may require additional sleep to manage stress, repair muscle tissue, and recover fully.

It's important to listen to your body. If you're consistently feeling tired, sluggish, or mentally foggy, it's an indicator that your sleep needs aren't being met.

---

9. Improving Sleep Quality

While quantity is important, sleep quality is equally vital. A poor night's sleep, even if it lasts 8-9 hours, can leave you feeling unrefreshed and impair recovery. Fortunately, there are strategies you can implement to improve both the duration and quality of your sleep:

10. 1. Stick to a Consistent Sleep Schedule

The body thrives on routine. Going to bed and waking up at the same time every day—regardless of whether it's a weekday or weekend—helps regulate your circadian rhythm and ensures better-quality sleep. Aim to keep this schedule as consistent as possible, even during off days or rest periods.

11. 2. Create an Optimal Sleep Environment

Your environment plays a significant role in your ability to fall and stay asleep. To optimize your sleep:

- **Cool Temperature**: Keep the room temperature cool (around 60-67°F or 15-19°C) to promote deeper, more restful sleep.
- **Darkness**: Use blackout curtains or sleep masks to block out any light. Light interferes with the production of melatonin, a hormone responsible for regulating your sleep-wake cycle.
- **Noise Control**: Use earplugs or a white noise machine to block out distracting sounds.
- **Comfortable Bedding**: Ensure your mattress and pillows support restful sleep. You should be comfortable and well-supported while you sleep to avoid waking up with aches and pains.

12. 3. Limit Blue Light Exposure Before Bed

Exposure to blue light from screens (phones, tablets, computers) can delay the production of melatonin, making it harder to fall asleep. Limit your use of screens at least 1 hour before bed, or use blue light blocking glasses or apps on your devices if you must use them.

13. 4. Relaxation Techniques

To signal your body that it's time to sleep, engage in a relaxation routine 30 minutes to 1 hour before bed:

- Practice deep breathing exercises.

- Engage in light stretching or yoga to release muscle tension.
- Read a book (preferably a physical one to avoid the use of screens).
- Meditate or practice mindfulness to clear your mind.

---

14. Active Recovery: Enhancing Your Rest Days

Recovery isn't just about getting enough sleep at night. It also involves taking active steps during your rest days to promote muscle repair, reduce soreness, and ensure that you're ready for your next workout or competition.

Active recovery involves low-intensity exercise that promotes blood flow to the muscles, reduces stiffness, and accelerates the healing process. Unlike high-intensity training, which breaks down muscle tissue, active recovery helps stimulate muscle growth and improve flexibility.

15. Effective Active Recovery Techniques

1. **Foam Rolling and Self-Myofascial Release**: Using a foam roller or massage tools can help release tight spots in your muscles and fascia. This helps alleviate soreness, improves flexibility, and promotes blood circulation to areas that may have become tight after intense training.

2. **Stretching and Mobility Work**: Spend time stretching your major muscle groups and working on your range of motion. Focus on areas that may be particularly tight, like the hamstrings, shoulders, and hips. Incorporating mobility exercises into your routine will not only reduce injury risk but also improve your overall movement quality, especially during high-intensity CrossFit movements.

3. **Low-Intensity Cardio**: Engaging in low-intensity cardio such as swimming, walking, light cycling, or rowing allows the muscles to recover while keeping the body active. These forms of exercise help remove metabolic waste products (such as lactic acid) from the muscles and provide a gentle challenge for the cardiovascular system.

4. **Ice Baths or Contrast Showers**: Cold water immersion (or ice baths) can reduce muscle soreness and inflammation following tough workouts or competitions. The cold constricts blood vessels, reducing swelling, while the subsequent warm-up (in a contrast shower) helps promote blood flow back into the tissues, aiding recovery.

---

16. Nutrition and Sleep: Supporting Recovery with Proper Fueling

To maximize sleep and recovery, it's important to fuel your body properly, especially in the hours leading up to bedtime. The right nutrition helps repair muscle tissue, replenish energy stores, and promote hormone balance during sleep.

17. Pre-Sleep Nutrition

- **Protein**: Eating protein-rich foods before bed ensures that your body has the amino acids it needs for muscle repair. Casein protein (found in dairy products) is ideal before bed because it digests slowly, providing a steady release of amino acids throughout the night.

- **Carbohydrates**: Consuming carbohydrates can help increase serotonin levels, which is a precursor to melatonin, the sleep hormone. Consider eating a small serving of carbs, such as sweet potatoes or fruit, alongside your protein before bed.
- **Healthy Fats**: A small portion of healthy fats (such as avocado or nuts) can help with the absorption of fat-soluble vitamins and provide steady energy for the body during recovery.

Sample Pre-Sleep Snack:
- Greek yogurt with berries and a handful of almonds.
- Cottage cheese with a tablespoon of almond butter and sliced banana.

18. Supplements for Sleep and Recovery

Certain supplements can support your sleep and recovery process, but they should be used in conjunction with good sleep hygiene and nutrition practices, not as a substitute. Some effective supplements include:

1. **Melatonin**: Melatonin is a hormone that regulates your sleep-wake cycle. While it is best to avoid relying on melatonin too often, it can be helpful in resetting your sleep schedule or aiding in sleep during times of high stress or competition.
2. **Magnesium**: Magnesium helps relax muscles, calm the nervous system, and improve sleep quality. It can also help with muscle cramps, tension, and post-workout recovery. Consider taking a magnesium supplement in the evening, especially if you struggle with sleep or muscle cramps.
3. **BCAAs (Branched-Chain Amino Acids)**: Consuming BCAAs before and after workouts may reduce muscle soreness, improve recovery, and decrease fatigue. They help reduce muscle breakdown during and after intense training, promoting muscle repair.
4. **Protein Shakes**: Consuming a slow-digesting protein shake (like casein protein) before bed can improve muscle repair and reduce catabolism (muscle breakdown) during the night.

19. Conclusion

Sleep and recovery are vital pillars of athletic performance, particularly for CrossFit athletes who constantly push their limits in training and competition. Prioritizing sleep by maintaining a consistent sleep schedule, creating an optimal sleep environment, and implementing relaxation techniques will help you recover effectively and perform at your best. Active recovery and smart nutrition also play critical roles in supporting your body's ability to repair and regenerate.

Incorporating these strategies into your routine can drastically improve your performance over time and ensure that you stay strong, healthy, and prepared for any challenge that comes your way.

Pre- and Post-Workout Nutrition

In CrossFit, the intensity and volume of your workouts can be grueling. To perform at your best and recover effectively, your pre- and post-workout nutrition plays a pivotal role in fueling your body for the tasks at hand, maintaining energy, and ensuring proper muscle repair. What you eat before and after your workouts is not just about providing fuel—it's about maximizing the outcomes of your training efforts and ensuring you're ready for the next session. This chapter will break down the science and best practices behind pre- and post-workout nutrition, offering clear strategies to help you optimize your performance and recovery.

---

1. The Importance of Pre-Workout Nutrition

Pre-workout nutrition is crucial because it helps fuel the body for the intense activity you're about to engage in. CrossFit workouts, or WODs (workout of the day), often demand explosive power, strength, endurance, and mental focus. If you don't consume the proper foods before your workout, you may run out of energy too soon, resulting in poor performance or early fatigue. Proper pre-workout nutrition not only provides the body with fuel but also primes it to perform at its best.

2. When to Eat Before Your Workout

The timing of your pre-workout meal is important. Ideally, you should aim to eat about **30-60 minutes before your workout**. This allows your body to digest the food, convert it into energy, and have it available when you start exercising. However, timing may vary slightly depending on personal preferences, the type of workout, and how your body reacts to different foods.

For those who have sensitive stomachs or prefer a lighter option, a smaller snack may work better. On the other hand, some people may need a more substantial meal, especially if they're doing heavy lifting or an endurance-based WOD. Keep in mind that you should avoid eating foods that are too high in fat or fiber, as these can cause digestive discomfort and lead to sluggishness during your workout.

3. Macronutrient Breakdown for Pre-Workout Nutrition

4. **Carbohydrates**: Carbs are the body's primary source of fuel during high-intensity exercise. When you consume carbohydrates, your body breaks them down into glucose, which is stored as glycogen in the muscles and liver. This glycogen provides the immediate energy required for explosive CrossFit movements, such as sprinting, lifting, and jumping.

- **What to Eat**: Focus on moderate-to-high glycemic index (GI) carbohydrates, which are easily digested and absorbed by the body. Examples include:
    o Oats or oatmeal
    o Whole wheat bread or toast
    o Sweet potatoes
    o Bananas, apples, or other fruit
    o Rice cakes

2. **Protein**: Protein is essential for muscle repair, recovery, and the prevention of muscle breakdown during workouts. Including a moderate amount of protein in your pre-workout meal will help support muscle tissue during the high-intensity efforts of CrossFit.

- **What to Eat**: A small serving of lean protein can help provide the amino acids your muscles need to prevent breakdown during exercise. Examples include:
    o Chicken or turkey breast
    o Lean beef or pork
    o Greek yogurt or cottage cheese
    o Protein powder (whey or plant-based)

3. **Fats**: Fats take longer to digest and provide a slower, more sustained source of energy. While it's essential not to overload on fats before a workout, a small amount of healthy fat can support endurance during longer or more intense WODs.

- **What to Eat**: Choose sources of healthy fats that are easily digestible and light on the stomach. Examples include:
    o Avocado
    o Nuts (almonds, walnuts)
    o Nut butters (peanut butter, almond butter)
    o Chia seeds

---

5. What to Eat: Pre-Workout Meal Examples

Here are a few examples of pre-workout meals and snacks to help fuel your CrossFit workout:

1. **The Balanced Pre-Workout Meal**:
    o 1/2 cup of oatmeal with banana slices, a spoonful of almond butter, and a drizzle of honey.
    o 1 small serving of chicken breast or turkey.
    o Hydrate with water or an electrolyte drink.
2. **Quick Pre-Workout Snack**:

- o   1 medium banana with a tablespoon of peanut butter.
- o   A small handful of almonds or walnuts.
- o   Water or coconut water.
3. **For a Higher-Intensity Workout**:
    - o   1 slice of whole-grain toast with 1 scrambled egg and a few slices of avocado.
    - o   A small protein shake mixed with water or almond milk.
    - o   Water or an electrolyte-rich drink.

---

6.   The Role of Post-Workout Nutrition

After an intense CrossFit session, your body enters a recovery phase where muscle repair, glycogen replenishment, and rehydration take place. Proper post-workout nutrition is critical to make sure your body gets the nutrients it needs to recover quickly and rebuild stronger.

Post-workout nutrition is about **replenishing glycogen stores**, **repairing muscle tissue**, and **reducing inflammation**. If you don't refuel properly, you risk muscle fatigue, injury, or inadequate recovery, which will hinder your progress and performance in future workouts.

7.   When to Eat After Your Workout

The best time to eat your post-workout meal is within **30-60 minutes of completing your workout**. This is often referred to as the "anabolic window," which is a period when the body is primed to absorb nutrients and replenish depleted stores. Though some research suggests that this window is not as narrow as once thought, eating within this timeframe ensures your body receives the nutrients it needs quickly to begin the recovery process.

If you can't get a full meal in right away, consider having a protein shake or a small snack immediately after your workout, then follow it up with a balanced meal later.

8.   Macronutrient Breakdown for Post-Workout Nutrition

1. **Carbohydrates**: After your workout, your body's glycogen stores will be depleted. To recover, you'll need to replenish these stores as quickly as possible. This is especially important after CrossFit WODs, which tend to deplete glycogen stores due to their high-intensity nature. Carbohydrates should be the bulk of your post-workout meal.

- **What to Eat**: High-glycemic index carbohydrates are ideal because they are quickly absorbed by the body. You can opt for whole food sources, such as sweet potatoes or rice, or quicker-digesting options like fruits and white rice.
    - o   Rice (white or brown)
    - o   Sweet potatoes
    - o   Quinoa
    - o   Fruit (bananas, berries, pineapple)
    - o   Whole-grain pasta

2. **Protein**: Protein is essential after your workout to repair muscle tissue that has been broken down during exercise. Consuming an adequate amount of protein ensures that muscle protein synthesis is activated, and muscle growth is optimized. Protein should be included in every post-workout meal.

- **What to Eat**: Choose fast-digesting sources of protein for quicker absorption. Whey protein powder is a popular choice post-workout due to its rapid digestion and high bioavailability.
  - Whey protein shake or isolate
  - Chicken, turkey, or fish (salmon, tuna)
  - Greek yogurt or cottage cheese
  - Plant-based proteins (tofu, tempeh, or legumes)

3. **Fats**: While fats are not the primary focus for post-workout nutrition, a small amount of healthy fats can be included for hormonal balance and nutrient absorption.

- **What to Eat**: Include healthy fats in moderation, focusing on sources that support recovery without overwhelming digestion.
  - Avocados
  - Nuts and seeds
  - Olive oil or coconut oil (used in cooking)

---

9. What to Eat: Post-Workout Meal Examples

Here are some examples of post-workout meals and snacks to promote recovery and replenish energy:

1. **The Balanced Post-Workout Meal**:
   - Grilled chicken breast with quinoa and steamed broccoli.
   - 1 small serving of sweet potato or brown rice.
   - Hydrate with water or a post-workout recovery drink (with electrolytes).

2. **Quick Post-Workout Snack**:
   - A whey protein shake with a banana.
   - A handful of almonds or walnuts.
   - Water or an electrolyte drink.

3. **For Optimal Recovery**:
   - Salmon fillet with roasted vegetables (carrots, zucchini, bell peppers).
   - 1/2 cup of quinoa or wild rice.
   - A small serving of avocado for healthy fats.

---

10. Hydration and Electrolytes: The Unsung Heroes of Pre- and Post-Workout Nutrition

Hydration is one of the most important aspects of pre- and post-workout nutrition that is often overlooked. CrossFit workouts are incredibly demanding, and sweating is inevitable. The loss of fluid and electrolytes can lead to dehydration, muscle cramps, and poor performance. Proper hydration should go hand-in-hand with fueling before and after your workout.

11. **Pre-Workout Hydration:**

- Aim to drink **500-750 ml (17-25 oz)** of water about 1-2 hours before your workout.
- If you're training in hot or humid conditions, or if your session is longer than an hour, consider drinking an electrolyte-rich beverage to replenish lost minerals like sodium, potassium, and magnesium.

12. **Post-Workout Hydration:**

- After your workout, aim to replenish the fluids you've lost through sweat. A good rule of thumb is to drink **1.5 times the amount of weight lost during exercise** (for example, if you lost 1 pound during your workout, drink 1.5 pounds of water post-workout).
- Electrolytes are also essential in your post-workout recovery drink, especially after high-intensity or endurance-based WODs. Sports drinks, coconut water, or electrolyte tablets can help balance your fluid levels.

---

13. **Conclusion**

Pre- and post-workout nutrition is a critical factor in the success of your CrossFit journey. By fueling your body properly before you exercise, you ensure that you have the energy and endurance to push through the demands of your workout. Similarly, by recovering correctly after your workout, you allow your muscles to rebuild, replenish your energy stores, and be ready for the next challenge. With the right balance of carbohydrates, protein, fats, and hydration, you'll not only optimize your performance but also promote faster recovery and progress in your fitness goals.

Be consistent with your pre- and post-workout nutrition, listen to your body's needs, and adjust as necessary to continue achieving your CrossFit goals. Proper nutrition will give you the edge you need to perform at your peak and recover like a champion.

Supplements

In the world of CrossFit, where intense training and competition are the focus, many athletes seek additional ways to support their performance, recovery, and overall health. While proper nutrition, adequate sleep, and a well-rounded fitness plan are the foundational pillars of success, supplements can serve as valuable tools to help fill in any nutritional gaps, optimize recovery, and enhance performance. This chapter will explore the most popular and effective supplements for CrossFit athletes, how and when to use them, and the benefits they offer when paired with a well-structured nutrition and training plan.

- **Understanding Supplements in CrossFit**

Supplements are designed to **supplement** a balanced diet, not replace it. They can help to enhance performance, promote muscle recovery, support immune function, and help CrossFit athletes meet their unique nutritional needs. However, supplements should never be viewed as a magic solution for success. They work best when incorporated into a lifestyle that includes proper training, a well-rounded diet, adequate rest, and effective stress management.

Before diving into the specifics of each supplement, it's important to note that the effectiveness of supplements can vary between individuals based on factors such as body type, age, goals, and training intensity. Supplements also have different levels of scientific support in terms of their effectiveness. While some are well-studied, others may have limited research, so it's essential to approach supplementation carefully and in conjunction with professional advice when necessary.

- **Essential Supplements for CrossFit Athletes**

There are several categories of supplements that can benefit CrossFit athletes. These include those that aid in **performance enhancement**, **muscle recovery**, **general health**, and **fat loss**. Let's break them down into their respective categories.

- **1. Pre-Workout Supplements**

Pre-workout supplements are designed to provide energy, enhance focus, and improve endurance during your workout. They are typically consumed 20-30 minutes before training and are formulated to help you perform at your peak.

- **Caffeine**: One of the most researched and effective pre-workout supplements, caffeine can enhance endurance, strength, and focus. It works by stimulating the central nervous system, increasing alertness, and reducing perceived effort, allowing you to push harder during your WOD. Caffeine also helps mobilize fatty acids, providing an additional energy source during high-intensity training.

- o **Dosage**: Aim for 3-6 mg of caffeine per kilogram of body weight. For a 70 kg (154 lb) athlete, this would be approximately 210-420 mg of caffeine.
- o **Considerations**: Be mindful of your tolerance to caffeine, as it can cause jitteriness, insomnia, or digestive discomfort in some people. Avoid consuming caffeine too late in the day to prevent interfering with your sleep.

- **Beta-Alanine**: This amino acid helps buffer acid build-up in muscles during intense exercise, allowing you to perform high-intensity work for longer. Beta-alanine is particularly beneficial for WODs involving short bursts of effort followed by rest, as it helps delay fatigue and improve endurance.
  - o **Dosage**: 2-5 grams per day, with a dose taken about 30-60 minutes before exercise.
  - o **Considerations**: Some people may experience a tingling sensation on the skin, known as **paresthesia**, when taking beta-alanine. While harmless, this sensation can be uncomfortable for some individuals.

- **Creatine Monohydrate**: Creatine is one of the most well-researched supplements for performance enhancement. It increases the availability of phosphocreatine in muscles, which is crucial for short bursts of power (think Olympic lifts or sprints). Creatine can improve strength, power, and overall performance in explosive activities common in CrossFit.
  - o **Dosage**: A typical loading phase involves 20 grams per day for 5-7 days, followed by a maintenance phase of 3-5 grams per day. Alternatively, you can skip the loading phase and start with 3-5 grams per day.
  - o **Considerations**: Creatine is safe for most people, but be sure to stay hydrated, as it can cause water retention in muscles. Some people may experience bloating or discomfort.

- **2. Post-Workout Supplements**

After an intense workout, the body needs to repair damaged muscle fibers and replenish glycogen stores. Post-workout supplements are designed to support this process, promoting recovery and reducing muscle soreness.

- **Whey Protein**: One of the most popular post-workout supplements, whey protein is a fast-digesting source of protein that helps stimulate muscle protein synthesis (the process of building new muscle). Because CrossFit can break down muscle tissue, consuming whey protein immediately after your workout helps promote muscle repair and growth.

- - **Dosage**: 20-40 grams of whey protein within 30-60 minutes post-workout.
  - **Considerations**: Choose a high-quality whey protein isolate with minimal added sugars. If you have lactose sensitivity, consider whey protein isolate or plant-based protein powders.
- **Branched-Chain Amino Acids (BCAAs)**: BCAAs consist of three essential amino acids—leucine, isoleucine, and valine—that play a significant role in muscle protein synthesis and recovery. Consuming BCAAs before or after your workout can help reduce muscle soreness, improve recovery, and prevent muscle breakdown.
  - **Dosage**: 5-10 grams of BCAAs, either before or after exercise.
  - **Considerations**: BCAAs can be helpful, especially if your protein intake throughout the day is insufficient. However, they may not be as effective if your diet already provides ample protein.
- **Carbohydrates (Post-Workout)**: High-intensity CrossFit workouts deplete glycogen stores, which are the primary source of energy for muscles during exercise. Consuming carbohydrates after your workout helps replenish these stores. Pairing carbohydrates with protein in your post-workout meal or shake can further enhance recovery.
  - **Dosage**: Aim for 1-1.5 grams of carbohydrates per kilogram of body weight post-workout. For example, a 70 kg (154 lb) athlete would consume approximately 70-105 grams of carbohydrates.
  - **Considerations**: Focus on fast-digesting carbs like white rice, sweet potatoes, or fruit. If your workout was particularly long or intense, consider adding simple sugars (like dextrose or maltodextrin) to your post-workout shake to speed up glycogen replenishment.

- **3. Joint Support and Inflammation Control**

CrossFit workouts often involve repetitive movements, heavy lifting, and high-impact exercises that can place significant stress on the joints. Joint support supplements can help protect against wear and tear, reduce inflammation, and promote overall joint health.

- **Fish Oil (Omega-3 Fatty Acids)**: Omega-3s have anti-inflammatory properties that can help reduce joint pain and stiffness associated with high-intensity workouts. They can also support heart health and reduce muscle soreness after training.
  - **Dosage**: 1-3 grams per day, with a focus on EPA and DHA content (the active forms of omega-3s).
  - **Considerations**: If you're prone to fishy burps or digestive upset, look for high-quality, enteric-coated fish oil supplements.
- **Glucosamine and Chondroitin**: These compounds are found naturally in the cartilage of joints and are commonly used to promote joint health

and reduce pain or discomfort. They may help slow the breakdown of cartilage and support joint function.

- o **Dosage**: 1,500 mg of glucosamine and 1,200 mg of chondroitin per day.
- o **Considerations**: These supplements can take time to work, and results may vary depending on the individual.
- **Turmeric (Curcumin)**: Curcumin, the active compound in turmeric, has potent anti-inflammatory effects. It can help reduce joint pain, muscle soreness, and inflammation after a workout.
  - o **Dosage**: 500-1,000 mg of curcumin per day, often in combination with black pepper (piperine) to enhance absorption.
  - o **Considerations**: Take turmeric with food to improve absorption, and always choose a supplement that contains bioavailable curcumin.

- **4. General Health Supplements**

In addition to performance-boosting supplements, CrossFit athletes should consider supplements that support overall health and well-being. These supplements are often designed to fill nutritional gaps and ensure that the body is functioning optimally for training and recovery.

- **Multivitamins**: A high-quality multivitamin can help fill any gaps in your diet, ensuring you're getting a broad spectrum of essential vitamins and minerals. While whole foods should be your primary source of vitamins and minerals, a multivitamin can be useful for athletes with higher demands due to intense training.
  - o **Dosage**: Follow the recommended dosage on the supplement label. Look for a multivitamin that contains a broad range of vitamins and minerals, with particular attention to vitamin D, magnesium, and zinc.
- **Vitamin D**: Vitamin D plays a vital role in immune function, muscle function, and bone health. CrossFit athletes, especially those who train indoors or live in regions with limited sunlight, may be at risk for vitamin D deficiency.
  - o **Dosage**: 1,000-2,000 IU per day, or as recommended based on blood tests.
  - o **Considerations**: Consider getting a blood test to assess your vitamin D levels before supplementing.
- **Magnesium**: Magnesium supports muscle function, energy production, and electrolyte balance. It also helps with relaxation, making it especially useful for improving sleep quality after intense workouts.
  - o **Dosage**: 300-500 mg per day, taken in the evening to promote relaxation and better sleep.

- **Conclusion**

Supplements can be an effective tool in supporting CrossFit athletes in their pursuit of optimal performance, recovery, and overall health. While they should never replace a balanced diet, the right supplements can enhance your workouts, accelerate recovery, and help prevent injuries. As with any supplement, it's important to remember that quality matters. Always choose high-quality, reputable brands, and consider working with a healthcare professional or nutritionist to tailor your supplementation strategy to your individual needs.

Incorporating the right supplements into your CrossFit routine—alongside proper nutrition, sleep, and training—will help you reach your full potential, recover more efficiently, and continue progressing in your fitness journey.

Recovery Strategies

In the world of CrossFit, where intensity and volume are paramount, recovery plays a crucial role in ensuring athletes can perform at their best, day in and day out. While training hard is essential for progress, it is during recovery that muscles rebuild, energy stores replenish, and the body adapts to the stress of intense workouts. Proper recovery strategies not only maximize performance but also help prevent injuries, reduce fatigue, and enhance long-term health.

In this chapter, we will explore the science behind recovery, discuss the various recovery techniques, and provide actionable strategies that CrossFit athletes can implement into their routines. Whether you're training for an upcoming competition, navigating the off-season, or simply trying to avoid burnout, understanding and prioritizing recovery will help you perform at your peak and stay healthy for the long haul.

1. **Understanding Recovery: The Science Behind Muscle Repair and Growth**

Recovery is the process through which your body repairs itself after intense exercise. During a workout, especially a high-intensity CrossFit session, your muscles undergo micro-tears, and energy stores (such as glycogen) are depleted. The body needs time to repair these tissues and replenish energy stores before you can train again at the same intensity.

Recovery is a multifaceted process that includes several key components:

2. **Muscle Repair and Growth**: After a workout, your body initiates the process of muscle repair by synthesizing new proteins to rebuild the micro-tears caused by exercise. This process is critical for muscle growth and strength development.

3. **Glycogen Replenishment**: Intense CrossFit workouts deplete the glycogen (stored carbohydrate) in your muscles and liver. During recovery, your body works to restore these glycogen levels to ensure that you have sufficient energy for future workouts.

4. **Fluid and Electrolyte Balance**: Sweat loss during CrossFit workouts can lead to dehydration and imbalances in electrolytes like sodium, potassium, and magnesium. Rehydrating during and after a workout is essential for optimal recovery and performance.

5. **Central Nervous System (CNS) Recovery**: High-intensity training can put significant stress on the central nervous system, which controls muscle movement and coordination. CNS recovery is crucial for avoiding burnout and overtraining.

6. **Hormonal Balance**: Exercise influences hormone levels in the body, including stress hormones (like cortisol) and recovery hormones (like testosterone and human growth hormone). Recovery helps restore hormonal balance to allow for optimal performance.

With these processes in mind, let's explore the strategies that support recovery in CrossFit.

---

7. 1. Rest and Sleep: The Cornerstones of Recovery

Rest is the most important component of recovery, and sleep is the cornerstone of rest. Without adequate rest, the body cannot effectively repair muscle tissue, replenish glycogen, or restore energy levels. CrossFit athletes, especially those who train at high intensities or multiple times per day, must prioritize sleep and adequate rest days to prevent overtraining and promote recovery.

- **Sleep**: Sleep is when the body undergoes its most significant repair processes. Growth hormone, which plays a key role in muscle repair and fat loss, is released predominantly during deep sleep. Lack of sleep can impair recovery, leading to increased fatigue, decreased performance, and higher injury risk.
  - **Optimal Sleep Duration**: Aim for 7-9 hours of sleep per night. Athletes training intensely or on a high-frequency schedule may need more sleep (up to 10 hours per night) to fully recover.
  - **Sleep Quality**: It's not just about quantity but also the quality of sleep. Prioritize deep, restorative sleep by minimizing light exposure before bed, reducing caffeine intake, and creating a comfortable sleep environment (e.g., dark, quiet, cool room).
- **Active Recovery Days**: While rest days (complete days off from exercise) are crucial, active recovery days can also be highly beneficial. These are low-intensity days where you engage in activities like light jogging, swimming, or yoga to keep your body moving without overloading it. Active recovery aids circulation, reduces muscle stiffness, and speeds up the removal of metabolic waste products like lactic acid.
  - **Frequency**: Incorporating 1-2 active recovery days per week is ideal, depending on your training volume.

---

8. 2. Nutrition for Recovery: Fueling Your Body for Repair

Proper nutrition is essential for supporting recovery, and what you eat immediately after a workout can have a significant impact on how quickly your body heals and rebuilds. Post-workout nutrition should focus on replenishing glycogen stores, repairing muscle tissue, and providing the body with the nutrients needed to promote recovery and reduce inflammation.

- **Protein**: Protein is the building block for muscle repair. After a CrossFit workout, muscle tissue is broken down, and consuming protein helps initiate the repair process. Aim to consume high-quality protein sources to maximize recovery.

- o **Protein Sources**: Whey protein, chicken, fish, eggs, and plant-based protein powders (such as pea or rice protein) are all excellent options.
- o **Post-Workout Protein Intake**: Aim for 20-40 grams of protein within 30 minutes to an hour post-workout. This window is critical for maximizing protein synthesis and muscle repair.
- **Carbohydrates**: CrossFit depletes your glycogen stores, which are your muscles' primary energy source. To replenish glycogen, it's essential to consume carbohydrates after your workout. Complex carbs such as sweet potatoes, quinoa, and whole grains are great options for steady glycogen replenishment.
  - o **Post-Workout Carb Intake**: Aim for 1-1.5 grams of carbohydrates per kilogram of body weight post-workout. A 70 kg (154 lb) athlete should consume between 70-105 grams of carbohydrates after a workout.
- **Fats**: While fats are not the primary focus of post-workout nutrition, they do play an important role in overall recovery. Healthy fats support hormone production and the absorption of fat-soluble vitamins, such as vitamins A, D, E, and K.
  - o **Healthy Fat Sources**: Include avocados, olive oil, nuts, seeds, and fatty fish (like salmon) in your post-workout meals. However, be mindful not to overconsume fats immediately post-workout, as they can slow down digestion.
- **Hydration**: Proper hydration is critical for recovery, as dehydration can impair muscle function and increase the risk of cramps and injuries. After a workout, it's essential to replace fluids lost through sweat and maintain proper electrolyte balance.
  - o **Electrolytes**: Consider supplementing with an electrolyte drink or consuming electrolyte-rich foods (e.g., bananas, coconut water) to help restore sodium, potassium, and magnesium levels.
  - o **Water**: In addition to electrolyte drinks, continue to drink plenty of water throughout the day to stay hydrated and support cellular function.

9. 3. Foam Rolling and Stretching: Reducing Muscle Tightness and Improving Flexibility

Foam rolling and stretching are two of the most effective techniques for alleviating muscle tightness, improving flexibility, and reducing muscle soreness (DOMS – Delayed Onset Muscle Soreness) following intense CrossFit workouts. These techniques can increase blood flow to muscles, help break down adhesions in muscle tissue, and enhance overall recovery.

- **Foam Rolling**: Foam rolling is a form of self-myofascial release (SMR) that targets muscle knots and tightness. Rolling over tight or sore muscles can help release built-up tension, improve circulation, and reduce post-workout soreness. Aim to foam roll for 5-10 minutes after your workout, focusing on major muscle groups like your quads, hamstrings, calves, and back.

- o **Technique**: Roll slowly over each muscle group, pausing and applying pressure on any particularly tight or sore spots. Avoid rolling over joints or bones, and always maintain control to avoid overstretching or injury.
- **Static and Dynamic Stretching**: Stretching helps to improve flexibility, release muscle tension, and increase range of motion. Static stretching involves holding stretches for 20-30 seconds, while dynamic stretching involves moving through a range of motion to actively stretch muscles.
  - o **Static Stretching**: Perform static stretches after your workout, focusing on key areas that may have become tight during exercise, such as the hip flexors, hamstrings, and shoulders.
  - o **Dynamic Stretching**: Incorporate dynamic stretching into your warm-up to improve mobility and activate muscles before a workout. Movements like leg swings, arm circles, and hip rotations can help prepare your body for action.

10. 4. Contrast Therapy: Hot and Cold Treatments for Recovery

Contrast therapy involves alternating between hot and cold treatments to promote recovery. This method has been shown to reduce muscle soreness, improve circulation, and speed up recovery time.

- **Ice Baths or Cold Showers**: After a tough workout, cold therapy (such as ice baths or cold showers) can help reduce inflammation, numb sore muscles, and prevent swelling. Cold exposure constricts blood vessels, reducing metabolic waste accumulation and flushing out toxins.
  - o **How to Use**: Take an ice bath for 10-15 minutes, ensuring the water is cold but not too uncomfortable. Alternatively, a cold shower can also provide similar benefits.
- **Heat Therapy**: Heat can promote blood flow, relax muscles, and reduce stiffness. Heat treatments such as hot baths, saunas, or heating pads can help relax tight muscles and improve flexibility.
  - o **How to Use**: After cold therapy, or on a rest day, take a warm bath or use a heating pad for 15-20 minutes to soothe your muscles.

11. 5. Injury Prevention: Listening to Your Body and Avoiding Overtraining

While recovery strategies can help your body heal and repair, injury prevention is just as important for staying in the game long term. Overtraining, lack of rest, and improper technique can lead to injuries that sideline your progress. Listening to your body, avoiding excessive training loads, and addressing small issues before they become larger problems are key aspects of injury prevention.

- **Signs of Overtraining**: Watch for signs of overtraining, including persistent fatigue, irritability, decreased performance, joint pain, and trouble sleeping. If you notice these symptoms, it may be time to reduce your training intensity or take additional rest days.
- **Proper Technique**: Always prioritize good form, especially when lifting heavy weights or performing complex movements. Poor technique can lead to muscle strains, joint injuries, and long-term damage. Consider working with a coach to ensure you're performing exercises with proper form.

12. Conclusion

Recovery is not just an afterthought; it is a vital component of any CrossFit athlete's training plan. By prioritizing rest, nutrition, sleep, and recovery techniques like foam rolling, stretching, and contrast therapy, you can enhance your performance, reduce muscle soreness, and avoid injury. Consistently taking care of your body will not only allow you to perform at your best but also promote long-term health and success in your fitness journey.

Remember, recovery is not passive—it requires active effort and a conscious commitment to listening to your body. Incorporating these recovery strategies into your routine will ensure that you recover faster, perform better, and stay injury-free as you progress in your CrossFit training.

Enhancing Performance and Recovery

CrossFit is a demanding and high-intensity sport that requires both physical strength and mental focus. Athletes push their limits day in and day out, seeking to maximize their performance, accelerate recovery, and achieve their goals. One way to help support these efforts is through the use of supplements. Proper supplementation can offer an edge when it comes to fueling performance, enhancing recovery, and improving overall health.

In this chapter, we'll take a deep dive into the world of CrossFit supplements. We'll cover the most commonly used supplements, discuss their potential benefits, and explore how to incorporate them into your training and nutrition plan. From pre-workout stimulants to post-workout recovery aids, we will help you understand which supplements are worth considering, how they can support your CrossFit goals, and how to use them safely and effectively.

---

1. Understanding Supplements in CrossFit

Supplements are products designed to provide additional nutrients that may be missing from your diet or enhance specific aspects of performance and recovery. They should never replace a balanced, nutrient-dense diet but can serve as valuable tools to support your training and goals.

When it comes to CrossFit, supplements can be categorized into two main areas:

2. **Performance Enhancers**: These supplements are intended to improve workout performance, such as increasing energy, endurance, and focus during your CrossFit sessions.

3. **Recovery Aids**: These supplements help the body repair itself post-workout by replenishing nutrients, reducing inflammation, and enhancing muscle recovery.

It's important to note that while supplements can offer benefits, they should always be used as part of a well-rounded nutrition and training program. No supplement can replace hard work, consistency, and a proper diet.

---

4. 1. Pre-Workout Supplements: Boosting Energy and Focus

Pre-workout supplements are designed to give you a boost of energy, focus, and endurance before hitting a high-intensity CrossFit session. These products often contain a combination of ingredients that stimulate the nervous system, increase blood flow to muscles, and provide the necessary nutrients to sustain high-performance efforts.

5. Key Ingredients in Pre-Workout Supplements:

- **Caffeine**: Caffeine is the most common and effective ingredient in pre-workout supplements. It is a stimulant that boosts alertness, focus, and endurance by increasing adrenaline and dopamine levels. Caffeine also helps reduce the perception of effort, making intense exercises feel slightly easier.
    - **Recommended Dosage**: 100-300 mg per serving, depending on tolerance. Start with a lower dose if you're new to caffeine.
    - **Side Effects**: Too much caffeine can lead to jitteriness, anxiety, or an upset stomach. If you're sensitive to caffeine, opt for a caffeine-free pre-workout formula.
- **Beta-Alanine**: Beta-alanine is an amino acid that helps buffer lactic acid buildup in muscles, delaying muscle fatigue and improving endurance during high-intensity exercise. It's especially beneficial during workouts involving short bursts of intense effort, like many CrossFit movements.
    - **Recommended Dosage**: 2-5 grams, taken 20-30 minutes before your workout. Be mindful that beta-alanine can cause a tingling sensation on the skin, which is harmless but may be uncomfortable for some individuals.
- **Citrulline**: Citrulline is an amino acid that helps increase nitric oxide production in the body. Nitric oxide improves blood flow, allowing more oxygen and nutrients to be delivered to muscles during intense workouts, which can enhance endurance and reduce muscle soreness post-workout.
    - **Recommended Dosage**: 6-8 grams per serving, taken 30 minutes before a workout.
- **Creatine Monohydrate**: Creatine is one of the most researched and effective supplements for improving strength and explosive power. It enhances the body's ability to regenerate ATP (the energy currency of the cell), which is used during high-intensity exercises like lifting, sprints, and jumps.
    - **Recommended Dosage**: 3-5 grams daily. Some pre-workout formulas may already include creatine, so make sure you're not taking excessive amounts.
6. **How to Use Pre-Workout Supplements:**
- Take your pre-workout supplement 20-30 minutes before your CrossFit session. This allows enough time for the ingredients to be absorbed and start working.
- Start with a small dose, especially if you're new to pre-workouts, to assess your tolerance and avoid any unpleasant side effects.

---

7. **2. Intra-Workout Supplements: Sustaining Energy During Workouts**
Intra-workout supplements are designed to provide your body with nutrients during your training, helping maintain energy levels, prevent fatigue, and improve hydration. While not everyone may need intra-workout supplements, they can be

especially beneficial during long or highly intense CrossFit sessions that push your body to its limits.

8. **Key Ingredients in Intra-Workout Supplements:**
- **Branched-Chain Amino Acids (BCAAs):** BCAAs, consisting of leucine, isoleucine, and valine, are essential amino acids that help reduce muscle protein breakdown during exercise. Consuming BCAAs during a workout can help preserve muscle mass, improve endurance, and reduce the onset of fatigue.
  - **Recommended Dosage:** 5-10 grams of BCAAs during your workout.
- **Electrolytes:** CrossFit workouts often lead to significant sweat loss, which can result in dehydration and a loss of vital electrolytes like sodium, potassium, and magnesium. An electrolyte supplement can help maintain fluid balance, prevent muscle cramps, and enhance performance.
  - **Recommended Dosage:** Follow the product's instructions, but most intra-workout electrolyte supplements are taken at a dose of 500-1000 mg per serving.
- **Carbohydrates:** During intense CrossFit sessions, the body burns through glycogen stores quickly. Carbohydrates consumed during a workout can help maintain blood sugar levels, sustain energy, and prevent fatigue. Fast-digesting carbohydrates like glucose or maltodextrin are commonly used in intra-workout supplements.
  - **Recommended Dosage:** 20-30 grams of fast-digesting carbs per hour of exercise.

9. **How to Use Intra-Workout Supplements:**
- Mix your intra-workout supplement with water and sip it throughout your CrossFit session.
- If your workouts are particularly long or intense, consider incorporating both BCAAs and electrolytes into your intra-workout routine.

10. **3. Post-Workout Supplements: Accelerating Recovery**

Post-workout supplements are designed to help your body recover after training by promoting muscle repair, replenishing glycogen stores, and reducing inflammation. These supplements are critical for maximizing recovery and ensuring that you are ready for your next training session.

11. **Key Ingredients in Post-Workout Supplements:**
- **Protein:** After a CrossFit workout, your muscles are in a state of repair. Protein provides the essential amino acids needed to rebuild and strengthen muscle tissue. Whey protein is a popular option because it digests quickly, but casein and plant-based proteins are also effective.
  - **Recommended Dosage:** Aim for 20-40 grams of protein within 30 minutes to an hour post-workout for optimal muscle repair.

- **Creatine Monohydrate**: Creatine plays a role in muscle recovery by replenishing ATP stores that were depleted during exercise. It's also known to reduce muscle soreness after intense training.
  - **Recommended Dosage**: 3-5 grams post-workout.
- **L-Glutamine**: Glutamine is an amino acid that helps support the immune system, reduce muscle soreness, and speed up recovery. While the body produces glutamine naturally, supplementation can be helpful after intense CrossFit sessions to restore levels and aid in muscle repair.
  - **Recommended Dosage**: 5 grams post-workout.
- **Tart Cherry Juice or Curcumin**: Both tart cherry juice and curcumin (the active compound in turmeric) have anti-inflammatory properties that can help reduce muscle soreness and inflammation after a tough CrossFit session. These can be especially useful if you experience delayed onset muscle soreness (DOMS).
  - **Recommended Dosage**: 8 oz of tart cherry juice or 500 mg of curcumin after your workout.

12. **How to Use Post-Workout Supplements:**
- Consume your post-workout supplement (such as a protein shake) within 30 minutes to an hour of finishing your workout. This is the optimal window for muscle protein synthesis and glycogen replenishment.
- If you're using creatine or other recovery aids, consider mixing them with your protein shake or taking them separately, depending on personal preference.

---

13. **4. Vitamins and Minerals: Supporting Overall Health**

While not specific to CrossFit, essential vitamins and minerals are crucial for overall health, immune function, energy production, and muscle contraction. Ensuring you get the proper micronutrients will support your training and recovery in the long term.

14. **Key Vitamins and Minerals for CrossFit Athletes:**
- **Vitamin D**: Vitamin D supports bone health, immune function, and muscle function. CrossFit athletes often train indoors, where sunlight exposure is limited, making supplementation important.
  - **Recommended Dosage**: 1000-2000 IU daily, especially if you're deficient.
- **Magnesium**: Magnesium helps with muscle relaxation, reducing cramps, and improving sleep quality, which is essential for recovery.
  - **Recommended Dosage**: 200-400 mg daily, ideally taken in the evening to support sleep.
- **Omega-3 Fatty Acids**: Omega-3s (from fish oil or plant-based sources like flaxseed) help reduce inflammation, support heart health, and improve cognitive function.
  - **Recommended Dosage**: 1000-3000 mg of EPA/DHA daily.

15. 5. Safety and Considerations

While supplements can be beneficial, they are not a magic solution for success in CrossFit. They should always be used in conjunction with a solid training program and proper nutrition. Additionally, it's important to use supplements that are third-party tested for quality and safety.

- **Quality Control**: Choose supplements from reputable brands that adhere to Good Manufacturing Practices (GMP) and are tested by third-party organizations like NSF or Informed-Sport.

- **Consult with a Healthcare Provider**: Before starting any supplementation regimen, especially if you have pre-existing medical conditions or are taking medications, consult with a healthcare professional.

16. Conclusion

Supplements can play a valuable role in enhancing CrossFit performance, improving recovery, and supporting overall health. However, they should always complement a balanced diet and training routine rather than replace them. By carefully selecting and using supplements such as pre-workouts, BCAAs, protein, creatine, and vitamins, CrossFit athletes can optimize their performance, reduce recovery time, and ultimately achieve their fitness goals.

Remember that supplements work best when combined with consistent training, proper nutrition, and ample rest. Always focus on the basics—hard work, a solid training program, and smart nutrition—before turning to supplements as a way to enhance your CrossFit journey.

Cornerstones

In the fast-paced, intense world of CrossFit, it's easy to fall into the trap of thinking that the more you train, the better your results will be. Many athletes focus exclusively on pushing their limits in the gym, constantly chasing that next personal best or striving for the ultimate physical condition. However, what many overlook is the critical role that **sleep and recovery** play in optimizing performance and ensuring long-term success.

Whether you are training once a day or multiple times, your body needs time to recover in order to adapt, grow stronger, and perform at its peak. **Sleep** is the most significant factor in recovery, as it directly influences muscle repair, hormone production, and overall mental and physical well-being. Without adequate rest and recovery, your progress can plateau, and you may even risk injury or burnout.

In this chapter, we will explore the science behind sleep and recovery, discuss how to maximize both for optimal CrossFit performance, and offer practical tips for integrating these crucial elements into your training routine. We will also discuss strategies for managing fatigue and avoiding overtraining, ensuring you stay healthy, energized, and ready for every workout.

1. **The Science of Sleep and Recovery**

Sleep is an often underestimated factor in athletic performance, but it is arguably just as important as the time you spend training. During sleep, your body undergoes critical processes that repair tissues, strengthen muscles, and restore energy stores. Without sufficient sleep, you are effectively sabotaging your progress, no matter how hard you work in the gym.

2. **The Stages of Sleep**

To understand how sleep impacts recovery, it is essential to know the different stages of sleep and how they contribute to muscle repair, growth, and overall health:

3. **Non-Rapid Eye Movement (NREM) Sleep**: This stage consists of three sub-stages (N1, N2, and N3) and makes up about 75% of your total sleep.

   o **Stage N3 (Deep Sleep)**: This is the most important stage for physical recovery. During deep sleep, the body's anabolic processes are at their peak, meaning muscle repair, growth, and regeneration occur. Human Growth Hormone (HGH), a vital hormone for muscle repair and tissue growth, is released in large quantities during deep sleep.

   o **Stage N2**: This stage also plays a role in muscle repair, but it is more focused on stabilizing the body's internal processes and consolidating memories, which is essential for cognitive function.

4. **Rapid Eye Movement (REM) Sleep**: REM sleep is critical for mental recovery, cognitive function, and memory consolidation. During this phase, your brain processes emotions, information, and skills, contributing to mental clarity and focus the next day. Though REM sleep is not directly tied to muscle recovery, it plays a role in cognitive function, mood, and mental well-being.

5. **Sleep and Muscle Recovery**

During your CrossFit workouts, your muscles undergo small tears, and it is during recovery (primarily while you are sleeping) that these tears repair and rebuild stronger than before. Without adequate sleep, muscle recovery is delayed or impaired, which could lead to chronic fatigue, injuries, and diminished performance.

Additionally, when you sleep, the body works to replenish its glycogen stores—your primary energy source during high-intensity workouts. A lack of sleep prevents the body from properly replenishing glycogen, which can leave you feeling fatigued during your workouts.

---

6. **How Much Sleep Do You Need?**

The amount of sleep needed varies from person to person based on factors like age, genetics, and training intensity. However, general recommendations for CrossFit athletes and active individuals are as follows:

- **7 to 9 hours of sleep per night** is ideal for most athletes.
- Some athletes may need more sleep (10+ hours) during particularly intense training periods or when recovering from an injury.
- Inadequate sleep, such as consistently getting less than 6 hours, can significantly impair performance, increase the risk of injury, and hinder recovery.

It's essential to remember that the quality of your sleep is just as important as the quantity. If you are getting 8 hours of sleep but waking up frequently throughout the night, your body is not experiencing the deep, restorative stages of sleep required for muscle repair and overall recovery.

---

7. **Sleep Hygiene: Tips for Better Sleep Quality**

Achieving high-quality sleep involves more than just lying down for a set amount of hours. It requires creating an environment conducive to rest and establishing habits that promote relaxation. Here are some effective strategies for improving your sleep quality:

8. **1. Create a Sleep Schedule**

Going to bed and waking up at the same time each day helps regulate your body's internal clock (circadian rhythm). Consistency is key. Try to wake up and go to sleep at the same time every day, even on weekends, to maintain a regular sleep pattern.

9. **2. Optimize Your Sleep Environment**

- **Keep your bedroom cool and dark**: A cooler room (around 60-67°F or 15-20°C) promotes deeper sleep. Darkness signals to your brain that it's time to sleep, so use blackout curtains or sleep masks if necessary.

- **Invest in a comfortable mattress and pillow**: Ensure that your mattress provides adequate support for your body and that your pillow keeps your neck aligned with your spine.
- **Limit noise**: Use earplugs or white noise machines if you live in a noisy environment.

10. **3. Limit Exposure to Screens**

The blue light emitted by phones, tablets, and computers can interfere with your body's production of melatonin, the hormone responsible for regulating sleep. Avoid screens at least 30 minutes before bedtime.

11. **4. Create a Relaxing Pre-Sleep Routine**

Engage in calming activities like reading, taking a warm bath, or practicing mindfulness before bed. Avoid intense physical activity or stimulating mental tasks close to bedtime.

12. **5. Be Mindful of Caffeine and Alcohol**

Caffeine and alcohol can interfere with sleep quality. Avoid consuming these substances late in the day, as they can disrupt your ability to enter deep sleep stages.

---

13. **Recovery Strategies Beyond Sleep**

While sleep is the foundation of recovery, there are other strategies that can accelerate muscle repair, reduce soreness, and optimize your CrossFit performance.

14. **1. Active Recovery**

Active recovery involves engaging in low-intensity exercises, such as light jogging, cycling, or swimming, on your rest days. This helps to increase blood flow to muscles, which aids in the delivery of oxygen and nutrients while also reducing muscle stiffness. Active recovery can also be used after a tough CrossFit session to reduce post-workout soreness (DOMS).

15. **2. Foam Rolling and Stretching**

Foam rolling is an effective technique for relieving muscle tightness, improving flexibility, and enhancing circulation. It works by applying pressure to trigger points in muscles to release tension. Additionally, regular stretching can improve flexibility, promote blood flow, and reduce muscle stiffness, helping you recover faster from demanding workouts.

16. **3. Nutrition for Recovery**

Proper nutrition is integral to the recovery process. Immediately after a workout, you should focus on refueling with protein and carbohydrates to promote muscle repair and glycogen replenishment. A post-workout meal or shake containing a 3:1 ratio of carbs to protein is optimal for recovery. Be sure to maintain balanced nutrition throughout the day, including plenty of fruits, vegetables, lean proteins, and healthy fats.

17. **4. Hydration**

Staying hydrated is critical for recovery. Water helps transport nutrients to muscles, regulate body temperature, and flush out waste products. Electrolyte-rich drinks or supplements can help replenish the minerals lost during intense workouts.

18. **5. Cold Therapy and Contrast Baths**

Cold therapy, such as ice baths or cold showers, has been used by athletes for decades to reduce muscle inflammation and speed up recovery. Similarly, contrast baths (alternating between hot and cold water) may also help increase blood circulation and reduce soreness.

19. **6. Massage Therapy**

Massage can be a great tool to relieve muscle tension, improve flexibility, and reduce soreness after a CrossFit workout. Regular massages can also enhance blood flow to muscles, helping you recover faster.

---

20. **Avoiding Overtraining: Listening to Your Body**

While it's important to train hard to achieve your CrossFit goals, overtraining can be counterproductive. Pushing yourself too hard without adequate rest can lead to burnout, injury, and setbacks. Signs of overtraining include persistent fatigue, difficulty sleeping, decreased performance, irritability, and an increased risk of illness or injury.

To avoid overtraining, it's essential to:

- **Listen to your body**: If you're feeling exhausted or sore, consider taking a rest day or doing active recovery.
- **Incorporate rest days into your weekly routine**: Make sure to schedule at least one or two full rest days per week to give your body time to recover.
- **Vary your training**: CrossFit often involves high-intensity and high-volume training. Mix up your routine with different exercises and intensity levels to prevent excessive strain on specific muscle groups.

---

21. **Conclusion**

Sleep and recovery are non-negotiable components of your CrossFit journey. Without proper rest, all the hard work you put into your training could be in vain, as your body won't have the chance to repair, adapt, and grow stronger. Sleep is the foundation of your recovery, but combining it with other recovery strategies like nutrition, active recovery, and self-care techniques can further enhance your results. Prioritizing sleep and recovery not only improves your performance but also supports long-term health and well-being, allowing you to continue achieving your CrossFit goals without burning out.

Make sleep a priority, listen to your body, and remember: rest is not a sign of weakness but a vital part of becoming the best version of yourself.

Macronutrients

When it comes to CrossFit, the workout itself is only one piece of the puzzle. Without proper **nutrition**, you may find yourself hitting plateaus, lacking energy, or struggling to recover from intense training sessions. What you put into your body plays a pivotal role in not just your performance during workouts, but also in how quickly you recover, build muscle, and maintain overall health.

The unique nature of CrossFit—combining strength training, cardio, and high-intensity workouts—requires specific nutritional strategies to fuel your body, maximize endurance, and promote muscle repair and growth. Whether you're a beginner or a seasoned athlete, understanding how to fuel your body for optimal performance is crucial.

In this chapter, we'll break down the principles of CrossFit nutrition, discuss macronutrients and micronutrients, provide meal planning tips, and explain the importance of timing your meals around your workouts. We'll also look into specific considerations for those in different stages of training, such as during the off-season, in competition mode, and in preparation for multiple workouts a day.

- **The Role of Macronutrients in CrossFit Nutrition**

At its core, CrossFit requires a well-balanced diet rich in **macronutrients**: proteins, carbohydrates, and fats. Each of these macronutrients plays a specific role in supporting energy production, muscle growth, repair, and recovery. Understanding the functions and importance of each macronutrient will help you design a diet that supports your training and performance goals.

- **Protein: The Building Block of Muscle**

Protein is a critical nutrient for muscle repair, growth, and recovery, making it the cornerstone of any CrossFit athlete's diet. CrossFit workouts, especially those that involve high-intensity strength training or functional movements, cause microscopic tears in your muscle fibers. Protein helps to rebuild and strengthen these muscles, ensuring you improve and recover faster.

- **How much protein do you need?** The general recommendation for protein intake varies based on your training intensity and goals. For CrossFit athletes, aim for approximately **1.2 to 2.0 grams of protein per kilogram of body weight** per day. This amount supports muscle repair, growth, and recovery. If you are looking to gain muscle mass, you may want to increase this intake to the higher end of the spectrum.

- **Sources of protein**: High-quality protein sources include lean meats such as chicken, turkey, and lean cuts of beef, as well as fish, eggs, dairy, and plant-based proteins like tofu, tempeh, and legumes.
- **Carbohydrates: The Fuel for High-Intensity Performance**

Carbohydrates are your body's preferred energy source during intense exercise. CrossFit workouts, with their high intensity and varied movements, deplete your glycogen stores (the stored form of carbohydrates in your muscles and liver). To ensure your body has the fuel it needs to perform at its best, consuming enough carbohydrates is essential.

- **How much carbohydrate should you consume?** A general guideline for CrossFit athletes is to consume around **3 to 6 grams of carbohydrates per kilogram of body weight** per day, depending on the intensity and frequency of your workouts. Higher carbohydrate intake is especially important on days when you perform multiple workouts or engage in high-intensity training.
- **Sources of carbohydrates**: Focus on whole-food sources of carbohydrates that are rich in fiber and nutrients. These include vegetables, fruits, whole grains, and legumes. Examples include sweet potatoes, oats, quinoa, brown rice, and leafy greens.
- **Fats: The Essential Energy Source**

Fats are essential for overall health, hormone regulation, and long-term energy needs. While carbs provide quick energy during workouts, fats serve as the body's primary source of energy during lower-intensity activities or longer-duration training.

- **How much fat should you consume?** Around **20% to 30% of your total daily caloric intake** should come from healthy fats. For CrossFit athletes, fats are used primarily for sustained energy throughout the day and to support the body's inflammatory response and recovery.
- **Sources of healthy fats**: Incorporate sources of unsaturated fats such as avocados, olive oil, nuts, seeds, and fatty fish like salmon. Additionally, omega-3 fatty acids found in fish oil and flaxseeds are especially important for reducing exercise-induced inflammation.

- **Micronutrients: The Unsung Heroes**

While macronutrients receive most of the attention, **micronutrients** (vitamins and minerals) play an equally crucial role in supporting CrossFit performance and recovery. These tiny nutrients are vital for energy production, immune function, muscle function, and overall health.

- **Magnesium**: Important for muscle contraction and relaxation, magnesium can help prevent cramping and improve sleep quality, which is essential for recovery.
- **Vitamin D**: Plays a crucial role in bone health, immune function, and muscle function. CrossFit athletes, especially those training indoors, may need to supplement with vitamin D to maintain optimal levels.

- **Electrolytes** (Sodium, Potassium, and Calcium): These minerals help maintain fluid balance and muscle function. Sweating during intense CrossFit workouts depletes electrolytes, so it's essential to replenish them through both food and supplements.
- **Iron**: Important for oxygen transport in the blood, iron helps improve endurance and overall energy levels. CrossFit athletes, especially women, may be at risk of iron deficiency and should pay close attention to their intake.

Incorporate a variety of colorful vegetables, fruits, lean meats, and legumes to ensure you are getting a broad spectrum of micronutrients.

- **Meal Timing: Fueling for Performance**

In CrossFit, meal timing plays an essential role in ensuring that your body has the fuel it needs for peak performance. The timing of your meals can influence energy levels during workouts, recovery afterward, and overall muscle growth.

- **Pre-Workout Nutrition: Preparing for Success**

Your pre-workout meal should focus on providing readily available energy without causing digestive discomfort during your workout. Aim to consume a balanced meal **1.5 to 2 hours before** your workout that includes easily digestible carbohydrates and moderate protein. Avoid high-fat and high-fiber foods immediately before a workout, as they can cause sluggishness.

- **Pre-workout meal example**: A serving of oatmeal with protein powder mixed in, or a banana with a scoop of almond butter.

If you're eating **30 to 60 minutes before** a workout, opt for a small snack like a piece of fruit (e.g., a banana or apple) or a smoothie with protein and carbs to provide quick energy.

- **Post-Workout Nutrition: Replenishing and Repairing**

Your body is in a heightened state of recovery immediately after a workout, and it's crucial to fuel your body with the right nutrients within **30 to 60 minutes post-workout**. This is often referred to as the "**anabolic window**," the period where your body is most receptive to nutrients for recovery.

Your post-workout meal should prioritize protein to support muscle repair and carbohydrates to replenish glycogen stores. Aim for a **3:1 ratio of carbs to protein** to maximize recovery.

- **Post-workout meal example**: A protein shake with whey protein and a banana, or a chicken breast with sweet potato and leafy greens.

In addition to protein and carbs, rehydrating after your workout is essential. Drink water and consider an electrolyte-rich beverage to replace lost minerals during your intense CrossFit session.

- **Hydration: The Fuel That Powers Every Workout**

Hydration is essential for CrossFit athletes to perform at their best. Dehydration can impair strength, endurance, and focus, leading to poor performance and increased risk of injury. Even mild dehydration can lead to reduced glycogen storage and slower recovery.

- **How much water do you need?** The general guideline is to drink **half your body weight in ounces** of water each day. However, CrossFit athletes may require more water depending on the intensity of their training and environmental factors like heat and humidity.
- **Electrolyte supplementation**: During intense workouts, you lose electrolytes through sweat. Replenish these minerals (sodium, potassium, magnesium, and calcium) by consuming sports drinks or electrolyte powders, or eating foods rich in electrolytes like bananas, spinach, and yogurt.

- **Supplements: Enhancing Performance and Recovery**

While a well-balanced diet should be your primary source of nutrients, supplements can help fill in the gaps, support specific goals, and enhance your performance and recovery. The key to successful supplementation is to focus on products that complement your diet and support your training needs.

- **Common Supplements for CrossFit Athletes**
1. **Protein Powders**: Whey protein is a fast-digesting protein ideal for post-workout recovery. Plant-based protein powders (e.g., pea or hemp protein) are great alternatives for those who follow a vegan diet.
2. **Creatine**: Known for improving strength, endurance, and muscle mass, creatine is one of the most researched and effective supplements for athletes. It enhances performance during short bursts of high-intensity activities like lifting or sprinting.
3. **Branched-Chain Amino Acids (BCAAs)**: BCAAs (leucine, isoleucine, and valine) help prevent muscle breakdown during long, intense workouts and support muscle recovery.
4. **Fish Oil (Omega-3s)**: Omega-3 fatty acids are vital for reducing inflammation and supporting heart health, making them a great addition to your supplementation routine.
5. **Multivitamins**: A high-quality multivitamin can help fill in any gaps in your nutrition and ensure you're getting all the essential vitamins and minerals your body needs to perform optimally.

- **Conclusion**

Proper nutrition is one of the most powerful tools in your CrossFit arsenal. By fueling your body with the right balance of macronutrients and micronutrients, timing your meals to optimize energy levels and recovery, staying hydrated, and supplementing smartly, you can maximize your performance, improve muscle recovery, and maintain overall health.

Remember, CrossFit is a marathon, not a sprint. Consistency with your nutrition will lead to lasting improvements in your training. As you refine your diet, keep track of how your body responds and adjust as needed. CrossFit is a unique sport, and your nutrition should be tailored to your individual needs, goals, and preferences. Through smart, strategic eating, you can unlock your full potential and continue to progress in your fitness journey.

Importance of Sleep and Recovery

In the pursuit of fitness, it's easy to focus entirely on the intensity of the workouts themselves, but one of the most overlooked yet crucial factors for performance, health, and long-term success is **sleep** and **recovery**. The common misconception is that progress comes solely from working hard and pushing limits during training sessions. However, **recovery**—especially sleep—plays a vital role in muscle repair, injury prevention, energy replenishment, and overall performance. Without proper recovery strategies, you risk burnout, injury, and stagnation in your progress.

This chapter will dive deep into why **sleep** and **recovery** are so crucial for CrossFit athletes. We will discuss how to optimize sleep, how to implement recovery strategies, and why recovery is a critical component of any CrossFit training regimen.

- **The Role of Sleep in CrossFit Performance**

Sleep is often referred to as the body's "most powerful recovery tool," and for good reason. Sleep impacts nearly every aspect of an athlete's performance, from muscle repair to mental clarity. CrossFit athletes, in particular, place immense strain on their bodies, and without adequate rest, they cannot recover properly or perform at their best.

- **Sleep and Muscle Recovery**

CrossFit training, which often involves high-intensity exercises like weightlifting, Olympic lifting, gymnastics, and cardio, causes microscopic tears in muscle fibers. These tears are repaired during sleep, allowing your muscles to rebuild and grow stronger. Most of this repair process occurs during **deep sleep**, when growth hormone levels peak. The longer and more restorative your sleep, the more efficient the muscle repair and recovery process will be.

- **Sleep stages**: Sleep consists of different stages, including **light sleep**, **deep sleep**, and **REM (Rapid Eye Movement)** sleep. **Deep sleep** (or slow-wave sleep) is particularly critical for physical recovery. During this stage, the body releases growth hormones that stimulate muscle regeneration and protein synthesis, both essential for rebuilding muscle tissue broken down during intense CrossFit workouts.

- **Growth hormone production**: A lack of sleep can significantly reduce the amount of growth hormone released, impairing muscle recovery and hindering muscle growth over time. For athletes, this means less effective training and less progress toward fitness goals.

- **Sleep and Performance**

Adequate sleep also enhances cognitive function, mood, and focus—all of which are essential for CrossFit. Sleep deprivation impairs decision-making, reaction times, and the ability to concentrate, which can reduce workout effectiveness and increase the risk of injury.

- **Reaction times**: Poor sleep affects your coordination and reaction time, which can be particularly dangerous during high-intensity CrossFit movements like Olympic lifts or heavy lifting.
- **Mental clarity and focus**: Sleep helps with mental sharpness and focus, which is crucial for performing complex CrossFit movements with proper technique. Sleep deprivation can increase the likelihood of errors in form, leading to poor performance and potential injury.
- **Sleep and Hormonal Balance**

Sleep also plays a pivotal role in maintaining **hormonal balance**. When you sleep, the body regulates the release of various hormones, such as cortisol (the stress hormone) and testosterone. Cortisol, in particular, is a major concern for athletes because chronic sleep deprivation can lead to elevated cortisol levels, which can have a catabolic (muscle-wasting) effect on the body. Conversely, sleep helps increase testosterone levels, which are essential for muscle growth and repair.

- **How Much Sleep Should a CrossFit Athlete Get?**

The general recommendation for adults is 7-9 hours of sleep per night. However, athletes involved in intense training, such as CrossFit, may need more to fully recover from their workouts and optimize performance. For CrossFit athletes, **8-10 hours of sleep** each night is ideal to ensure proper recovery and energy levels.

- **Sleep Tips for CrossFit Athletes**

To optimize your sleep for maximum performance and recovery, consider the following tips:

1. **Consistency is Key**: Try to go to bed and wake up at the same time each day. Consistency helps regulate your circadian rhythm, which is crucial for high-quality sleep.
2. **Create a Relaxing Bedtime Routine**: An effective sleep routine can signal to your body that it's time to wind down. This might include activities like stretching, light reading, or meditation.
3. **Limit Caffeine and Alcohol**: Avoid consuming caffeine at least 6 hours before bedtime, as it can interfere with the quality of your sleep. Similarly, while alcohol may initially make you feel drowsy, it disrupts sleep cycles and can decrease REM sleep.
4. **Make Your Sleep Environment Comfortable**: A cool, dark, and quiet environment is conducive to better sleep. Consider blackout curtains, earplugs, or white noise if necessary to block out disturbances.
5. **Avoid Electronics Before Bed**: The blue light emitted by phones, computers, and televisions can interfere with your body's production of melatonin, a hormone that regulates sleep. Try to limit screen time 30-60 minutes before sleep.

6. **Mind Your Nutrition**: Eating a large meal right before bed can disrupt sleep, but small snacks rich in protein and carbohydrates (e.g., Greek yogurt with berries) can promote restful sleep and prevent hunger from waking you up during the night.

- **Active Recovery: Balancing Intensity and Rest**

In CrossFit, recovery isn't just about sleep—it's also about active recovery practices that reduce muscle soreness, improve flexibility, and prevent injury. **Active recovery** includes low-intensity exercises or mobility work that promotes blood flow and muscle relaxation without adding further strain on the body.

- **The Importance of Active Recovery**

Active recovery helps flush out metabolic waste products like lactic acid from your muscles, which can accumulate during high-intensity workouts. By maintaining gentle movement and improving circulation, you can speed up the recovery process, reduce muscle tightness, and increase your range of motion.

Active recovery activities might include:

- **Light aerobic exercise**: Activities like swimming, cycling, or a light jog at a slow pace help increase circulation and promote muscle healing without overtaxing your system.
- **Mobility and stretching**: Incorporating dynamic stretching before workouts and static stretching after workouts helps maintain flexibility and prevent muscle stiffness.
- **Yoga**: Yoga can improve flexibility, mobility, and relaxation while reducing stress, making it a great addition to your recovery routine.
- **Foam Rolling and Self-Myofascial Release**

Foam rolling is a popular recovery technique for CrossFit athletes. It helps relieve muscle tension, reduce soreness, and improve flexibility. By applying pressure to trigger points, foam rolling helps release tightness in the muscles and fascia (the connective tissue surrounding muscles).

- **Injury Prevention and Recovery Techniques**

While CrossFit offers incredible benefits, it's important to remember that high-intensity workouts can increase the risk of injury if not approached with proper technique, warm-up, and recovery. CrossFit athletes often experience injuries such as strains, sprains, or joint pain due to the high-intensity nature of the sport. Fortunately, with proper recovery strategies and injury prevention techniques, you can significantly reduce your risk of injury.

- **Warm-up and Cool-down**

Proper warm-up and cool-down routines are essential for injury prevention. Warming up prepares your body for intense activity by increasing blood flow to your muscles and joints. A good warm-up should include a combination of dynamic stretches (such as leg swings, arm circles, and hip rotations) and light aerobic activity to get your heart rate up.

After your workout, take time to cool down. This includes static stretching, foam rolling, and low-intensity movements to gradually bring your heart rate back to baseline and help relax your muscles.

- **Strengthening Weak Areas**

CrossFit places significant strain on various parts of your body, especially your shoulders, knees, and lower back. Strengthening weak areas through targeted exercises (such as mobility drills for the shoulders and core work for the lower back) can reduce the risk of injury. Focus on building a strong foundation of mobility and stability to protect your body from unnecessary stress.

- **Rest Days and Deload Weeks**

Rest days and deload weeks (a week of reduced training intensity or volume) are also key components of a successful recovery program. These periods allow your body to repair itself, address any potential imbalances, and prevent burnout. Even during the off-season or when you're not actively preparing for a competition, rest is essential for long-term progress.

- **Conclusion: Recovery is Just as Important as Training**

In the world of CrossFit, recovery is not a luxury—it is an absolute necessity. The intense training loads, complex movements, and high-intensity nature of CrossFit demand proper recovery strategies to ensure you continue progressing, avoid injury, and maintain peak performance.

By prioritizing **sleep**, engaging in **active recovery**, practicing **injury prevention**, and giving yourself adequate rest, you will ensure that your body is fully prepared for each and every workout. Remember, recovery is not just about rest—it's about taking proactive steps to optimize your body's ability to repair, rebuild, and perform better than ever.

With these strategies in place, you will be able to train smarter, not just harder. CrossFit is a marathon, not a sprint, and learning how to properly recover will allow you to thrive for the long haul.

Putting It All Together

Now that we've covered the importance of sleep, recovery, and workout strategies, it's time to focus on the most crucial aspect of your training: **nutrition**. In CrossFit, proper nutrition is the foundation upon which everything else is built. Without the right fuel, your body cannot recover effectively, perform at its best, or make the most of your hard work.

CrossFit demands a combination of strength, power, endurance, and agility. Your nutrition plan must be tailored to support these demands. This chapter will provide you with a comprehensive guide on how to optimize your nutrition both on a daily basis and in alignment with your CrossFit workouts, recovery, and competition cycles. From **pre- and post-workout nutrition** to **macronutrient breakdowns**, **supplementation**, and **hydration**, we'll cover everything you need to know.

- **Understanding the Role of Nutrition in CrossFit**

Your body needs energy to perform during intense CrossFit workouts. Energy comes from the food you eat, and how you fuel yourself can have a significant impact on performance, recovery, and body composition.

- **The CrossFit Nutrition Pillars**

There are several key nutritional principles that support CrossFit athletes:

- **Macronutrient Balance**: Proper ratios of protein, carbohydrates, and fats are essential for muscle repair, sustained energy, and optimal performance.
- **Micronutrients**: Vitamins and minerals support overall health and performance, so your diet needs to be rich in micronutrient-dense foods.
- **Hydration**: Staying hydrated is essential for muscle function, recovery, and performance. Dehydration can drastically reduce performance and recovery time.
- **Timing**: The timing of your meals, particularly before and after workouts, plays a critical role in fueling your body and aiding recovery.

We will explore each of these aspects in detail, so you have a well-rounded understanding of how nutrition impacts your CrossFit performance.

- **Macronutrient Breakdown: Fueling Your Body for Performance**

The three primary macronutrients—**carbohydrates**, **protein**, and **fat**—are the building blocks of your diet. Each of these plays a specific role in supporting different aspects of CrossFit performance and recovery.

- **Carbohydrates: Your Primary Source of Energy**

Carbohydrates are the body's primary source of energy, especially during high-intensity activities like CrossFit. They are broken down into glucose, which is used as energy during exercise. Since CrossFit workouts often involve high-intensity movements and circuits, carbohydrates are the most important macronutrient for fueling performance.

- **Complex vs. Simple Carbs**: Complex carbohydrates (such as whole grains, oats, quinoa, and sweet potatoes) provide sustained energy because they are digested slowly. Simple carbohydrates (such as fruits and honey) provide quick bursts of energy, which can be useful right before or during a workout.
- **Carb Timing**: Eating carbohydrates before a workout can help provide energy during intense training, while post-workout carbs help replenish glycogen stores that are depleted during exercise.

Carbohydrate Recommendations:

- Pre-workout: 30-60g of carbs, focusing on complex carbs for sustained energy.
- Post-workout: 40-60g of carbs to restore glycogen levels and enhance recovery.
- **Protein: Repairing and Building Muscle**

Protein is essential for muscle repair and growth. When you engage in intense CrossFit training, you cause micro-tears in your muscles that need to be repaired to grow stronger. Protein provides the building blocks—amino acids—necessary for this process.

- **High-quality protein sources**: Opt for lean meats (chicken, turkey, lean beef), fish, eggs, and plant-based options like lentils, beans, tofu, and quinoa.
- **Protein Timing**: Consuming protein before and after your workouts ensures that your muscles have the necessary nutrients to repair and rebuild. A protein-rich meal post-workout helps accelerate muscle recovery.

Protein Recommendations:

- Pre-workout: A small protein-rich snack, such as Greek yogurt or a protein shake, 30-60 minutes before training.
- Post-workout: 20-30g of protein immediately after exercise for optimal muscle recovery.
- **Fat: Supporting Long-Term Energy and Hormonal Health**

While carbohydrates are your primary fuel source for intense CrossFit training, **fats** are an essential part of a balanced diet, helping to support hormonal balance, brain function, and long-term energy. CrossFit athletes need healthy fats to keep their body functioning optimally, especially during lower-intensity workouts or recovery periods.

- **Sources of healthy fats**: Avocados, nuts, seeds, olive oil, coconut oil, and fatty fish (salmon, mackerel) are excellent sources of healthy fats.

- **Fat Intake**: Fat should make up approximately 20-30% of your total daily calorie intake.

Fat Recommendations:

- Fat intake can be more flexible around your workout times, but it is essential to include in all meals to support overall health.

- **Hydration: The Foundation of Performance and Recovery**

Hydration is often underestimated, but it is one of the most critical factors for performance and recovery. CrossFit workouts involve high-intensity movements that make you sweat, and losing fluids can impact your ability to perform well, recover efficiently, and avoid injury.

- **Hydration Guidelines**
- **Pre-workout**: Aim to drink at least 500-600ml of water 2-3 hours before your workout. This ensures you're well-hydrated going into the session.
- **During the workout**: Hydrate throughout the workout with water. If you're doing a longer workout or sweating excessively, consider adding an electrolyte drink or sports drink to replenish lost electrolytes.
- **Post-workout**: Replenish fluids after the workout. A good guideline is to drink about 500-750ml of water for every pound of body weight lost during the workout.
- **Electrolyte Balance**

When you sweat, you lose not only water but also electrolytes such as sodium, potassium, magnesium, and calcium. These minerals are essential for muscle function and overall hydration balance. Consider including electrolyte-rich foods like bananas (potassium), spinach (magnesium), and coconut water (potassium and sodium) in your post-workout nutrition.

- **Pre- and Post-Workout Meals: Timing is Everything**

The food you consume before and after a CrossFit workout has a direct impact on your performance, muscle recovery, and energy levels. Understanding **meal timing** will help you maximize your results and fuel your body correctly.

- **Pre-Workout Nutrition**

The goal of pre-workout nutrition is to fuel your body with enough energy to power through the workout. The ideal pre-workout meal includes a balance of carbohydrates for energy, protein for muscle preservation, and a small amount of fat to keep you satisfied.

- **When to eat**: Eat your pre-workout meal 1.5-2 hours before your workout for optimal digestion and energy.
- **Meal ideas**:
    - A bowl of oatmeal with protein powder and berries
    - Whole-grain toast with almond butter and banana slices
    - A smoothie with spinach, protein powder, berries, and almond milk

- **Post-Workout Nutrition**

Post-workout nutrition is critical for muscle recovery and replenishing the energy you've expended during exercise. The primary goal is to restore glycogen levels (with carbohydrates) and repair muscle tissue (with protein).

- **When to eat**: Aim to eat your post-workout meal within 30-60 minutes after your workout.
- **Meal ideas**:
    - Grilled chicken with quinoa and steamed vegetables
    - A protein shake with a banana and a handful of spinach
    - A whole-grain wrap with turkey, avocado, and greens

- **Supplements: Filling the Gaps in Your Nutrition**

While a balanced, whole-food-based diet should be your primary source of nutrition, supplements can help fill the gaps and optimize performance. Some supplements can enhance strength, endurance, recovery, and overall performance for CrossFit athletes.

- **Common Supplements for CrossFit Athletes**
1. **Whey Protein**: Helps ensure you meet your protein needs for muscle recovery and growth.
2. **Creatine**: Supports high-intensity activities like weightlifting and sprinting by enhancing the body's energy production.
3. **Branched-Chain Amino Acids (BCAAs)**: Help prevent muscle breakdown during exercise and promote muscle recovery.
4. **Fish Oil (Omega-3s)**: Reduces inflammation and supports overall joint and heart health.
5. **Electrolytes**: Replenish sodium, potassium, and other minerals lost through sweat during high-intensity training.
6. **Multivitamins**: Ensure that you're meeting your daily micronutrient requirements, especially if your diet is lacking in certain areas.

- **Supplement Timing**
- **Pre-workout**: Consider a pre-workout supplement containing caffeine or beta-alanine for increased energy and endurance.
- **Post-workout**: After your workout, a protein shake and creatine can help jump-start recovery.
- **Throughout the day**: Fish oil and multivitamins are great supplements to take with meals for long-term health.

- **Putting It All Together: A Sample Day of Nutrition**

Here's an example of what a balanced day of CrossFit nutrition might look like:

- **Breakfast**: Scrambled eggs with spinach, whole-grain toast, and avocado.
- **Mid-morning snack**: A protein smoothie with protein powder, almond milk, banana, and spinach.

- **Lunch**: Grilled chicken breast, quinoa, and a mixed salad with olive oil dressing.
- **Pre-workout snack**: A small bowl of oatmeal with protein powder, topped with berries and a teaspoon of almond butter.
- **Post-workout**: A protein shake with a banana and a handful of walnuts.
- **Dinner**: Grilled salmon with sweet potatoes and steamed broccoli.

- **Conclusion: Nutrition is Key to Success**

When it comes to CrossFit, nutrition isn't just about what you eat; it's about when and how you eat to maximize your performance, recovery, and overall health. By following the principles outlined in this chapter—balancing your macronutrients, optimizing hydration, timing your meals properly, and utilizing the right supplements—you'll be giving your body the best chance to perform at its peak and recover fully.

Remember, training hard is only half the battle. Proper nutrition is what allows your body to adapt, recover, and improve. With the right nutrition plan, you will be able to perform at your best, stay injury-free, and make long-term progress on your CrossFit journey.

Conclusion

As you embark on your CrossFit journey, it's crucial to understand that **nutrition** is not just a supplement to your training but a central component that dictates your progress and overall success. Your diet fuels your workouts, aids in recovery, and ensures your body has the necessary building blocks to handle the intense demands CrossFit places on it. Without the right nutritional strategies, even the most rigorous training regimen can fall short of delivering the results you desire.

This comprehensive guide has provided you with all the tools necessary to optimize your CrossFit nutrition. From **macronutrient breakdowns**—how to balance carbs, protein, and fats for energy, muscle growth, and recovery—to **timing your meals** to fuel workouts and enhance recovery, every step has been designed to help you improve performance, stay healthy, and recover faster.

However, understanding nutrition in theory is only part of the equation. The real challenge lies in **applying** this knowledge consistently and strategically. It requires discipline, mindfulness, and a deep understanding of how your body responds to different food types, timing, and hydration levels. But rest assured that once you get the hang of it, you'll begin to see tangible improvements in your performance, recovery, and overall well-being.

1. **Creating a Solid Nutrition Foundation for Your CrossFit Goals**

In CrossFit, every workout you complete should build upon the last. Your nutrition plan needs to mirror this mindset. A solid nutritional foundation is built on consistency, balance, and smart choices. Throughout this book, you've learned that there is no one-size-fits-all approach to CrossFit nutrition. Your unique needs—based on your goals, training schedule, body type, and metabolism—determine how you should fuel yourself. What works for one person may not work for another, and that's why it's so important to pay attention to your body's signals and adapt your approach as needed.

From the moment you step into the gym to the minutes after you've finished your workout, every aspect of your training cycle benefits from nutrition. It's not just about getting enough food; it's about eating **the right** foods, at the **right times**, in the **right amounts**, to keep your body performing at its best. And this can't be overstated: **Nutrition is not just about weight loss or muscle gain—it's about optimizing health and performance across the long term**.

2. **Mastering Nutrition for Different Training Phases**

CrossFit involves multiple phases: **off-season**, **in-season**, and **competition season**. Each phase demands a specific nutritional focus.

3. **Off-season**: This is a time when you can focus more on recovery and building strength. The focus during this period should be on maintaining a

well-rounded diet that prioritizes **muscle building** and **fat loss** while maintaining your energy levels. You may also have the freedom to indulge in some flexibility, allowing for experimentation with different meal plans, macronutrient ratios, and supplements.

4. **In-season**: During this time, the intensity of your workouts increases as you push toward achieving your performance goals. Your nutritional intake should mirror this intensity with an emphasis on **consistent energy**. A balanced approach is key, with an appropriate focus on carbohydrates to fuel energy demands, protein to support muscle recovery, and fats to maintain overall health.

5. **Competition Season**: Leading up to a competition, your nutrition needs to be fine-tuned for peak performance. This means **higher carb intake** to replenish glycogen stores for maximal energy output and **adjusted protein levels** to ensure optimal muscle preservation. Additionally, **timing your meals around your workouts** can make a significant difference in sustaining peak performance throughout the competition.

By adjusting your nutrition based on the phase of training you are in, you ensure that your body is receiving exactly what it needs to maximize performance, endurance, and strength, while also allowing for sufficient recovery.

6. The Importance of Consistency and Flexibility

Consistency is critical. By making the right nutritional choices consistently, you build habits that will last a lifetime, helping you continuously improve and progress as an athlete. But just as important as consistency is **flexibility**. Life, personal schedules, and even your body's natural rhythms will sometimes require adjustments to your meal plan. Whether you're traveling for a competition or dealing with an injury, being able to adapt and modify your nutrition without stress or guilt is an essential aspect of a successful long-term approach.

Think of your nutrition as a dynamic, evolving system that requires regular check-ins and adjustments. While you should aim for consistency, don't be afraid to modify your approach as your body changes, as your workout intensity fluctuates, or as you discover new techniques and strategies that work for you.

7. The Role of Hydration in Nutrition

One of the most common yet overlooked aspects of nutrition in CrossFit is hydration. Every training session, especially those involving high-intensity exercises, results in significant fluid loss. As we discussed, staying hydrated isn't just about drinking water—it's about **maintaining the right balance of electrolytes**. Proper hydration supports every cellular function in your body, and when you're properly hydrated, you experience better endurance, strength, and recovery. Additionally, you reduce the risk of injury and fatigue. Staying hydrated will also help with muscle recovery and prevent cramping, ensuring that you can maintain peak performance day after day.

8. Supplements: Enhancing Your Progress

While a balanced diet should provide the majority of your nutritional needs, supplements can fill in the gaps. They're not a magic bullet, but when used appropriately, supplements can enhance your recovery, endurance, and strength. It's essential to understand that **supplements are meant to complement, not replace** a solid nutrition plan. Proper supplementation with protein, creatine, BCAAs, fish oil, and other compounds can help optimize your training cycle, recovery, and overall well-being.

Remember that no supplement can replace hard work, good nutrition, and consistency. If you're already committed to those three pillars, supplements can serve as the cherry on top, accelerating your results and improving your athletic performance.

9. The Psychological Impact of Nutrition on CrossFit

A healthy body requires a healthy mind. Nutrition is not just about the physical benefits—it can also have a huge impact on your mental health. When your body is properly fueled, you experience fewer mood swings, more mental clarity, and increased focus. Proper nutrition can help combat the stress and fatigue that often accompany intense physical activity. As you fuel your body with wholesome foods, your overall sense of well-being improves, reducing stress, enhancing focus, and helping you to maintain motivation throughout the ups and downs of your CrossFit journey.

Additionally, CrossFit often requires mental toughness, especially during challenging workouts. Having the right fuel to maintain energy levels can help you stay mentally sharp and focused, enabling you to push through even the most grueling sessions.

10. Nutrition as a Lifestyle

Ultimately, your CrossFit nutrition plan is not something to be followed rigidly and then abandoned. It should be seen as part of your overall lifestyle—a lifestyle centered around long-term health, sustainable performance, and continual improvement. The habits you form now will pay off in the years to come. Just like your workout routine, your nutrition plan should be seen as a lifelong commitment, one that evolves with you, your goals, and your progress.

---

11. In Conclusion: The Key Takeaways for CrossFit Nutrition

- **Balance is key**: A diet rich in balanced macronutrients—protein, carbohydrates, and healthy fats—ensures your body has the fuel it needs for training, recovery, and optimal health.
- **Meal timing is essential**: Proper pre- and post-workout nutrition ensures you maximize energy for performance and recovery for muscle growth.
- **Hydration supports every system**: Drink enough water and replenish electrolytes to support muscle function, endurance, and recovery.
- **Supplements can enhance your results**: While not a replacement for good nutrition, supplements can boost performance and recovery when used wisely.
- **Adjust as you go**: CrossFit is a dynamic, ever-changing experience. Your nutrition plan should evolve based on your goals, training phases, and individual needs.

Remember that **nutrition is a powerful tool** that, when used correctly, can help you push your limits, recover faster, and see tangible results from your hard work in the gym. With the right mindset and strategies, you can not only optimize your performance but also live a healthier, more vibrant life outside of the gym. Embrace this journey, and let your nutrition be a guide to becoming the best version of yourself—physically, mentally, and emotionally.

Printed in Dunstable, United Kingdom